THANKS
Rony

Nev

Focus Your Mind On Success
Create And Follow Your Dreams
Turn Them Into Goals

All The Best

Neville Wright

WARNING
THIS BOOK CONTAINS REVERSE PSYCHOLOGY SO LOOK OUT FOR IT.

I feel my book is best read from front to back in order to gain the most value out of it, as the time line can feel a bit inconsistent any other way.

With having dyslexia and ADHD, I probably have thought of something that is not always related to the paragraph but it has been in my mind at the time and I have thought it is appropriate that the reader should know.

That is where you will find 'sidetracked' and 'back' along my journey.

# Dedication

## This Book Is Dedicated To My Family

My mother and father, without whose abundance of unquestionable love, and my father's rather strict guidance, I would not have pursued my goals in life. I am so deeply grateful.

My sister and brother, Carol and Terry, who completed a balanced family. They taught me, being the youngest, to know my place. I look up to both, thank you.

My mother and father-in-law; without knowing it, you pushed me to achieve under some very difficult circumstances. I will always be grateful.

My sons-in-law; it doesn't matter how old you get, you are continually learning; you have both taught me more than I could ever have imagined.

To my beautiful girls. My school reports used to say, "Neville could do better;" then I knew, when you two came along, I had achieved top marks.

I have written this book for Marilyn; you have made my life complete.

*I have tried to remember all of the correct dates, prices and conversations, but please forgive me if I have some wrong - it's been a long and exciting journey.*

*Thank you.*

## *Neville Wright.*

http://www.fast-print.net/bookshop

THE ANSWER IS YES – NOW WHAT'S THE QUESTION?
Copyright © Neville Wright 2016

A catalogue record for this book is available from the British Library

ISBN 978-178456-336-3

First Published 2016 by
Fast-Print Publishing of Peterborough, England.

# Contents

# Reflections

The day was Monday, 9th April 2012, 40 days into our 49-day holiday. We had taken eleven flights, and there were just two more to go before we ended our tour that had taken us to Singapore, explored Australia, sailed to Tasmania then on to New Zealand, back to friends in Brisbane, then stopping in Thailand before home.

Sitting next to the pool at the hotel just a few feet from the golden beach, this was the first time in 419 days since leaving Kiddicare that I had had the mental strength to put pen to paper "without stopping before starting," as had been the case up until now, because of the pain inside my head screaming, mostly in silence for the loss.

The loss of not being wanted or needed, being forgotten, tossed onto the scrapheap of life to fade away quietly, without fuss or bother but, most of all, the loss of not continuously building a life with the ones who meant more to me than any amount of money or success, and along with all the things that happened in our lives that had gone, never to be known by generations to come.

By this time, after having 419 days to reflect on the last 60 years of my life, I now started writing and, as they say, time is a healer, which is probably true, but I think it's more like time teaches you to hide those feelings.

So these are my reflections, my thoughts and my memories; there have definitely been some challenges and, as they say, "far too much information." Some I have deleted from this book but, anyway, this should give the reader a real look into the life of a family business from the first day, through, unfortunately, to the last.

# Our Backgrounds

### *School photos of Marilyn and me*

We were just two ordinary kids, from ordinary backgrounds. Arthur, my father, had a hard upbringing, and in turn he was very strict with me. When Dad left school he was an apprentice carpenter and cabinet-maker; like everyone in the 1930s, once his apprenticeship was over he was dismissed to find his own way in life.

Times were hard; he found work on building sites, and at one time he painted tar on the undersides of coal wagons. He said that he went home every night with more tar on himself than he had put on the wagons. Eventually he got a job with the Electricity Board in the Peterborough Power Station, then, a year later, he was called up into the Army and spent six years in the Burmese jungle, fighting the Japanese. After that he went back to the Power Station, where he stayed until retirement aged 60, when the plant was shut down.

My mother, Winifred Mary, came from a very sheltered background. She worked in a factory throughout the war, then, in 1946 they adopted my sister Carol. The doctor said that Mum would never have any children after having so many miscarriages but, on 3$^{rd}$

February 1948 Mum had my brother Terry; then, on 18<sup>th</sup> June 1950 it was my turn. My mum said that she shut the door after having me; maybe it was because I was so good that they thought they would never find another one to compare with me, or maybe not!! She said that I was a little sod; to me, my mum was the most precious thing in my life and was constantly there for all of us.

Marilyn's parents, June and David, came from Chatteris, a small market town in Cambridgeshire where her dad had worked from the age of 12, making meat pies in his father's bakery business. He, like my father, was called up into the Army, but luckily he got posted to the Tower of London, where he worked in the Catering Corps.

When the war was over he returned to Chatteris and carried on working in the bakery. After some time his mean and unforgiving father tried to sell the business, but without any luck; subsequently, David rented the now failing business from his father at the worst time possible, causing David to have a nervous breakdown in 1954. Marilyn was three years old by then, and her brother Michael was one; the family then moved to Peterborough.

David struggled to hold any job down for more than a few weeks but eventually landed a job as a progress chaser in Hotpoint, and then in Baker Perkins, a company in Peterborough that manufactured confectionery and tobacco machines. Then, by 1966 when I met Marilyn, he had got a job as a computer operator through his brother's connections, as he worked as a computer programmer in the same factory. In those days computers were new, and operating them did not require any degrees; he stayed there until his retirement at the age of 62.

Marilyn's mum, June, had worked in the bakery and then, arriving in Peterborough, she took up hairdressing. She worked in hairdressing salons and, in the last 15 years of her working life, she worked from home in an extension on their house that I built for her; it was my first large job after being in business for only a few months, which helped me enormously.

Marilyn was born on 21<sup>st</sup> April 1951; she was a very quiet, intelligent girl, brought up in an environment where children should be seen but not heard and, very often, if she was heard, a "good" smacking would put paid to that, which showed the unfortunate mental state of her father. She flunked her 11+, going to pieces with nerves on the day of her exams, the school system ignoring the underlying coursework and intelligence of the girl before them.

When I met Marilyn she was fifteen, and worked as a Saturday girl in the same hairdressers as her mum. She went to be an apprentice after leaving school and, in 1969 Marilyn became the top apprentice hairdresser of the year in Peterborough.

**Burghley Park, Stamford, Lincolnshire 1966**

As for me, I was born on 18th June 1950, the youngest of three. If you had to sum me up in a word in those early days it would be "trouble". I only know now why it was - I was dyslexic and I didn't see what everyone around me saw, as every time I blinked my eyes the letters of a word would change places, leaving me bewildered. I did not know how others could understand what was going on, and I couldn't explain what was happening because I didn't know what or how to explain it, so frustration led me to become, as my mum would say, a little sod and, of course, I did not want to let my mum's expectation of me down.

Also, I always managed to bring out the worst in my father and, after spending six years in the Burmese killing-fields, Dad had no hesitation in beating the shit out of me to make me conform but, unfortunately, that couldn't alter my brain. My poor mum would be screaming, "Stop hitting him, Arthur, you will kill him," and many a time he came very close to wiping that cheeky smile off of my face forever.

Yet Dad was my hero and I loved him so much. He inspired me to work, and this has been ingrained in me forever; my first job was at the age of seven, delivering milk before the school day started. One of my first thoughts to help compensate for my differences was that, as far as I knew, the whole class could read, yet at the age of seven I think that I was the only one with my own money in my pocket.

As soon as Marilyn and I met we instantly became inseparable, wanting to spend every minute together. Subsequently, I got banned by her father from seeing Marilyn on a Monday, Wednesday and Friday, so we could see each other only on Tuesday and Thursday, and at the weekends; this only resulted in making our bond grow stronger.

Unbeknown to him we used to see each other every day, even if it was only for a few minutes; I would wait until they had all gone to bed for the night, and then I would go from my house, which was on the other side of town, stopping my motor scooter down the road as they knew the sound of it, as I had put a hole in the exhaust pipe to make a horrendous sound which I thought was cool. I would climb over their back fence and Marilyn would open her bedroom window so we could talk, being careful not to make too much noise.

Other days I would get up at 5am to deliver a note through her door before going to work on the pig farm, which was 10 miles the other way. Marilyn has kept all of those love letters, well, notes that mostly said the same thing; a typical one that I have just found while looking for photos said:

"To Miss M Todd" **"Dear Marilyn, I love you very much I could not see you last night because I did not finish work until 9.30, and it is 5 to 7 time for work, all my love Neville xxx"** I was writing this before I went to work the next day; that was on 24th June 1967. I am amazed she kept them, silly girl, and I must confess now that I still have hers as well.

# The Answer Was Always Yes

## *"Well what would you prefer it to be?"*

It was 26th September 1974 when we set up in business cleaning windows, not because I liked window-cleaning, I had never cleaned a window in my life; it was because there was a recession and I couldn't get a job, so I thought that window-cleaning would be the easiest and cheapest way to get into business. Back then, most people who worked as a window cleaner did this to subsidise their normal incomes, but for us this was going to be our living.

Within a few days of starting the business, people asked me if I would do other jobs such as cleaning out gutters, unblocking drains or mending fences. Because of my overwhelming desire to prove to myself that I could look after my family without the government's hand-outs; the answer was always "yes", even though I could not do some of the jobs - with help and guidance from my father, who was a very practical person, I quickly learned. I didn't realise at the time that I was touching people's hearts; there I was, young and vulnerable, never refusing a job; I started off cleaning their windows and, as I did, I would talk to the customers about Marilyn, my wife, and our baby girl, Elaine, with such pride and emotion.

I couldn't hold my feelings back about my dreams of creating a business to look after my family myself, and without ever going back to being unemployed ever again in my life. I now believe that a lot of these people really wanted to help me; they found me jobs that they could have easily done themselves, but they chose to employ me. I will always be so deeply grateful for that.

## A Feeling of Despair, Standing In That Line

SIDETRACKED

Standing in line in the dole office feeling humiliated, my stomach churning with anxiety; then, and only then, standing in that dole queue I realised that I had disrespected some of my previous employers by taking their time, taking liberties and, above all, taking their generosity in giving me an opportunity to prove that I was as good as I said I was in the interview.

Then failing miserably with complacency and, as they say, the chickens came home to roost and I got what I deserved - I got fired. Standing in line each week, I prayed to my god to give me another chance. I said that I would be a role model employee if he just got me another job, but he had obviously had enough of me by then, so he thought it was time for me to stand on my own feet. It was payback time, and my attitude had to alter.

BACK

The customers responded by giving me other work and recommending me to their friends and neighbours, all through just expressing my true feelings. Maybe I was naïve, but people could see that I was genuine and they opened up their hearts and helped me. Very soon the income from the window-cleaning side of the business became smaller in comparison to the other jobs, which were more rewarding, both financially and mentally for me and, of course, for the business.

I learned very quickly that when starting a business having just scraps of experience like I had, the customer is king and, if I did what they asked, I would win; if not, then I would fail. Life is full of lessons; you will see mine over the following pages.

## Teachers, Bullies, and Bullshitters

As soon as I started the business it felt like it was the very first time that I was in control of my own destiny; I found the whole self-employment thing a bit strange, as I had so many times in the past been put down by teachers, bullies, and bullshitters, **(but not now!)**. Looking back, I know those people gave me the determination to succeed. I thank them all, the bullies and bullshitters, for teaching me, and the few cruel teachers who were very often just not nice to the children in their care. I say "not nice" - some delighted in inflicting pain, mentally and physically and at the age of 15, when I left school,

*I wished them all diarrhoea for the rest of their lives.*

I wanted to start the business in the correct way. I was lucky I had a dad. I now know I took him for granted and, as normal, if I wanted something I would ask him to point me in the right direction. He took me to his friend Mr Harrison, an accountant who we had lived near when I was five years old.

## SIDETRACKED

I could remember Mr Harrison because, at the age of five, my sister Carol dressed me up as a girl, called me Susan and took me to the neighbours to show off her skills. I think the Harrisons gave Carol some sweets; and what I got was an inferiority complex. Then, when I was twelve, the Harrisons gave me some work in their garden. Mr Harrison had seen my father one day and Dad had told Mr Harrison that I was working in people's gardens. I remember that when I went to their house their grass had been left to grow too long before they decided that it needed cutting, and all they had was a hand mower that was bigger than me at the time; I could hardly push the mower, let-alone cut the grass.

To top it all, they had a daughter named Jennifer who was a bit older than me. My hormones were kicking in at that time, so I had the embarrassment, in front of her, of not being strong enough to push the thing. Then when Mr Harrison came home he could see what the problem was, so he pushed the mower for me. That day I felt so bad; he did my job because I wasn't strong enough and so I was embarrassed in front of his daughter and him; I was standing there getting paid while he did my work. I learned so much that day that has stayed with me ever since; that day taught me to start to think ahead for myself, and the consequences of not being organised.

## BACK

When I met with Mr Harrison in 1974 I explained to him what we were doing, my dreams of working on building maintenance, and to buy and renovate houses in the future. Unfortunately, I got the impression by the look on his face that he did not think that we would be successful in business. He told me to go to Woolworths and get a book and, on one side, put down what I spent and, on the other side, what I had received; he also told me to take £20 a week for wages. I entered the £20 in the book because he told me to, even though I never had that amount of money to spare. I still put it in the book and probably paid tax on it, even though I hadn't received it; that's how naïve I was.

Although Mr Harrison was very good to me when I first started; and I did a lot of painting and decorating for him, by the time the first year was up I had changed my accountant to one that I thought would take me more seriously, Paul Temple. He lived next door to us when I was a child. He was our accountant for about 30 years until he sold his business.

I had taken my business away from Mr Harrison with no hesitation or thought of what his feelings would be; this never crossed my mind. Looking back now, this attitude seems ruthless to me; I was focused on what I wanted and blinkered to the consequences of my actions on other people's lives. Well, as the saying goes, what goes around comes around, as I would be on the receiving end of this attitude some 35 years later.

I never actually stopped the window cleaning, it just got to be one of those jobs I did if there was nothing else that was better paying. I would never turn down a job just because the money was low; it could always lead to a better-paying job in the future.

## Don't Let Yourself Down

I used knowledge from one job to get the next job, and so on. Don't be afraid to change jobs, because you will find something incredible that you would not have if you had just waited until the right job had come along. And what if it's not the right job, then what? Don't waste time by doing nothing. From the moment we started the business, there hasn't been a wasted moment ever since.

SIDETRACKED

I believe that when people are young and full of energy, they must work every hour they can regardless of the amount of reward they get, not forgetting the amount of money they receive is going to be 100% more than nothing, for doing nothing. Also, the experience they get will be worth far more in the future than the amount of money they have just received and, if they have taken notice, they will be able to sell their experience to other employers later on in their lives.

There are lots of people who would dispute this; these people have an opportunity to work but prefer to sit on their backsides, saying "Why should I work for a pittance?" My answer is that a pittance is better than nothing and, if you think about it, every hour that you don't work, when you could, is taking you further from your goals in life; well, that's if your goals include being wealthy forever.

I hear stories from people about their children, or their friends' children, who have never had a job; they want to get a job but can't. In my eyes in a lot of cases it's not a matter of can't, it's more of won't. These people won't go out of their comfort zone; they certainly won't, or have not been taught to, think outside of the box. They have pigeonholed themselves and got into a rut and the only way to describe a rut is an open-ended grave. I say to people, especially the young people: you should get out and live, prove to yourself, and I really do mean prove to yourself, that you are worth something. Don't go with the crowd, grasp life; it's the only chance you will ever have, don't let it go, don't let yourself down, don't be an **"If only, I had done that"** type of person in the future.

## Chess and Life Are the Same

BACK

At around the age of twelve my interest in chess started. I learnt to play as I could do this because it didn't involve reading, as reading was a subject I didn't understand - all those jumbled up letters that moved about every time I blinked my eyes; what was that all about, and how did my friends understand where to move the letters to?

The worst thing about reading was the slap I got around the head when I couldn't read the ever-changing fcuking letters that just keep on changing places. I remember one day, when I was about fourteen, everybody in the class was taking turns to read a book. I did not know the page, let alone the sentence. The teacher walked up to my desk, grabbed my hair at the back of my neck and twisted it as he lifted me off my chair.

I had long hair at the time, so there was plenty to get hold of. He was shouting in my ear, "Read it boy, read it." Well of course, I couldn't. By this time I was in tears, everyone was laughing, and there was a large, excruciating lump now protruding from my head. Today that sod would be in jail for that. I remember, when the lesson was over, walking to the next classroom; other kids were saying that I was dumb; I said that when we all left school they would get jobs and I would employ a secretary. I was amazed that I had said that; it was something in my subconscious. I desperately wanted to leave school and, like a lot of kids, I could get a job. I think kids should be able to leave at fourteen, giving much better opportunities in life.

I found chess was a great leveller of kids; the chess club made me feel normal. There were no arseholes there to put you down, it didn't matter what was **"wrong"** with you - fat, thin, glasses, stutter, dyslexic, posh, lanky, short, big ears, no ears, limp, shy, or what, it was only all about the game. I have just realised that I didn't include different nationalities; well, it was because there weren't any in my school in Peterborough in the 1960s and besides, if there were, then my brain, as it is now, was nationality-blind; but I would have included them with the rest of us in the chess team.

Chess made me look at life as though it were a game; you can't go straight to where you want to go without overcoming the hurdles and challenges that both the game of chess and the game of life throw at you. Whatever you do in life you are learning; you are learning to go either forwards or backwards. I found that I would only go forwards if I got off my backside and did something, otherwise I was in limbo, no-man's land, and then all of my life would be wasted. Everybody has dreams, and most of us have excuses why we don't follow them. Usually it's some other person's fault but not ours, or it's not the right time, or some other reason why we can't.

SIDETRACKED

I learned from my Zig Ziglar's motivational tapes that I listened to, but this was not until I was in my 30s. I listened to them until I wore them out. By the way I bought some more then, when they were worn out, I just bought some more. Zig said: describe a "can't". You can't. Now describe a "can"; you can, in a hundred different ways. There are tin cans, copper cans, metal cans, big ones, small ones, round … well, you get it. So "can" is a word I have used ever since, as it's a positive word and not a negative one.

# Can or Can't, Positive and Negative

There is only one letter difference between these two words, yet it divides siblings, families, friends and people up into groups, a million miles apart. In general terms these words divide the haves and the have-nots up but, if you are negative like I was in parts of my life, just take the "t" from can't and say "I can be positive for 30 days," and carry on, seeing there is a positive in everything in life; you just have to look for it, so say, "I can be positive."

# Dreams or Goals - What's the Difference?

BACK

My dreams included one of spending my life with the girl I met in 1966, Marilyn, because when I was with her she made me feel that "I liked myself". Also, my dreams included doing what we liked, when we liked, then doing the same with our family that we would have in time. I also had a dream that one day my dad and mum would live with us in a big house where I could look after them as they got older and, at the same time, look after our children and our grandchildren that we would have in the future.

Although this was common in places like Italy it wasn't in England and, as you know, everybody has different agendas, priorities and commitments at different times of their lives. Although not all of my dreams came true, a lot more than I had expected did, and many more would have if I had made more effort in that direction, but that's down to me not seizing opportunities when they appeared.

Another one of our dreams was to be financially independent and free of all debts, something that we really did not believe could happen to us. How could it? We had no right to even think like that. That kind of thinking is common in people telling themselves that they are not worthy to be successful.

Well, we had to force those thoughts out of our heads. We did this over time by telling ourselves that everyone, deep down, has the same opportunities as everyone else; we just have to believe in ourselves and not continually compare ourselves to everyone else. I did this until that deep-seated fear of not being as good as everyone around me had gone. Back then, apart from those things, I personally did not know what I liked; I had to figure that out over time. One thing I learned was to tell myself that the job that I was doing that day was the best job in the world; I had to do the job, so I might as well enjoy it - the day went quickly and it gave me a positive mind.

## Falling Down Is an Inevitability in Life

Looking back, our dreams, wants, and ambitions were easy; the hard part was keeping focused, especially when things didn't go to plan.

Maybe because there were no plans, as **"You don't know what you don't know,"** sometimes until it's too late, and sometimes it's a good thing in disguise that you don't know what you don't know because, if you did know, you probably wouldn't step on that stone to get over the river. Falling down and getting wet is an inevitable part of life.

I say "dreams", but I think they really turned into goals. When goals are achieved they complete the dream. I do know that, for us, having a dream was the catalyst to the journey of fulfilment, with the never-ending thought of not taking each other, or anyone else in this world for granted as, once you do, you become an arse and, I am ashamed to say, I've been one.

Obviously, when you have been brought up in a constrained way like we both were, and as millions of other people are, your mind is somewhat restricted as to what you can do. I would dream each day of being better than I was, so I would always be on the lookout to learn more and to do more, which in turn meant that I would eventually have more. I do think this was deep-seated within me, as I was always wanting to find something different when I was working for other people; I could never settle completely into any job for long.

## My Life in Some Stranger's Hands

This was very difficult for me when I worked in companies that had unions, because in that situation you were not allowed to think or do things that helped the company that you worked for, consequently bringing you down to a "gun fodder" level all of your life. Very often I would go to work not knowing whether the factory would be on strike that day and whether I would have any money that week. In the 1960s and 70s I thought the unions had gone too far. It was plain to see that pushing for more money was destroying jobs and companies alike. For companies to survive, they brought in automation and then decided to ship a lot of production abroad so, as I saw it, the unions ended up shooting themselves in the foot, and creating mass unemployment.

## Follow Your Own Dreams

Don't think you have only one go at life. Every day you are given another chance; most of us never realise this until we think it's too late, so don't be afraid to follow your dreams. Dreams do come true, except for the Lotto, so don't waste your time on that dream because that's all it will be. Concentrate on what you can be in control of and ask yourself what's the worst thing that could happen. Then, if it did happen, what would you do?

We all worry about these things and quite rightly so but, as I sit here in our camping car in Normandy, France, writing this on Friday 6th June 2014, 70 years after D-Day when thousands of poor sods got shot to pieces on the beaches that day, that puts your life into perspective. Some of them didn't even make it far enough to be shot as, when the landing-craft opened their doors some of them were still a long way from the shore, and the troops jumped out thinking they were on the beach, only to be drowned in a few feet of water by the 90lbs of kit on their backs taking them down to the ocean floor. ***"God rest their souls"***

*1974; Marilyn, Elaine and me - a day trip to the seaside*

## Money Is Not the Only Thing

There are hundreds of examples where people have not gone into business because things might be a bit hard for them, and then they spend the rest of their lives saying "I could have", or "I should have", and the classic is, "But I'm not risking my money." I think most people are too frightened to become millionaires.

So without us following our dreams, we would have not gone into business and wouldn't have worked together, which has been great. Also, it gave us the opportunity for Elaine, Scott, Joanne and Andrew to join us, spending our lives working with our children.

# Mind Over Matter

*"Or does it mean determination?"*

I found out only after we became millionaires in the 80s that the only way we did it was because we got off our backsides and did something, anything that we were capable of, then some more, *"every hour of every day."*

Keeping our eyes and ears open for opportunities that just seemed to be everywhere if we looked for them, we have always had the passion and desire to look for and seek out deals where there didn't appear to be any; we didn't know or realise that, at the time, we were on a journey of highs and lows, and everybody knows that a journey of 1,000 miles starts with one small step. That's where we all procrastinate so, very often, we will not make that first step until someone pushes us to do it.

*"Working for yourself is like leaping into a very cold swimming pool - you are all right once you have got in."*      Neville Wright

I think our country needs another one million more self-employed people to boost the economy. There is a type of person generally known as a self-employed entrepreneur; they can be a single, one-man band but, in some cases, in their minds they are acting and thinking like a large company and consequently, in many cases, naturally grow to be a big company.

These people often have the mind of a one-man band when it comes to customer service, being very reliable and efficient by putting themselves into the customer's shoes at all times. I remember that I had made that transition in my mind, and had also carried it through into the business as it just became natural, but I found the only way that I could make that transition scalable was to have compatible people around me. Without these people I couldn't have done any of what I did; it's a very hard transition and, without having those people around, most will fail.

Firstly, having Marilyn around encouraged me to want stability for her; secondly, we wanted to give our children a secure life. After that, everything fell into place with the people whom we attracted.

# To Have More Is Quite Easy

*"You can get everything in life that you want as long as you just help enough other people get what they want."* Zig Ziglar

So, just to summarise: for me to get more I had to motivate myself to do more and, when I did more, that motivated me even more to have more. Some words of caution:

*"Understand and know why you are doing it."*

One day recently when I was on a plane, I was working on my laptop and I had a fellow passenger start talking to me. She asked what I did for a living so, to keep it short, I said that at the moment I was writing a book on how we built a successful business; I shouldn't have told her that, as she said to me that so many businesses that had outlets in every shopping centre were exploiting children, making them do menial tasks for minimum wages. I said to her that that was building a more educated person for the realities of life.

I said that they should let their bosses educate them, for example, to clean toilets with pride and enthusiasm, and that she shouldn't be afraid to let their managers, co-workers and bosses teach and encourage her children, and she should too. I said that I had taught my children to do any job that was asked of them with pride, as long as it was not immoral or illegal.

I would have loved to have told her that my children are multi-millionaires in their own right through having this great attitude towards work, but I wouldn't because she would come up with some excuse as to why it's all right for some, but not for others. I now go Business Class on long-haul flights; 10 hours are too valuable if you are sat next to a negative person - actually 10 minutes are. Having said that, you can learn a great deal from negative people; they do help me with my exercising and keep-fit programme. I don't walk away from them any more, I run away from them as fast as possible.

# Where Am I? Where Do I Want To Be?

I said in the last chapter that, at the age of 12, chess changed the way I thought, from thinking that because I wasn't as clever as other people and, as the teachers said, I would not amount to anything, to thinking of different ways to get from where I was to where I wanted to be. I came to realise this by using the same principles as in chess, thinking that if I made this move, what the outcome would be and what the consequences would be. I learned quickly that I had to do more than I was doing.

## Speculate To Accumulate

When I was thirteen, my parents and I were staying with some relations who lived in Leominster. The man's name was Arthur Dye. I remember saying to him when I saw him drive up to his house in a brand-new Land Rover, "How can you afford a new Land Rover?" Maybe I had overheard my dad and mum talking - why else would I have said it? Arthur's reply to me was, "Neville, you have to **"speculate to accumulate".** I said nothing, apart from all the usual stuff like "wows" and "cors". I had never ever had the chance to sit in a new vehicle before. I made up my mind there and then that I wanted to speculate to accumulate just like Arthur, even though I hadn't got a clue what it meant. But I kept on thinking what this sentence meant. If only I could really understand what it meant.

SIDETRACKED

We paid £260 for the truck; the following week the engine blew up; this cost another £250!!

Marilyn had told me not to buy it, so now she could tell me what she had already told me the week before.

I loved that truck, and now I was a real builder, well, odd-job man!!

When the business started we used our car then, after a few days, we progressed to the car and Dad's trailer. Then the day came when I got the opportunity to buy an old VW milk delivery wagon from Horrell's Dairies where Ray, our next-door neighbour worked; it was a pick-up, great for the sort of work that we had started to do; we bought it for £260. It was a lot of money to us and, when the engine blew up and the cost was another £250, I knew what was going to happen. Marilyn had told me not to buy it; I was becoming good at selective hearing, but now I thought that I was a real builder.

When I said that most people are too frightened to become millionaires, I mean they think that they could lose what they have to the point that they won't give themselves a chance to start, although wanting to be successful. Investing what they have is not part of their thinking, as they are afraid of losing it or living below their standards.

The vast majority of millionaires look after their money; they respect it and nurture it to make it grow. They don't hoard it and haven't buried it; they use it to the good and, in doing so, attract even more. But getting over the first hurdles in business life to become substantially wealthy can be so easy, as the first step is in your mind.

From the age of thirteen my dream of having a new Land Rover didn't go away, nor did Arthur's words that were constantly in my head: ***"speculate to accumulate."*** Another goal was achieved.

# Empathy or Sympathy

## *"I know how you feel, but I'm not feeling the same"*

When I was employed, Marilyn was at home with Elaine. I just hated going to work, leaving them at home, but once at work I had sympathy with everyone for everything. Why not? I wanted friends, I wanted to be liked, I wanted to be the same as the person that I was being sympathetic to. I felt their feeling through and through; it cost nothing; well, that's what I thought at the time. Now I know it was costing me a great deal in wasted energy and emotion; it was bringing me down to their level of despair and destruction.

## Man Down, Carry On

Once I became responsible for my family I had to solve problems each day and sometimes not eat, so I had a paradigm shift. From then on I could understand how others felt, but I didn't feel their feelings. I could back away from the problem and offer a solution. I think now that the shift went too far; I became so hard that it looked like I had absolutely no feelings whatsoever but, deep down I did have lots of feelings. I was also proud that I could offer a solution, but my solutions came across as cold, hard, and not caring; **"Man down but don't stop; the customer comes first."**

When you are building any business like ours from scratch with absolutely no knowledge at all about employing people, with all their wants, needs, emotions and fears. It was very hard for me to understand why someone would just not turn up for work, or be off sick with a bruised leg after playing football, when they had a job sitting down at a desk, as I would still have to work even if I broke my leg. I didn't see or understand the difference between us.

I had empathy for people, but it certainly did not come out that way. If someone cut their finger on pieces of paper and was off work, my thoughts were, "How can they afford to do that?" I had sympathy for them, but what came out of my mouth was, "Why have you been off with that? My wife and both daughters worked up until the day they had their babies and were back to work the next day; you are off for nothing.", However, they were a minority of our staff.

Our personal assistant, Andrea Jarvis, would say to me, "Neville; if you think that everybody is going to be like you and your family, they would be doing what you are doing, so be grateful they're not, as you might not have a job." Oh Andrea, if only you knew what a calming influence you were on me; I dread to think what would have happened if you hadn't have been there for me.

## Everyone Was a Loser

It did make me a very hard person, and frustrated when those same people who had been off work said they hadn't got enough money. We all lost out - they never got enough money and I lost a worker and the money they should have earned for the company for the time they had off, and the customers never got the attention they deserved.

Luckily, when the retail baby business grew to well over seventy staff in 2006, we had our family, brilliant managers and core staff to look after that kind of thing for us.

The more successful we got, the more I realised that our dreams were coming true and all the things that we wanted were within our grasp. It was like a drug; I got so focused on the outcome, I forgot about everything else around me. I imagined that everyone around me was thinking the same but, of course, they weren't, something I still have a problem to accept. There are people who want more, but they don't do more and can't bring themselves to give more to receive more.

I was being driven by a hate of myself from my childhood, to prove to myself that I was not the idiot that people portrayed me as when I was at school. Also, I hadn't gone through all of those beatings just to be a taker in life; I wanted to be a giver, and that made me blinkered to things around me. Every day I would find myself repeating over and over in my mind:

***"I must do the most productive thing possible at every given moment."***

Things obviously get easier as time goes on; people who want to work with you stay with you, and others go for greener fields. That's life, and luckily in the UK at this time we are free to do what we want, but I predict things won't stay this way for the majority of people in the future.

# Don't Be a Mental Loafer, Neville

I told myself not to be a mental loafer, not even for one moment; so, when people came to work with us my thoughts were that, if they leave, they should go with more knowledge than they came with. Then I was happy, because they had taken notice and been of use to both the company and themselves but, if they left with no more knowledge than they came with, I blamed myself for not inspiring them enough to learn more.

Then, in 2010 Marilyn & I made a life-changing decision when we decided to sell our last Kiddicare retail baby nursery equipment business that Marilyn had started and nurtured for 35 years, along with the children and grandchildren, the business that we loved and all of the people that were involved with it. I found that the people around us who we had worked with for years had so much empathy for our situation. They were so kind and considerate towards our feelings; they felt our feelings as theirs, although they understood what was going on in our lives, to the extent that they could back away, giving a solution with so much warmth and kindness.

## *"Why hadn't I been like that?"*

Well, probably, as all business people who have built businesses from nothing to well over £40 million turnover and £30 million in assets by 2010, through probably the worst recession in modern history will know, it's been done by juggling balls and spinning plates for years and years, perfecting your craft to create the golden goose that produces those golden eggs every day, day in, day out. That's why I was so tough,, not only on others but mostly on myself.

Knowing how people feel, but not feeling the same, is a great way to solve other people's problems, which is great if that's what they want. It took me years to understand that a lot of people don't want solutions, they just want sympathy. Some want you to agree that they are right; the last thing they want is a solution to their problems - that would be a whole new ball game for them, forcing them to create another lot of excuses for why life has dealt them a bad hand. Which is why they have failed to be successful in their eyes but, from my perspective, not necessarily in anyone else's eyes.

# Management Responsibility

I think the responsibility of management is to provide a safe and secure job for their workers by helping them create a working environment and life of stress-free happiness, although it's seldom achieved in the ever-changing competitive world of today; but that must be the aim and, although our business seemed to change every day, it was always with the thought of these principles, striving to make a better place to work in. I can hear people saying, "What a load of old shit," but there you are, they didn't know everything that we were thinking in our hearts and heads.

Some of our lovely staff; this picture was taken around 2007. Many of these people helped me in 2010/11 in my darkest days, and I will always be so very grateful to them for the help and understanding that they showed.

*On the shop floor in 2007; another move and the inevitable changes*

I always wanted to understand people, why they did things that seemed to hurt themselves, especially when they were successfully going up the ladder. It taught me very early on to help others as you are going up because, with the unpredictable way of the world, you could just find yourself working under a person that you have disrespected in the past, and that wouldn't do, would it? I have found that there are some people who are motivated in life to help others, but some only to help themselves, and there are people who distrust everyone, even the person that they see in the mirror each morning. *(Sad)*

# A World of Our Own

## *"We thought that it was normal"*

It was 1968 and we had just bought our first house. Well, I say "bought" - we had agreed to buy and the sellers had agreed to sell. That was good enough for us, we were 17 and 18 at the time, and we were very naïve. The next day, we got into the house and started to take the wallpaper off the walls.

There was a knock on the front door. We couldn't open it as we didn't have the key; I got out of the back downstairs window thinking that I was in trouble. When I opened the side passage door, which was situated next to the front door, I was met by a rather large lady holding a tray with a teapot, cups, and biscuits. "My name is Sylv - I live two doors away. Welcome to the street."

Her husband Albert was a self-employed painter and decorator - what a stroke of luck. So, long before I went into business, I started working with him in between my shifts. He taught me the skills of painting and decorating. Albert used to tell me how to do jobs that I was unfamiliar with, which was most of the jobs.-sorry, all of the jobs; then I was able to teach Marilyn.

It took Marilyn and me from 1968 to 1970, together with the help from my father, to completely renovate our first house. My dad was a great help to us. Then, on 4$^{th}$ July 1970 we were married, and moved in. I started working with Albert most days after that; I was able to do this because at the time I worked on a 2000-acre land reclamation project. This was for the Electricity Generating Board. Situated on the outskirts of Peterborough, it was a project that filled in the London Brick Company clay pits with coal ash from power stations; the clay had all been excavated over the last one hundred years or so for brick-making. Once the pits were filled, which would take around twenty years, a new township would be built there and, in fact, our offices were built on the reclaimed land, together with five thousand houses.

I was on a shift pattern, which was great for me; I worked for 21 days straight off, doing a three-shift system - nights, mornings, and afternoons, then the next seven days off. Every day when I was working mornings or afternoons, I could work with Albert for about four hours a day. Then, when I worked seven nights, I could work with him all day; the reason was because we used to sleep for about

4 or 5 hours a night on that shift. I think that's where I got into the habit of working through the night.

Fortunately for me, there wasn't too much work to be done in the middle of the night on this reclamation project, but we had to be there for security and other essentials like water-level readings on the site, etc. On the night shift we clocked on at 10.00 pm; we then raced around doing the jobs that needed to be done. Like me, most of the staff had other part-time jobs to go to in the morning. It took around three hours to do the necessary work, and we were then able to sleep before the day started again.

It was a wonderful opportunity for me to be semi-self-employed, which probably contributed to giving me the bug to become self-employed later on. One man on my shift cleaned windows in his spare time. I asked him how he did it, and he showed me a piece of cloth, called scrim, that absorbed water then dried instantly, and the secret ingredient that he put in the water to clean the windows.

## My First Lesson in Leveraging Time

Looking back, it was probably the first time that I was using a method of leveraging, by which I mean creating more out of a situation, whether it be time or money; basically, a goal within a goal. Over the years, I continuously used money or time twice, three, or even four times; in other words, a goal within a goal, when you can utilise something twice or more. For example, I was sleeping and getting paid for it by the Electricity Board, then I was working for Albert and getting paid by him at the time when I should have been sleeping.

I would be completely free on the fourth week, so I could work with Albert every day; that meant I was working around 300 hours a month.

Without us buying that house we would never have met Albert, I would never have learned painting and decorating and probably would still be cleaning windows, although it wouldn't have mattered because we probably would have been running, by now, the biggest window-cleaning business in the UK. I just fancy cleaning The Shard; how exhilarating would that be?

## 72 St Martins Street, Millfield, Peterborough; it cost us £650 in 1968.

This picture was taken in 2014. It was our first house back in 1968, when we bought it for £650. It was part of a row of houses and the windows were in the right places then. I find it sad that people don't look at a building before destroying the character and, in my opinion, at the same time devaluing the property. There was nothing wrong with the sash windows that had been in there for a hundred years; although double-glazing and plastic have taken over, the originals were in the right places. Our first home, it holds such lovely memories.

SIDETRACKED

Fate takes us on a mystery tour in life; what's next? Every day was different; we took our luck as it came, and we also learned to fit ourselves to it; if we couldn't change it, we had to accept it, but there was not a lot that we accepted. I think our strategy at that time was "Fire". Oh yes, "Take aim" and then we would take stock of the situation. We had to think outside of the box and take advantage of whatever situation arose. It was so exciting, we were young, free in our minds, and very adventurous in the things we took on, with always "The answer is yes, now what's the question?" This carried on when we owned the nursery shops, doing all the things that defied convention.

BACK

When I was working on the reclamation project and some other places, I found that there would be some colleagues who would talk about management, saying things like:

**"You can't do enough for a bad boss, and you can never do too much for a good one."**

This one sentence can destroy trust between workers and employers. It destroys motivation and learning if you take notice of it. It can destroy your future success in life; it certainly affected me for a while - I am ashamed to say I listened to that crap. Sometimes, when you are young, it happens, but there is no excuse as you mature into your mid 20s, when your brain has become fully grown, allowing you to be responsible for your own actions without blaming others.

Obviously I didn't know that but, in the future I would be employing hundreds of people and, of course, I had done my time as an employee. So when I became an employer I had the knowledge of knowing what some employees (but sadly not all of them) were thinking, so I felt that I was able to understand things a bit better. I could put myself in their shoes and feel their feelings, whilst not necessarily agreeing with their thoughts. I could empathise with staff and, at the same time, explain how the system worked to accomplish the best results for everyone concerned. Most people understood and took it on board.

There were always the ones that didn't let the sound of my voice penetrate their eardrums. It takes about 27 hours for the sound of your voice to go around the world, which is approximately 24,900 miles. After the sound of my voice had travelled all that far for so long, it just hovered a centimetre or two away from some of the recipients' ears, and I found out that, unfortunately, it can take a lifetime for the sound to travel the next few centimetres into the ear and brain and, in some cases, it never does, even when it's in their own interest.

# It Was So Easy To Get a Job

Up to 1974 I had walked into jobs; it was so easy for me to get a job. Then the economy changed. People were wondering why they had not been offered jobs, and it was because all the jobs had disappeared.

The world had changed, a recession was upon us, and thank goodness I had met Albert when I did, some six years earlier. Albert taught me a trade that I could use but, at this time I did not have the confidence in myself to do it and, besides, my attitude was all over the place - ***"life is not fair."*** Not only that, I wanted a job, but at the same time I had disrespected the situation when I had one. This taught me, when I became self-employed, to be interested in learning new things, as you never know when you will need them and since then I have never stopped learning, every day, without fail. There is never a day goes by without learning something of interest; even negative things teach us.

Everybody wants to get the best out of their job. The worst thing in any job is boredom and, if you stay because it's easy, this will destroy you and your life. Whatever job I have had, I have tried to motivate myself to find something good in the job that I was doing, and then I might even like it. I say I tried, but it never worked.

Unfortunately, it never happened for me, as I was not in control of things. Apart from the job that I had on the pig farm when I first met Marilyn when I was 16 years old, I couldn't settle on anything before, and then after this. By 1974 I needed to have my back against the wall to motivate me, a situation that's followed me through life.

## Soul-Destroying

Between 1972 and 1974 I worked for the Ministry of Defence; we were waiting for the next war to start, and I thank my God it didn't. It was the most soul-destroying job that I could ever have had, as it was in a forgotten outpost, literally a massive hole in the ground, where the only contact we had with the outside world was on a Friday.

We would turn on a radio that had been there since the start of war in 1939 to hear someone say a one-liner, like "The dog barked three times today." Charlie, our boss, took it very seriously and wrote it on a postcard and sent it off to wherever but to me, in 1973, it seemed ridiculous doing this sort of thing; but this was the norm - even now there are companies that are still in 1973 mode.

Within a few days of getting the job I found I was mentally climbing the walls. I just couldn't sit there talking shit with the other staff all day long. I would have to exercise my mind and body; I would run every morning around the camp for about an hour, up and down the grass hills which contained tanks with millions of gallons of jet fuel in them.

Part of my job would be to take readings every day to see how much water had leaked into these old, rusty, million-gallon tanks, but even putting a tape measure down into a fuel tank was something that I was not allowed to do, because of Health and Safety; I might cause a spark and blow everyone up. But then I would go into the underground tunnels and release the water from the tanks; inevitably there would be some fuel escape which was to be disposed of.

I was allowed to take open buckets of fuel out of the tunnel because Charlie didn't want to do that; that's how H&S worked then. After some processing, the wasted fuel would go into employees' cars, something I avoided as I thought my engine would blow up if I was to put jet fuel in it; what would I do then? I hadn't got any money to fix it if it did blow up.

SIDETRACKED

Then, after the running, I would spend the next two hours in the locker room doing yoga, which I had practised from the age of thirteen. I said earlier that some teachers at my school were bad, but there were one or two that were working, or came to work at the school, that were really nice. The first day when a new teacher came, everybody was determined to piss him off, trying him and testing him to see what his limits were. This was normal when someone new started.

New teachers daring to come to our school were in for a challenge so, when he walked into a rowdy class, we expected him to start shouting at us, and then the fight could begin. But instead, he said, "Sit crossed-legged on top of your desks; we will see who is fit." Up to then, nobody had been allowed to sit on their desks; if you were to do that in any other teacher's class it would be instant punishment.

This was brilliant. He then proceeded to talk about yoga; I don't know what the subject was that we were supposed to be there for;

in fact I never knew what most of them were, as my best subject every day was my thought of leaving school as soon as possible, going to whatever job I had got going at the time. I not only had got a job after school, I always had several in the holidays.

That teacher never had a problem with us; he saw positive things in negative children, he inspired me to see the good in myself and be 1% better at everything that I did all of the time, and then he left. If only he could have stayed until I had left school; I needed positive role models because positive can soon turn into negative without getting inspiration from a teacher, mentor, or coach. 1% is an incredible amount; watch Formula 1 racing - one tenth of a second can be worth millions to the winner.

BACK

Albert was one of my role models. He had taught me and, in turn, I taught Marilyn. I found out that one of the secrets of success is to share your knowledge with other people. I have worked in so many places where staff, and even bosses, would not tell me their little secrets of how to get the job done more easily or quickly. They unfortunately were, in my eyes, insecure; I thought that if they told someone else, that would make their job easier for them, the company and, ultimately, the customer would benefit.

*Albert was a perfectionist when it came to painting and decorating. One day he taught me a lesson. I was keen to get finished, he let me put the ladders on the car, and I was all ready to go home. He said, "Let's just look at the job" and, to my amazement, I had missed painting the size of a fingernail in the corner of a stairwell. I had to unload the ladders, sheet down, and put it right, all for being lazy. I opened my eyes after that.*

**Albert and Sylvia at our wedding, 4$^{th}$ July 1970**

The diagonal stripe across the left-hand side contained the photograph number that we were supposed to order the pictures from. With having very little money, we just had the proof samples that were included in the price. As a boy I thought there was nothing wrong with that, but Marilyn felt sad that we couldn't afford proper photos.

I remember seeing her crying one day as she was looking at the pictures after visiting some friends who had bought the proper ones. I felt like shit because I was the breadwinner in the family, but we literally had no money, and, on top of that, Marilyn wanted stability and security in her life. I knew that getting into debt buying things that we could not afford was not on the agenda. I knew that if we spent our money as quickly as it came in, we would be poor and, if we saved and invested from the start we would be wealthy. These things all go to building determination; having said that, at that time we really didn't have a penny.

I thought that one day I could have a business with Albert, painting and decorating for customers and renovating houses for ourselves. But that wasn't going to happen, as he was happy staying the way he was, not getting any bigger or, as he said, not risking his money on property. Maybe he was afraid of change, or maybe he was dyslexic like me, or maybe he was content with his lot in life. As far as I knew he didn't have any children, so probably didn't have any motivation to leave a legacy. I will never know because I never asked him, which I regret, but would he have told me the truth? I don't know, or maybe he just hadn't thought about it, or didn't care.

Whatever business I have had, I have encouraged staff not to be afraid to show others how to do their job. It opens up opportunities for them to expand their own knowledge and, at the same time, become more valuable in the company, freeing them to take on more interesting roles doing things that they wouldn't normally have time to do if they had not shared their secrets. In doing so, they would open up opportunities for others who wouldn't normally have a chance or opportunities to explore new avenues, roles and areas of responsibility.

Now I'm not talking about giving away a secret scientific formula that belongs to the company, only a basic sharing and overlapping with the teaching of jobs to make it more interesting, productive, and inspiring for all who work there. I find it most infuriating as a customer when I can't get my needs dealt with because someone is on lunch, or is sick, or on holiday, when no-one else knows what to do, or can't make a decision. In our Kiddicare business we had staff that thrived on responsibility; they were making decisions themselves without any fuss or delay.

# One Thing Leads to Another

***1966 Terry, the champion cyclist; I am second from the right***

Without my brother Terry, in the middle holding the trophies for racing champion of the Peterborough Cycling Club in 1966, Marilyn would never have met me; I am second from the right. By the way, the lads in the club used to say that there was a chap in the club who was a shirt-lifter; I was 16 years old and I thought he worked in a shirt factory, loading lorries!

This picture was in the window of a newspaper in Peterborough city centre. One Saturday, Marilyn and some friends were in town shopping, and looked at the photos; one of them said, "I know that boy; his name is Neville, he was the one that Julia introduced to you last week." Marilyn obviously made a comment; so one of her friends said, "Let's go to his home so you can have a look at him." With that, they set off to see me so Marilyn could take a look!

At the time, my boss was Mr Mancer (a farmer). I was friends with his daughter, Julia. Each day I used to see her walking down the track after getting off the school bus. I made a point of finding a job nearby so we could talk; this got as far as holding hands until her mum spotted us and, in no uncertain terms, said I should find a job, not stand about talking. Maybe she meant find a job somewhere else.

Having said that, sometimes we used to see each other in Peterborough on a Saturday afternoon when she was in town with lots of her friends. One of her friends had another friend called

Marilyn. Julia introduced me to her; it was at the same time as pop stars Paul and Barry Ryan were just going into the Embassy Theatre to perform, so I asked this girl Marilyn, that I had only met one minute ago, if she wanted to go to the show. She said no, as she had to get home. That was good, as I never had the money for the tickets anyway, so I would have had to think quickly if she had said yes.

With nothing coming of that, I never thought anything of it. Even the next week, when she saw the photo in the window, and then she sat there in my mum's lounge with the other three girls, her head down, her long, black hair covering most of her face, saying nothing. I remember thinking that she was gorgeous but, as she wasn't talking to me, she obviously wasn't interested. I didn't know they had seen the picture and they had brought her to look at me.

It wasn't until the next weekend, when I was outside the home of her friend, Claire D'Arcy (14), chatting to her, and Claire said, "I can't see you any more; my mother says you should be with boys, of your own age (16), not girls." Then she said, "But Marilyn likes you." I said, "Who's Marilyn?" She said, "The girl we were with at your house - she wanted to see you - and the same girl you met outside the Embassy."

With that, I asked Claire where Marilyn lived. The second she told me I was off, leaving Claire's house and going straight to Marilyn's. I'm glad to say she approved. I am writing this at 2 am on 4th July 2014; it is our 44th wedding anniversary, forty-eight years after we first met, all thanks to Julia, Claire, and especially Terry - without your effort to win that trophy I wouldn't have been with Marilyn all of these years.

## Mad, Foolish or Dreamers?

Were we mad, foolish, or just two more dreamers? Actually, I think we were all of those things; mad, because we had never had any experience of business whatsoever; foolish, because we had no money at all, nothing that we could lay our hands on and, yes, we were definitely two of the world's greatest dreamers.

## Just Don't Give Up

By 1974 our dreams of becoming wealthy overnight just disappeared and realistic dreams took their place, thinking of what we wanted to have, to be, and do, in ten, twenty, thirty, or even fifty years' time. This took us into a different place as far as our minds were concerned; we couldn't get upset if things went wrong, because instant, short-term success had gone from our minds.

It was all about long-term goals, so setbacks didn't upset us any more; in fact they gave us a boost, propelling us to the next level. We actually thrived on them, whereas we saw others give up along the way after only one failure and, after seeing others fail, we never saw ours as failures; we saw them as just another way not to do things. Imagine if inventors gave up on their first attempt - we would still be in mud huts with no electricity, not too dissimilar to the caravan we lived in at the same time as we went into self-employment.

Unfortunately, I didn't have any certificates for painting and decorating, so I thought no one would give me any work. Looking back, I think that it was not a certificate that I needed, it was just confidence. I also didn't have many tools or the equipment necessary for that type of work plus, of course, not forgetting, I had no money to buy them, and no chance of borrowing any more money. On top of all that, I was a 'dyslexic'. By that time I hadn't told anybody about this, not even Marilyn, because I didn't realise there was a name for the problem. I have just asked Marilyn when was it  she had first realised that there was a problem with me; she said,

**"It was right from the start; I always knew there was something wrong with you."** Thanks, Marilyn.

I've had so many jobs and learned such a lot, but I always managed to get out of any paperwork; I always made sure that I was doing practical things that others didn't want to do. This was so my bosses used me for those things instead of paperwork. If I knew I had to do any paperwork in front of anybody, I would just leave that job instead of suffering the embarrassment if ever my problem was found out.

# A Pig Farm Is All We Ever Wanted

Although I found things that I liked doing in the majority of the jobs that I had, the one job that I had when I met Marilyn in 1966 was the one that I loved the most of all; it was working on a pig farm. I remember when Marilyn's grandma found out that I was a pig man, she told Marilyn's dad to stop us seeing each other because I would have been watching the pigs, and I would have got some ideas from them; REALLY!! I was 16 years old; I would have had sex on the brain 24/7 whatever job I was doing.

Marilyn and I decided that we wanted to have a farm of our own. Unfortunately, there was no way we could get enough money together when suitable properties came along, as the average price was around £7,000 for a pig farm, and to get a Council farm was impossible as they were reserved for farmers' children.

When I left school I worked on a chicken farm that had a few pigs. A friend, Richard Corfield, who was also a pig man who lived across the road from us with his mum and dad, above his dad's garage, had just got a new job working for Norman Mancer in Crowland, Lincolnshire. He asked me if I wanted to work with him, which I did.

There were about twelve sows and seventy offspring; over the next two years this went up to sixty sows and five hundred offspring. Richard got another job and I was now the manager at seventeen; this was great, as this was my life. Marilyn and I were going to get married and we were hoping to live on the farm so I could be available at all times for the pigs. We thought that maybe we could get a caravan to live in, and then Mr Mancer would see what a great asset I was to his business and he would then build us a house on the farm. ***Funny what you think sometimes.***

I was going away on holiday with Marilyn and her parents to the Isle of Wight, so I wrote instructions ready for Mr Mancer's son, Phillip. This took what seemed to me like hours to do, listing jobs, and what food the pigs needed each day. He was a couple of years older than me. I really looked up to him; he was a role model for me. Not only was he well-educated, he was really good-looking, taking after his dad, and had the features that any guy of my age would have liked to have had. He and his friend, who went to agricultural college at that time, were off for their summer break, and they were going to look after the pigs for me.

The day I got back from our holiday, they were both looking at my instructions, laughing; then they asked me who "Mac Shaw" was. I thought that I had written "make sure"; then I had put the quantity of food that each lot of pigs needed. My spelling was wrong. Here I was, the manager; I wanted to be looked up to for doing a good job. This took me back to my school days, that feeling of humiliation.

I had been found out, and now I felt like running away, although I stayed because I loved that job. I felt, with what they had said to me, that I was a complete failure. I now know they didn't mean any harm; most people would have thought nothing of it, after all, they just saw it as a joke, which it was, but then with my insecurity I saw it as a putdown and, if I couldn't spell, then I was no good at being a manager.

The pig business was increasing so much that it was impossible to house all of the pigs in a conventional manner, so Mr Mancer made compounds out of straw bales, which held sixty pigs in each, but without any wire fencing around them to keep the bales secure **(hindsight)**. Pigs being inquisitive animals, some escaped one Sunday afternoon; they got into the boss's garden, and guess who got the blame? Me. Mr Mancer telephoned my dad to ask him to come to the farm for a meeting, what for I don't know; probably it was to get my dad to tell me off.

## My Dad Instantly Changed

I remember he came to the farm at 4.00 pm on the Tuesday after arranging to have some time off work, which did not please him; I was cleaning out some pigsties at the time. Dad told me to come with him. At the door Mr Mancer said, "Neville doesn't need to be in the meeting." My dad said, "Oh yes he does." I thought, "Shit, I am going to get a bollocking from both of them now," as, up to this point in my life, I had always been wrong as far as my dad was concerned.

We sat in Mr Mancer's study. I was very quiet, expecting a wallop at best from my dad but, before Mr Mancer got out many words about how I had let him down by not doing the job properly my dad told him, in no uncertain terms, what a bad employer he was. You see, my dad worked in the electricity industry, where the unions were involved, the health and safety rules were paramount, and all of the other facilities were excellent.

If you worked on a farm in 1966, the toilet was in the nearest dyke. You hoped you would never need to go as in the summer you were likely to have got stung with stinging nettles, and in the winter you would get wet by falling in the water as the banks of any dyke are not made for people wanting to have a poo. Dad said that he should be ashamed of the non-existent facilities, but it didn't bother me; I loved being there but, at the same time, I was so proud that my dad was now sticking up for me, saying that I was a credit to Mr Mancer's business, and that he didn't deserve to have me working there.

# I Left the Job That I Loved

The next day I handed in my notice. Mr Mancer told me that he had never been spoken to in that way ever before in his life, as my father had spoken to him. He then said that because I had given my notice in, he would not be paying me the bonus for the year, as I had only done eleven months of it. The bonus was 6 pence a pig on the quantity of pigs going to market; up to that month we had sent 220 to market. I had worked my socks off for that £11.00, but I wasn't going to let that affect me. I carried on that week as though nothing had happened.

At 4.30 pm on the Friday I attended to the latest litter of fifteen piglets, clipping their razor-sharp teeth and then giving them 1cc of oramycin orally and 2cc of iron that was injected into the muscle. That done, I then went home on time, probably for the first time ever since I had started working there.

I was on my motor scooter; I stopped at the end of the farmyard, turned around and spat on the floor in defiance, just like in the cowboy films, like saying, "Sod you," but I felt stupid doing that because I didn't want to leave. I was thinking, "Who would look after the pigs now?" That worried me, as no one had bothered to work with me to see at what stage everything was being left. I have to admit, I had tears in my eyes going down that track for the last time. Well, I did go back a few years later when passing with my mum and dad in one of our Bentleys, to find there were no pigs any more.

I think that if that incident had not come about I would still be there today. And by now, Mr Mancer and I would probably have the biggest pig farm in the UK. Well, that would have been my dream, and I have no doubt that we would have made him a fortune.

## Someone is always there for you

That evening around 7.00 pm there was a knock on the door; it was Richard's dad from across the road. He owned the garage there. He was a friend of Mr Mancer's and said to Dad that he had heard that I had "left" and would I like to work for him, which I did the very next day. I was there for six weeks as a grease monkey. I hated every minute of it as, when I served petrol I couldn't write properly on the till receipt what the customer had had; once again it brought it home to me that I needed to be working for myself.

Every week, when Mr Corfield was doing the accounts he would come into the garage shouting at all of the lads who worked there about writing clearly so he knew what we had sold. He knew it was me, not them; he should have just sacked me. Anyway, I applied for a job at the Co-op bakery and, when the manager found out that I had worked for Mr Corfield and Mr Mancer, he rang them as he was in the same motor club as them. There was obviously something they liked about me because he gave me the job there and then; or maybe he was just desperate for staff.

In every job I learned something; I had learned that a grease monkey got all of the dirty jobs, and I hated oil on my hands. And when I complained they just said that it had to be better than pig shit, which I disagreed with. The other thing I had learned in that first week in the garage and, in fact, every week: when the lads were talking they would come out with a phrase, "The Eagle shits on Friday."

I hadn't got a clue what they were on about, until Friday lunchtime when all the lads were sitting on the bench telling me to look out for the Eagle, as it only has a shit on a Friday; then Mr Corfield walked in with our pay packets. I could have never seen myself staying there talking bollocks all day; I thought there must be something better in life, but I needed to find it.

## We Wanted Our Own Safe World

SIDETRACKED

Even after leaving and going to the Co-op bakery, I was still looking for a pig farm for ourselves and, in 1969, we found a derelict property with two acres of land worth no more than £800; well, it was 1969. It had some old pigsties on the land that needed rebuilding; we could put chickens and pigs in the house as it was too far gone to live in; we would live in a caravan. It went to auction and, in the weeks leading up to it, we had taken all of our friends and relatives around to look at where we were going to live.

At the auction the bidding started; never being at an auction before, I was in there bidding. It started at £250 and went up by £50 a time; up and up it went until it got to our limit, which was £1,100.

Everyone that I had been bidding against was out, so I thought that was it, I had got it; I had bid nine times, of course it was mine, I deserved it. Oh shit, a new bidder came forward just as the auctioneer said what they say: "For the first time, for the second, for the third and final time, all done." The hammer was just ready to fall; "£1,150," someone shouted. It was a man who had just walked in.

All eyes were on me; fcuk! We had no more money; in fact we didn't have the £1,100 we had just bid, and we thought that if we got the farm we would sell off our half-renovated house in town - we thought it was worth the £1,100. I looked round in desperation, my face obviously telling a story. Marilyn's dad said, "I will lend you £200." The auctioneer could see that I was struggling. "I'll take £25," he said. I think that he felt sorry for me, a nineteen-year-old kid desperate to get this property; he knew I had been to see the property about 20 times in the last 6 weeks.

Unbeknown to me, the man that was bidding against me at the back of the room was one of the biggest farmers around there, and the auctioneer knew that he had only seen the property at 6 pm that night.

I bid £1,175; £1,200 immediately came from the back. Then I bid £1,225; "£1,300," the man shouted. I was out of money again. My dad tapped me on the shoulder. The room was packed like sardines. The auctioneer was saying, "I have £1,300, I will take £25." My dad whispered, "I will give you £100."

I knew he really hadn't got it to give; I knew he would have to borrow it. How could he put himself into debt over me, after all the grief I had caused him? I bid £1,325; "£1,400," the man said. My brother then said, "Nev, I've got £50 you can have." £1,425 I bid, then £1,500 rang in my ears; that was it - I had nothing left. The hammer went down. The tears are in my eyes now as I write this, just as they were in that auction room all those years ago, and all that we both wanted was to create our own safe world where we could look after ourselves.

That was a sad day, as we all lost the property called Fern Villa, in Guntons Road, Newborough. A month later, I heard that the man who bought it had fallen off a tanker lorry in his yard and died. How sad is that?

## Stuck With Nowhere to Turn

BACK

When I got the sack in June 1974 I tried to sell our house or get another, bigger mortgage. We couldn't raise any money as the recession was in full swing, and we certainly could not sell the house in the state it was in at any price; we were in negative equity. We constantly talked about starting a business; any and every business idea went through our heads. We would talk ourselves into, and then we would talk ourselves out of, every idea that we had; hairdressing was one idea, as Marilyn had been a hairdresser.

Maybe she had been a hairdresser, but that was never going to be for me because I thought in the 70s that you were classed as gay if you were a man that did hairdressing; well not me, matey. Ironically, a year later when we opened a shop selling baby stuff, customers would say to me when I worked there on a Saturday, "What's a boy doing working in a baby shop? It's a girl's job; are you a girl?" In the 70s people still thought that men did men's jobs, and women did women's jobs. It made me think that I should have been a hairdresser, and then I wouldn't have got those sorts of comments every week. Marilyn experienced the same problems when she started to work on the building sites.

Questions went through our heads. What if we failed? Would our parents be ashamed of us? What if we didn't earn enough? Would we be able to afford a holiday? A hundred problems and two hundred excuses ran through our brains constantly. At the end of the day I had got the sack and couldn't get a job so, in the end, I opted for window-cleaning, the advantage being we needed no money to start.

I borrowed my father's wooden ladder, Marilyn gave me a bucket that she had in the house and we bought a piece of scrim - a piece of absorbent cloth - for 37p. It is an essential piece of equipment for window-cleaning. Just to put the money situation into perspective the scrim cost 37p.

In those days the seller would cut a length of it from a roll, and leave a frayed edge. If I had used it as it was, it wouldn't have lasted very long. Marilyn put a hem on the cloth with her sewing machine; this type of thinking has saved us thousands of pounds over the years. Just a word of caution; it works only as long as you're not spending more on doing these things than you are saving, as this can get a hold of you. Now, the scrim is probably in a pound shop already hemmed.

I thought that, with this kind of work, if I made a mistake the customer would immediately tell me and it wouldn't cost any money, only a few minutes of my time to put it right. But to be quite honest, I didn't envisage any mistakes cleaning windows. I do think now that, if I did make any mistakes, it was the fact that I not only cleaned the glass, I also cleaned their dirty window-frames, which on some houses hadn't been cleaned for twenty years.

My thoughts were to do more than I was paid to do, and that obviously worked. Looking back now, I see there was a business opportunity cleaning paintwork, as a lot of my customers said to me, "Now you've cleaned the frames, it looks as though I've had the house painted." Pity, I should have capitalised on that as another job. I am sure if someone wanted to start a business now without any money, or didn't have any education, they could revitalise windows and doors.

By the time we could afford a pig farm we didn't want one any more. Our hearts' desires were to work together, and we realised it didn't matter what we did; although I loved working with pigs, the downside was that every day I would be committed to looking after the animals and, by that time, our lives were changing.

## *"If you can't find a job, create one."*
Neville Wright

As we went along, always having our backs against the wall, following our hearts' desires to build a business together that would not only survive but also grow, along the way we would see people who made failure a crutch for the rest of their lives. This taught us to carry on and expect that, if you do the same things tomorrow as you have done today, the same results will happen. So we learned by our triumphs as well as our failures. Flexibility is one of the main keys to success; be like a tree, learn how to bend in the wind and, at the same time, be tough on yourself.

# Wrightway Decorating

## "And Property Maintenance"

As my confidence grew I began to promote my decorating skills to my now established customers, so, within three months of starting my business, I was now taking on jobs worth hundreds of pounds instead of the 30p for cleaning windows.

As soon as Elaine went to Auntie Pearl's child-minding, Marilyn was able to work with me, something we had always wanted to do since meeting each other in 1966.

Now she had joined me we thought we had better give the business a name, so we decided on Wrightway Decorating and Property Maintenance. We thought that the right name was essential for us; it had to say who we were, and what we actually did in a very few words, without confusion.

We had two magnetic signs made to go onto the car doors. If we exceeded 30 miles an hour the bloody things would fly off. We would have to stop the car and go and retrieve them. This only lasted for so long as, when I got home one day I found one had come off without me noticing - it had flown away, never to be seen again.

After that I just put the one sign on the car when we arrived outside customers' houses, but really, at the end of the day we didn't need signs, we were getting our jobs from recommendation, and we knew who we were dealing with. This was better for us at that time, as having a connection was more of a guarantee of getting paid for our work.

## The Weather Was Our Boss

Every day was new and exciting; I always wondered what it would bring. As soon as I had opened my eyes I was up at the window looking to see what the weather was like. The weather was crucial to deciding what I would do that day, the weather was our boss; 40 years later the ritual is still the same.

It taught us so much in running a business; I learned a great deal about time and motion, and making sure that we always had work that was conducive to the weather conditions. It meant juggling inside and outside jobs at the same time; however, our priority was always the customer. One thing that was on our minds constantly was to eventually have enough of our own work so that we did not have to rely on other people's work schedules, or the weather, to make a living.

## Peterborough's First Girl Builder

We established the business in the Peterborough area through friends and family. When we were doing jobs it would be a matter of course that the customer would recommend us to someone they knew, their next-door neighbour, a relative, or a friend. Advertising was too expensive for us but, with the standard of work and attention to detail, plus our attitude towards the customer, it was not needed; that is, until we took on people to help, and then we decided to advertise.

Ray, our next-door neighbour, a milkman, would put homemade leaflets through his customers' doors for us. Of course the inevitable happened, some people did not pay. I thought that there had to be a better business model than this, and hopefully one day I would find out the secret.

The first large job that I got was from Marilyn's mum and dad. Marilyn's mum had been working as a hairdresser for years for someone who decided to close their salon; she needed an extension building onto their house so she could carry on working as a hairdresser from home; the cost of this job was £1,000.

Another large job was from my mum and dad. They had gone on holiday to see my sister, who lives in Switzerland. It was in the winter; their water pipe burst and flooded their house. This job cost, £1,600. I wasn't very sharp here; I should have got Dad to get a quote from an established builder and then charged the same.

I ended up doing this job as cheaply as I possibly could for Dad, and hadn't taken into account that it was for the insurance company who, in turn, employed a loss adjuster who then screwed Dad on the prices for his possessions, even though they knew that I had saved them money on the building work; they had also saved on rent for accommodation that I had provided free for Mum & Dad. It was the first time that I realised how big companies had processes that did not interact with each other, and didn't give a toss about the customer.

Luckily, for the last 20 years we have had a good friend, Neil Towns, who has taken care of all our insurances for us. It's very rare to find someone like Neil; he is on the same wavelength as me. I have always believed that my customers, in whichever business we have had, could give me a blank cheque and leave it to me to fill it in. I felt that I could do that with Neil from the first time that I met him.

**Neil and Dawn, Marilyn and me in the beautiful Maldives 2014**

## What Should We Do?

SIDETRACKED

Mum and Dad had been away for three weeks and Terry, my brother, and I had said that we would look after the house. It had been very cold, freezing in fact; we weren't too bothered because Dad had said he had turned off the cold water into the house but, like so many stop-taps, it was under the sink out of the way, and it was old.

Unfortunately Dad did not turn it off. He did not leave the heating on either, because he wanted to save money; consequently, the whole house was flooded. When we went inside the house the ceilings were coming down; the water had destroyed virtually everything.

We should have left it and let the insurers and Dad sort it out, but we panicked and thought we could salvage things; we couldn't. All we succeeded in doing was to throw everything into a heap in the garden; carpets, furniture, most of the personal stuff like pictures and photos; books, etc., all had been soaked.

Years later it dawned on me, when I was able to put myself into other people's shoes, how they must have felt when they came home. We thought we were doing the right thing. We should have left it to Mum and Dad to see what had happened; then they could have made the decision about what things to throw away, as they were so personal to them.

BACK

Mum and Dad came to stay with us for a few days and ended up staying for six weeks while we renovated their house. I loved having them stay with us; Dad used to come with me to work and, in the evenings, they looked after Elaine while Marilyn and I went out working.

I didn't want them to leave once their house was finished; I wanted us all to live together but in a bigger place. Years later, in the late 90s when Elaine and Scott stayed with us for a while when they were having their house renovated, the same thing happened, as I just loved cooking for a family and just wanted them to be around. And once again, in 2008-2010, when Joanne and Andrew lived with us, we got used to it, as all of these times made us very happy.

## Seize Opportunities

Pete, my posh mate (I say that because he was the only person I knew at that time in the 70s who talked with what I thought was a really nice accent) dressed smartly for work, whereas I wore overalls and, to be honest I just wanted so much to be like him. He worked for an estate agency called Norman Wright and Hodgkinson. This was where we bought our first house; they had a branch in Millfield, an area in Peterborough. Pete worked as the Manager.

I used to call in most weeks when I was window-cleaning along Lincoln Road. I would get so excited approaching the estate agency; I couldn't wait to see what new properties they had on the market. I would be cleaning the estate agency windows as fast as I could, as normal, but at the same time trying to take notice of what new properties were in the window that week. They were the only windows I have looked into as a window-cleaner, as I made a point of never looking through people's windows when cleaning, only looking at them to make sure they were clean. That was after seeing a man in bed having sex ... with himself!

PRUDENTIAL
Property Services

Incorporating Edward Bailey & Son

**P Haycox**
FNAEA
Branch Manager

Tel 0636 703141
25 Stodman Street
Newark
Notts NG24 1AR

One day when I went into the estate agents, Peter was looking at some quotes for a new window for one of the tenanted properties he was looking after. He said to me, "Do you do stuff like this, Nev?" I said, "Of course I do," full of confidence, and with the thought that it couldn't be that hard to do, and besides, my dad was a carpenter and he would help by telling me how to do it if I got stuck.

With that, Peter gave me the address. I looked at the job and gave him a quote of £52, which I think, by the look on his face, was a lot cheaper than the ones he had got. I did that job for him; it was the first of many. He obviously had more faith in me than I did in myself. I will always be grateful to Peter for giving me that opportunity and all of the work that followed; it just shows you how one 30p job can turn into thousands of pounds.

I used this as an advertising tool by telling people that I did work for Peter Haycox, the branch manager of Norman Wright & Hodgkinson. Everybody in the town knew it was a prestigious estate agency; it was a big deal for me, it was the best advertising I could have. Pete gave me an opportunity and I seized it.

# Peterborough's Culture Was Changing

As time went on we bought lots of houses from Pete and did lots of deals involving house swaps. One was a couple who owned a corner shop; they had been held up at gunpoint, and wanted to leave the shop as it had put them off being shopkeepers. They wanted a detached house in a nice location; we had just bought one from Pete to break a chain so six people could move.

We told them where it was. The man said to me, "I'm not going there, that area is full of Pakistani people. I want an area that is white." I thought, "That's funny, because you're a Pakistani yourself," but I was wrong - he was an Indian. To be quite honest, in those days geography and race never entered my head. In Peterborough in the 50s, I understand, there were a few Italians who once were prisoners of war and who stayed on to live there.

The 60s brought the West Indians then, in the 70s, came the Ugandans and Chinese. After that, it seemed to be a free-for-all. I think Peterborough has around one hundred different nationalities, all making for an interesting, diverse culture and economy. Anyway, three months later the man came back to us and did the deal; they moved into the house and, thirty years later, we still have their shop.

***Pete, Harriet, Marilyn and me after a long lunch 40 years on.***

We lost contact with Pete when he left Peterborough to work in Newark, about 40 miles away. We just exchanged Christmas cards as you do but, with everybody being so busy with their everyday lives, connections fade. Years later we got a phone call from him; he said he had come back to the area, and our friendship resumed.

He is still connected with the property scene, relocating people who are moving with their work, but he doesn't sell houses any more and, if he did, he wouldn't have any £650 houses to sell as in 1968. That's how much our first house cost us, and people ask me all of the time if property investment is a good bet; well, in this case it was, but it does depend on many factors so there's not a blanket answer to that question.

## Stop Right Now, Look Back, Look Forward

If our first house had just been our home it would now, 45 years on, be worth £150,000. If it had been an investment property, after renovation we could have let it out for £16 a month, giving us a return of 20%; and now the rent would be £450 a month, returning the initial £1,000, including renovation, every 62 days. On top of this, we could have mortgaged it and invested that money in other properties, with the rents paying the mortgages.

But we didn't do that, as we needed the money to buy the next house and home, or rather investment, as at that time I did not earn enough money to get a mortgage, so buying and selling was the answer for a start. Throughout those forty years, that £650 turned over into other properties and has increased to ... get ready for it ... £16 million!!! That is what compounding does for you if you work the assets. I will explain more about that later.

Another person who came into our lives was Ray; around 1975 he arrived in Peterborough and became my next-door neighbour. Ray came with Karen, his wife, 5 children and his mum and dad, and then quickly had his 6th child. He got a job as a milkman.

## Opportunities Are All Around

Ray soon joined us part time. He was a Londoner, and had moved because his landlord had given him money for a deposit on a new house. Forty years later, landlords in London are still doing that because the houses in some areas are worth so much more without a tenant in them. Ray would finish his milk round at 8 o'clock in the morning and work with me for the rest of the day; you could only describe him as a grafter - he worked continuously. I could get on and do any job more quickly, because he would be running round getting whatever I needed to do the job and clearing up; he was a great asset.

*In the 80s: Karen, me, Ray's mum, Ray and some of their children.*

Later on he worked full time in the shops with us. He had got the gift of the gab, and the customers loved him. He had got six children, so it would be easy for him to transfer his feelings to the customer. He taught me not to expect everyone to know everything, but to understand that everybody is great at something. We employed hundreds of people like Ray over the time, and I certainly know that everybody played a part in developing the business.

We recognised every resource there was available around us, and then didn't let opportunities go to waste. We respected all of the people that gave their time and energy to us. Ray was one of the original team, along with our fathers, who together made a really great team; sadly, Ray had a heart attack and died in December 2003.

# My Dad, My Hero

## *"He taught me to have pride in everything that I did"*

Within a few months of us starting our business my dad, Arthur, took early retirement from his job. He divided his time working with both my brother Terry and me; without him working alongside us and teaching us, we would never have got so far, so quickly.

If only my dad and mum could be here now to reap the rewards that they deserve; there's not a day goes by that I don't think about them. They would have loved seeing the success of the business, and how their grandchildren have developed into parents now. Mum and Dad both helped us enormously, Dad renovating houses with us, either for ourselves or for customers, and Mum doing work in the evenings for the shop. They both looked after Elaine at the drop of a hat when we had to work in the evenings, and always on a Saturday; then, when we had closed the shop and were ready to collect Elaine, Dad would always have a meal ready for us.

# My Brother Started Business at the Same Time as Us

SIDETRACKED

Terry had a cycle shop business called *Terry Wrights Cycles* which incredibly, unbeknown to either of us, he had started on 1$^{st}$ October 1974, the same week we started ours.

My father had quite a few passions in life. One was to bring his children up with respect for other people; he would tell us that all the time so we knew not to forget it, and he was extremely strict with us but loving at the same time. As I didn't know any different, it became normal.

How I survived some of his beatings I will never know. My poor mum would be screaming at him to stop hitting me before he killed me. It took me so long to comprehend and, to some extent, understand what state his mind was in to do that to me. I suppose your mind changes when you have been fighting in the Burmese jungle, in a kill-or-be-killed situation for so long; maybe he was teaching me how to survive, but I do think that I obviously pressed the wrong buttons with him.

Another passion was cycling; he was the Penny Farthing Champion of Great Britain and went from Land's End to John O'Groats on a vintage tandem with his mate, Tom Young, aged 72, and Dad at the age of 66. They were raising money for *Help the Aged*. He knew exactly what he was doing when he helped Terry in his cycle shops.

Dad would have done well if he had owned his own cycle shop. He could talk to people with passion about cycling, as he was a cyclist right from a boy up until he was well into his 80s. Selling is just transference of feeling about a product; a potential customer who is in two minds about whether to buy a product or not will make up their mind based on not only what you say, but how enthusiastic you are when you say it.

## "If I had a problem he would know what to do"

BACK

Another of Dad's passions was building. He'd been in the building trade all of his life; he had trained to be a cabinet-maker and French-polisher. I can't tell you enough about how much he helped me in those critical months after starting our business; working with him was incredible, each of us knowing what the other one was doing and thinking; it made the job so much easier and faster - we literally worked as one.

# He Never Talked About the Atrocities

He had survived for six years in the war, most of which was in the Burmese jungle. He had been fighting the Japanese, so to me he wasn't afraid of anything, mentally or physically, with probably only one exception - going into business for himself. You see, he was dyslexic like me. However, Dad was a very practical person.

If he had gone into business, he would have had to get someone to do the bookwork. Mum said that she did not want to do the bookwork and accounts; it would have been totally alien to her to do that as she would have been too concerned about what other people thought. And, to be fair, she had not even remotely come from a business background and, in the 1930s, there were so many uncertainties in life, so I think she erred on the safe side.

Looking back now, Dad could have gone into business. He had an accountant living next door and his brother was a very skilled engineer who wanted to work with Dad manufacturing caravans, something that Dad had done for himself. He built a caravan so we could have holidays; we would stay in the caravan at Mablethorpe, Lincolnshire all through the summers, from the mid 50s and 60s.

Dad's brother was a different character from Dad. He never went to war, managing to live the high life and, although I think they could have made a good business being two different characters, Dad was having none of it. Dad did not see eye to eye with his brother, as he would have spent all of the money, yet Dad was the opposite way. They would have needed someone in the middle to balance things up. Dad got a letter from his sister which read: "I hope you are having a lovely time in India. Your brother and his wife have just won a dancing competition dancing to Victor Sylvester's band." It was monsoon season and Dad was entrenched under gunfire. He never got over the feeling of unfairness that he felt. Although Dad chose security for himself and our family, he always regretted not going into business after the war. If he hadn't had a job to go to, I think he would have looked after himself and we would have had a family business. Terry and I would probably be manufacturing caravans now, which I would have loved to have done, working together with him.

The fact is that once you are in a job it is very hard to leave and risk everything, especially when you have three children to bring up. Dad was dyslexic; that can push you in many directions, like getting the job in which you can hide your dyslexia; but, most of the time, you get found out and you move on. That's what happened to me several times.

Eventually people end up being forced to become self-employed, as you can't keep under the radar indefinitely. Dad worked himself up to be a chargehand; nowadays it's called a facilities manager. There was very little writing to do in those days, and he kept under the radar because they had inkwells and pens that spilled ink, which my Dad said was very convenient - if he could not spell a word, he would just shake out a blob of ink onto the paper over the misspelled word.

Another way not to get found out, if you were dyslexic in the 70s, was to become a bad boy; but again, you knew that eventually you were going to get caught, and then the consequences were even worse. I think meeting Marilyn when I did saved me from going in the wrong direction. I will re-phrase that; I know that I would have gone the wrong direction in life. Nowadays there is a program called *Dragon Dictation* that corrects your spelling mistakes. I just have to speak into a microphone and, hey presto, out comes the words on the screen. Without *Dragon* I would not be writing this book.

I learned from Dad not to whinge or whine and just get on with it (**just do it**). This was in the 50s and 60s; then, in 1988, I heard it again. Nike had its campaign, "Just Do It" which, in 10 years sent their turnover up from $877 million to $9.2billion. **"Did they hear my dad"?** If I complained about time dragging, Dad used to say it to me.

Another thing he would say was, "Do the job slowly until you can do it right, then speed will come. And don't worry about the money; it will come along as a by-product of doing the job right."

When he was en route in the war, the lorry that he was in broke down. He was left behind, as the convoy had to keep going because they needed to get onto a ship. That ship he should have been on was torpedoed, and hundreds of men were drowned. Many times, through fate, Dad survived, and I believe surviving everyday occurrences like this made him a very hard person.

I usually ended up in the wrong place at the wrong time, which taught my brain to think quickly and duck. I also remember the days my poor mum was putting her head into the gas oven to kill herself when things got too much for her. I would be screaming, "No, don't Mum, I love you," as I tried to pull her out. The gas was deadly in those days.

*My dad and my lovely mum in the 1930s*

## *"The only way to kill time, is to work it to death"*

Arthur Wright

*Carol, me and Terry at Mablethorpe, where we spent all of the summer holidays in Dad's home-made caravan. 1958.*

Dad got back home from the war and returned to the power station, and stayed there until retirement at 61. Over the years I could tell he had a yearning to do things for himself; he wanted to look after his family. The war had taken something from him; he used to use the words "I should have" a lot, which taught me not to say that.

## Born in the 50s

To be born in the 50s and brought up through the 60s was such a magical time for most children, if you were to put the over-use of corporal punishment to one side. There was an air of Great Britain; we had won the war, people felt free and the youths in their teens thought they were changing social history, mostly because of the music, as it was the era of the Beatles, full employment, and free speech. Everyone had optimism; ***and old gas masks in their sheds.***

Really it was the older generation that changed things, by bringing to the masses the television, the telephone and all kinds of domestic products never seen before. Rationing was a thing of the past and there seemed to be an abundance of food in the shops. But there was an underlying need to be frugal with everything, just in case this stability was to be short-lived. For us kids, every day was an adventure, playing in fields, climbing trees, lighting bonfires, looking after our animals and always finding ways to earn pocket money.

# Open Your Eyes

## *"His mind was like a coiled spring"*

Not long after I started in business, my father-in-law, David Todd, came to work with us in between his shifts that he did working as a computer operator for a company called Baker Perkins, in Peterborough. David always wanted to earn extra money, we had just started the business, and we needed people who would work when we needed them, also people that we could trust 100%. He worked for the good of the business; he ticked all of the boxes for us.

*When I started to go out with Marilyn, a chap that I knew said, "There's an easy way to tell if you will stay with a girl! "Just look at her mum. Now that's what you are going to be sleeping with in 30 years time; would you like that?"*

**Marilyn's mum and dad in 1966, the year I met Marilyn.**

He was a bundle of nervous energy, like a coiled spring ready to be released. There was no hanging about; he wanted to know what to do and, when that job was done, he wanted another one. He couldn't stand still for a minute. It was so much easier working with him like that than to have someone that you have to push all of the time; not only did he do the job quickly, he did it with pride.

He also looked at ways to do it more easily or more quickly, and better. He had worked as a baker in his father's bakery business from leaving school, which was really hard work, something he wasn't afraid of; if there was anything that he was afraid of, it was the tyrant of a father he had, as he was a really nasty person, especially when it came to David; he was a very unforgiving man.

I understand that throughout and after the Second World War, his father had a fantastic business. This was way before supermarkets were around. In fact, other businesses from outside the area tried to buy him out but he was too greedy to sell, even though he was being offered the equivalent of ten years' profits; he thought that the money would just roll in forever.

Unfortunately, a lot of business owners fall into this trap of refusing to sell. David's father should have gone through a simple process of looking at his business, and then he would have seen that his profits would soon be going down; he needed to replace all of the old worn-out bakery equipment and the transport. Also, the larger bakeries were starting to expand into small towns like theirs and undercutting the prices.

## Don't Let a Business just Run Its Course

The other thing that some business owners don't consider, David's father included, I suspect, is that if they reject approaches from buyers they will only buy some other business nearby, or start another one themselves, and then there is the risk of the new people putting them out of business. Anyway, in 1954 his father decided to retire from business, because it had run its course; he took a job as a caretaker in Peterborough Technical College.

David took on the business at the time when all of the machinery, vans and equipment was ready to be renewed and as it was all just starting to break down, but with no money to replace it.

At the same time the supermarkets were moving in, undercutting the price of bread. His father had not trained him to run the business, only to be a baker; there is a big difference when you take on a business. David could bake bread and make cakes, but the business still needed someone to buy the stock, do the calculations to determine the price to sell at, and look after all of the hundreds of other things that go into running a business. His father left the business one day, leaving David to fend for himself; consequently the business failed, David had a breakdown and then, unfortunately, had to have prolonged hospital treatment.

It's a great shame that it happened, because every day when I started in business, he would be coming up with moneymaking ideas that he used to talk to me about, saying, "You should do this" and, of course, I hadn't got the money to do these things. I used to think, "Why doesn't he do it?" But I now realise his thoughts and ambitions were still there inside of him, although he would never go into business again because of the experiences he had encountered.

BACK

So many people have fantastic offers for their businesses, but they refuse to accept them because they think the business will just keep going up in value. Of course businesses, like all things, go around in circles and can end up being worthless. Timing is the key; there are always times when businesses are worth selling. One point is to sell when there is a great deal of opportunity for the buyer to expand the business; another is to be ahead of your competitors, then they will want to buy an existing business instead of taking time to develop the same. Some people just want to diversify into complementary businesses and, in some cases, a totally different business, and a lot want to buy an established business just because they have the spare money.

## Don't Look Through Windows

When windows of opportunity appeared, like people wanting to buy one of our businesses, sometimes we just ignored the offer out of hand; but we realised we had to think of all scenarios surrounding the offer, putting ourselves into the shoes of the interested party, playing the game of chess. If we reject them, what move will they make? What will they do next? Do you think that they will just forget about it? No, the chances are they may buy a competitor, or set up as a new competitor and then wipe you out, leaving your business worthless.

I have seen this happen. We have taken so many windows of opportunity along the way, knowing there has been plenty of scope left for the new owners if they just carried on in the same way as we had built that particular business. Some windows of opportunity we didn't take, to our cost, as you don't know what you don't know.

When David's father realised the business was going downhill and he couldn't sell it, he rented the premises and the machinery to his son knowing the business was likely to fail; this was the nature of that nasty person. Not only did the business fail, David's health failed as well, which in turn affected the whole family. I will always be grateful to my father-in-law for sharing the stories with me.

It gave me a much better insight on just a few things that can go wrong in a family business.

***This was the baker's shop in Chatteris, Cambridgeshire***

David started here in his dad's business at the age of twelve, in 1941, working for five hours each day after school making meat pies, a scheme introduced in wartime; he then rented it in 1954.

His father had built a great business; unfortunately, when the time was right he was too greedy to sell to a competitor with lots of money. When he had the opportunity to make the business stronger by diversifying, he didn't make the changes and investment to replace his machines and so, when the inevitable came along and the competition took the business away with new technology, the bread-slicing machines that churned out sliced bread in factories, he had made his exit, dumping the business on to David. Over the years, David has learned a great deal about life. I asked him what one piece of advice he would give people thinking about going into business and he said:

## *"Open your eyes."*

David Todd

# The Philosophy

## *"Do more than you get paid to do"*

Marilyn had got her driving licence, and so drove the truck; I did not want any of the men driving when they could be working - digging holes, mending roofs, replacing windows, things like that. We had a roof on the back to protect the goods, but it had open sides, so we put the ladders on the roof and all the materials in the back. If only I had kept it... I sold it for £500 - now it's a classic worth £25,000.

Marilyn would go to the rubbish dump and dispose of the rubbish, as well as picking up building supplies from the merchants each day. She would be a lot quicker than the men, as they would have to wait about in line to get served; not only had Marilyn got the attention when she went into a builder's merchant, she also would get the truck loaded by them as well, *"a goal within a goal"*.

I was fanatical about time and motion; for those people who don't know what this means, it's doing things in a manner that saves time every time you do something. So everyone had a job from the minute they came to work and, if you were going to the rubbish tip you would not go until you had some things to collect on the way back. This way of thinking saves you 50% of your time, and we all know time is money. When we had offices with forty staff, each person had their own stapler, calculator, etc. I used to say that if you had to go to another person's desk to get equipment then it would be cheaper to buy it, and save the time moving from desk to desk.

Renovating a house was like a production line and, when Marilyn wasn't driving the truck she would be hands-on, mixing concrete, or painting and decorating.

# A Hair-Raising Experience

SIDETRACKED

In most old houses, people would wallpaper over existing paper. Consequently, it was common to have twenty layers of paper to get off. We used to hire steamers that were run on gas; one day the thing wouldn't light. The gas had been on for ages; this was a big, heavy machine with a massive water tank on top.

I had to lie on the floor to see where to light it and, as soon as I lit the match the gas exploded in my face, taking every hair off of my face, hand and arm. In that fraction of a second my eyes closed and my eyelashes had fused together; I couldn't see, but I could smell burning hair. In those days we didn't think about complaining to the supplier, we just got on with it. The next two weeks were irritating, especially up my nose as the hair grew back, and it was embarrassing going around with a patch of burned hair on the front of my head and no eyebrows.

It made me realise that this could have disfigured my good looks forever, but my brain, and the person who I was, would still be inside that new-formed body. This episode instantly changed my perception of people trapped in bodies that didn't reflect the person.

BACK

At the end of each job that was for a customer, not one of our own jobs, Marilyn would be sitting in the truck with her typewriter typing out the invoice and, before presenting it to the customer she would have already gone around the site to make sure everything was in order.

## Don't Leave a Stone Untouched

If we painted a customer's house, part of the job for us was to rake over the borders underneath the windows so they could not see any of the flakes of old paint and we would sweep the paths and generally tidy up, so the property would look nice. This took only a few minutes; and made the presentation of the bill much easier and, although each person knew exactly how much they would have to pay before the job started, we wanted a situation where there would be no excuses for not paying.

I remember the first time when somebody said to me after presenting them with a bill for painting their house, "Do I get 30 days in which to pay it?" I had never heard of this before, so I said to him, "Do you get paid each week"? He said, "Yes, I do," so I said, "Do you buy your groceries on Friday?" He said, "I do," so I said, "I would like to buy my groceries this Friday as well, so I am like you. I've done the work you asked me to do, and I would like the money now, please." I wasn't rude or nasty, I was just hungry; he got his cheque book and gave me the money. We got our groceries, and that's what we said to everybody who asked for credit after that.

# Magnetism That Draws People Together

There are certain times in life when a group of people, for whatever reason, just happen to work well together and everything runs as it should. This was one of the times in our lives when we couldn't have wished for anything better - to have got a business established with such enthusiastic people.

I have found throughout business that people will be drawn in, or will be scared off, by your style, enthusiasm and ethics in your particular field; it works just like magnets. People either want to work and be with you, or they don't. Obviously I had no problem with the first lot, they could get and have practically anything they wanted, but the second lot are the trouble. That's if they stay; there is nothing worse in business than when you employ people with no thought or interest for the business that pays for everything in their lives; they are just coasting, and wasting their lives into the bargain.

## Do More Than You Are Paid To Do

Another thing that came naturally to us, and which we thought was unique to this business, was the philosophy which put us in good stead for when we started our shops.

Marilyn would take the client around the job before presenting the bill, pointing out what had been done and asking if they were 100% happy with the job. She would say, "We have cleaned out your gutters and this normally would cost so much (telling them a price), but we have done this for you for free because we appreciate your custom."

Sometimes a client would see a fence or a gate that had been mended; in their mind they would think it was going to be an extra on the bill. Sometimes they would see we had done a job and, before Marilyn could say anything they would invariably say, sometimes in an abrupt voice, "I did not ask for that." Marilyn would say, "No, you didn't; we saw it was broken and thought we would do that for you as a gift for our appreciation." This was better than spending money on advertising, plus, people invariably paid their bills immediately; the philosophy worked.

When we had the shops we would give the customer a bottle of sparkling wine after they had purchased their pram - a gift to wet the baby's head. They knew nothing about this gift until they were going out of the door; it wasn't to encourage them to spend more, it was our gift to them to say, "Thank you, and we really appreciate you."

# I Thought That I Would Be Eaten Alive

We always seemed to have enough maintenance work to keep us going; usually between three to four weeks in front of ourselves but, as in any business, more work was needed. I was always looking for more work; I learned a valuable lesson. One day I was working for a lady, her name was Mrs Corton and she lived opposite to my mother and father; I had known her since I was about eight years old. Mrs Corton was one of the first people to give me jobs when I started the business window-cleaning, then painting, etc.

When I was working in her house on a Friday, her lodger, "Leonard", would always get fish and chips from the local chip shop at 12:30 pm. Mrs Corton would shout to me, whether I was mending a fence or on her roof, "Neville; your dinner is ready." She would shout and expect me to be there in a minute; if I didn't arrive immediately she would shout again and, the longer I left it, the louder she got. On the one hand, Mrs Corton could be the nicest person on this earth, giving me so much work, yet on the other hand she could be a tyrant; she wouldn't care what she was saying to you.

Well, on this particular day I forgot it was a Friday. I had a telephone call the night before; this was well before we had mobile phones; in those days we worked in the day with no interruptions and had telephone calls in the evening. Can you imagine that now? The phone call was from a person who was something to do with a church in a village called Fotheringhay, about 15 miles from Peterborough.

The person said he wanted all the new radiators and pipe-work in the church painting, and could I give them a quote? I was not used to this, as I only gave quotes in the evenings. I used to like to leave the daytime totally free for working, as every extra hour in the day meant more money and most customers don't want you working evenings in their houses. He insisted it had to be at 12.30 and I wasn't strong enough to say no; also, I thought a job of that size was probably worth losing a couple of hours' pay so, at 12.00, off I went. I didn't get back until 2.30 pm. I could see that Mrs Corton was absolutely furious. She said to me, "Neville; where have you been?" I said I had been to look at a job to give an estimate and I had hurried back.

I learned such a valuable lesson that day. She said to me, "When you're working for somebody, that's what you're doing; you work

for them and you don't go off looking for other work in their time."
She told me that if I were to expect any more work from her, those
were the terms of my engagement, and it wasn't only the words
that she said - it was the tone of voice she said them in.

I was 25 years old, I was married with a child, I had got a house
and I was in business for myself, yet she made me tremble. I felt so
bad and I thought I'd lost all of the work from her; she was a very
valuable customer. Then she turned round as though nothing had
happened and said, "Your fish and chips are in the oven; I hope
they're all right," and carried on.

There is a moral to this story. The person whom I met at the church
just wanted me to give him a price for painting the radiators. He
wanted to knock that amount of money off the bill he had received
from the plumber because, in his words, he thought the plumber
should have provided radiators that were painted, so I was being
used. It was a very valuable lesson, really, about respecting people
and, from then onwards, I questioned people as to whether they
wanted the job doing, and whether they were the decision-maker,
or if a committee would be making the decision. This sorted the
chaff from the wheat, and I would meet people only when it was
right for my existing customers; a bird in the hand.

## Think About Your Customers' Feelings

We carried on getting new contracts, but in a more caring way. I did
not want that fiasco again; also, that situation made me more
determined to do work only for ourselves. One contract we did get
was with the local Education Authority; this was doing maintenance
work in schools during holiday periods. This contract was to put
paving around outdoor swimming-pools; the specification that was
given was for 1m x 600mm x 100mm, the largest, heaviest and
thickest slabs that you could get at the time.

Nowadays, companies would use machinery to handle them but,
together with our team of untrained part-timers, we laid them down
by hand. It would have been backbreaking work for two people to
handle 20 slabs, enough for two strong men, but we had to handle
600 over the summer holidays, and Marilyn was there alongside us
helping too, working like everybody else. I can still feel the pain in
my back just talking about it.

Another time, I got a contract for adjusting schoolroom doors. There
were so many doors to adjust, and so little time to do it in, that I
literally ran with my bag of tools and step ladder from one

classroom to another, virtually not stopping every day for two weeks.

This, then, set the scene for the way to work in the future, if achieving our goals was to be a reality.

## Are You Buying Or Selling Your Business?

Very early on in business, I learned that you are either buying your business or selling your business every day. So, at the end of every day, I would ask myself, "Have you bought, or sold your business today?" In other words, has what I have done today increased the value of the business? If it has increased, I am making it easier to sell, so I am selling; but, if I have not increased the value, I am then buying it myself, and is that what I want?

## Preparation plus Opportunity

SIDETRACKED

Now, it's immaterial whether your goal is to eventually sell, or just to keep it forever. And, by the way, nothing lasts forever, things just evolve. If you try to keep the business the same as it was when it started, you will be driving it into the ground. I think that 99.99% of businesses that are run this way may be for nostalgia, failing to produce enough income to sustain a lifestyle that they would have liked, until the owners die.

You don't have to sell, but just work on the business so you are ready to sell at any time as, when an opportunity appears you will be glad that you spent the time and effort on the preparation. If you never look for opportunities, and you want to pass the business on to the next generation, at least you will have had the foresight to, and the fun in building a business that can be sold in the future.

## It's Easy to Predict Business Failure

BACK

If your business by the end of the day is exactly the same as it was when you started this morning, you are starting to lose out, you are buying it, because things in your business haven't moved forward; someone else has taken a tiny piece of your business away without you knowing about it, and with your permission and, in doing so, you are helping them to sell their business and you don't even know who they are until it's too late.

It is easy to lose the passion when things are going well. Having an abundance of money is nice but, if you get complacent and forget your business, thinking it will take care of itself, you will be mistaken. Businesses don't run themselves; yours may coast for a little while after you have stopped working on it but, as sure as eggs are eggs, the business will crack and inevitably it will have broken beyond repair.

*I ask myself every day: What am I doing with my business? Is it good or bad, is it right or wrong? Am I going nearer to or further away from my goals and my heart's desires?*

## Everything Is Great

Of course, there are other things to take into consideration, especially in a business that you have involved family in, or those who have other skills that are needed. Once the honeymoon is over, which can take only weeks, but mostly years, the cracks will appear as everyone has their own agenda. I would recommend a clear strategy and frequent updates on the progress, and have a get-out option for everybody concerned, together with rules of the business that should be adhered to. Most family businesses don't have that kind of thing; they just evolve along the way, like ours did.

## Passion

Both our businesses were built with passion, enthusiasm and focus, which is highly attractive when people are associated with it, whether it's through employment or supplying goods and services and, at the same time, it is addictive for the owners, but with lots of consequences along the way.

I found that the passion in what I was doing could get so addictive that I would just keep going, irrespective of everything or anybody else in my life. There was a driving force inside of me pushing to challenge and beat myself at what I was doing; I was competing against myself.

# Setting Our Goals

***"We all need goals to succeed, so why don't people have them?"***

***"No goals! No life!"***
Neville Wright

We have always been the kind of people who have done more than one thing at a time; well Marilyn, being a girl, multi-tasks anyway, but it was a bit alien to me when going into business. But again I had a paradigm shift. I found this out of necessity, but I also found it to be fun. I've got a very short attention span, and I think the older I get the more I want to do, so time is very precious to me; something that I had to learn because I had a choice. I could abuse my time on earth, like so many people wishing and wanting to be millionaires, or I could repeat to myself what I had learned.

## The Attention Span of a Gnat

SIDETRACKED

At this present time, sitting here writing this, I have four screens in front of me. I am doing my emails on one, my book on another, a university course on a third and I am researching on the fourth or working on *nevillewright.com*; my attention switches. If I could have more space I would probably have six screens, but Marilyn says no, because we have a small office just off our lounge, and she doesn't want our home to look like an office. She says I can go to our main office in town if I want six large screens, but I like working from home and besides, I have a plan that Marilyn will love, when I do it. I know that I can split the screens, but then I have a job to see them.

I think that I am this way at this moment in my life (2014) because I am still searching for a position where I know what I want as a person who has passion to contribute to things. You see, I am mentally still in limbo (shitworld) after 2010 - more about that later.

BACK

Here below are the twelve words that are in my mind constantly. These twelve words I would urge you to put into every aspect of your life, not just in your work or home. Everything could change.

## *"I must do the most productive thing possible, at every given moment."*

Our number-one goal was financial independence, our second goal...There wasn't a second goal until the first one was accomplished.

## Use the Kiss Principle

"Keep it simple." This saying is a classic that's been around forever, and why? Because it's true - there are lots of complicated things in life. The simpler you can make a business, the better the chances are that it will be around for a long time, and the more valuable it will get; and, when it does get valuable to someone, don't be afraid to capitalise on your hard work.

I hear people saying, "I work in my business because it's a lifestyle. I love doing it but I will never make any money." This means, in other words, that the business is not working for them - they are working for the business. Making money is all about making the business work for you; consequently, they are buying their own business every day.

We were always aware of this trap. Very often, people will work all of their lives then close their business, because they haven't thought about selling it and putting things into place like developing the business five or even ten years beforehand, so they can keep up their lifestyle until they pop their clogs.

If your business is not working for you, just think before you throw the towel in: Are there other businesses around in your sector that are successful? I remember that we had to be only 1% better than the nearest competitor to take their business.

## Have You Got a Prize-Winning Racehorse?

From the first day in our business, we thought that first we would create a business that would sustain our lifestyle; this was no problem as we didn't have one yet; secondly, a business the family could make a living from and sustain all of their needs and, thirdly, one which could be around and passed on to generations to come, or be sold for a substantial amount of money. To be honest, that was never a thought at that time; that came a lot later. So in 1974, to do that, we had imagined our business was a foal which, with the right care, would one day turn into a prize-winning racehorse.

So we treated our business like you would a prize-winning horse, nurturing it every single day to keep it on top form, preparing for the day it wins the gold cup and is auctioned off to the highest bidder for stud. Or you could keep it until it dies, because one day it will; whether it's a horse or a business, it's the same principle.

## The Last "S" Is For Stupid

I was not afraid to call myself stupid. It was a bit strange at first, putting myself down, that's what other people had been doing behind my back and even to my face in the days that I attended school, so why should I not do it as well, especially if it were to make me think of how to do things better, more easily, quickly, cheaply, or not at all? When I say "stupid", I mean that if I am not in control of my own life then I must be stupid, and then stupid is something that motivated me to be in control.

### *"I Know That I Am Intelligent, Because I Know That I Know Nothing."*
Socrates

With our goal set to be financially independent, the conclusion was that the business would have to go through some radical changes over the next couple of years; the strategy as it was, "working for other people," obviously couldn't continue. To be a viable proposition for us we needed to earn a lot of money, not only in the daytime but also whilst we were sleeping. Also, we needed to use what money we obtained better and more productively. In the long run, if the goal were to be achieved, a strategy had to be put in place; we would build a portfolio of properties that would eventually give us all the income that we needed to live a financially independent life without needing to work.

## Ridiculously Hard Work, Was Fun?

If only we had known when we set this goal, a few months into our business, that it was going to take us the next twelve years of ridiculously hard work, investing every penny back into the business before we would have enough money to retain the first few properties for an income stream, let alone financial independence, we probably wouldn't have even started. *"Ignorance is bliss."*

After setting that one large goal we soon realised that we had to set thousands of very small goals along the way if we were to achieve our major one. I set month-to-month, week-to-week, day-to-day and, incredibly, hour-to-hour and then sometimes minute-to-minute goals along the way. All this was done in my head as I was working - I couldn't waste time trying to write them down.

As most people probably know, once one goal is set and achieved it's only a matter of time before the next one is set. For us there was no exception to the rule, goals are set and achieved, new ones are made and the process is repeated. But for me it was timing. I had goals set up in my head ready to slot into place immediately we had achieved the last one; in fact, we wouldn't leave the new goal until the next day. It would be that once one goal was achieved the next goal would be implemented in the next second. It was in my head, never-ending; it was like we were on a treadmill.

Although I describe it as a treadmill, and it probably looked like one, it didn't feel like it. We had our goals, our hopes and our dreams; we knew we had got to sacrifice so many things to achieve them, and that's what we were always prepared to do. We were totally focused, and ruthlessly hard on ourselves.

## Why Not Coast through Life?

We knew that we could just coast through life doing the bare minimum and be relatively poor for evermore, struggling to make ends meet, always having too much month at the end of the money.

We had the choice if we really wanted to; we could set to and work our butts off, sacrificing virtually everything for the next ten years, and then become financially independent for the rest of our lives, having abundant wealth from passive income until we died.

To me it was a no-brainer; we really had not experienced any of life's good stuff by then, so we would not miss what we had never had. I knew that most people have to perform at 95% in their jobs to keep them, or face getting fired, so all I had to do was work 5% more than the average person and just 1% more than any competitor who was around at the time.

For us to be successful and, on top of that, if we wanted to be really, really successful, we had to work every day just like normal people then, on top of that, work early, work late, work at the weekends and through break times that most people take. Plus we would have to work more quickly and smartly. It helped that we made our work our hobby in our minds, so then we were getting paid for our hobby.

## I Mentally Treated Work as a Game

I mentally treated the business as a game; a competition with imaginary players all competing against me. Losing wasn't an option. I had said in that dole office to that man behind the counter who verbally gripped my balls and my life, not to think that he was in control of my life. I said that I would look after my family myself; there was no way on this earth that I would ever go cap in hand to him, or anyone like him, ever again. Unfortunately for most people, life is just too easy; I should emphasise this.

## *"If life was harder, it would be easier to make the sacrifices needed to become rich."* Neville Wright

Security was Marilyn's number one priority in her life, so all decisions were made with that criterion in mind. Will this decision take us nearer to, or further from our ambitions and goals in life? As we wanted to be secure in the long run, I repeat, the long run, it didn't matter about the short run to us. Marilyn needed a great deal of money to make her life secure, or so she thought at the time, having started with nothing at all. A great amount in 1966 was £25,000; now, in 2014, it's £25 million. Just imagine, and project into the future, how much will be a great amount in another 48 years time.

My priority, on the other hand, was to prove to myself that I was capable of looking after us, so working harder and longer became normal. The more I did this, the more I wanted to do it; it was like I was hooked. I just could not stop myself from working, then investing the money into the business without a thought of easing up on myself. Every day, push, push, pushing myself, and I found that everyone around me did the same; really, it was just using time efficiently, that's all. That is until one night in 1977, three years into the business. I got home late, as usual; Marilyn said, "Neville, if you keep working like this you will come home one day and we won't be here." SHIT! I thought to myself, "Why am I doing this, anyway?" After all, I was doing it for Marilyn and Elaine and, if I was going to lose them, what was the point of all the hard work?

*"I am where I am because of what I have done in the past. If I want to be somewhere else, it's simple: I must change now, and do things differently to alter the future."*

## Don't Just Work Hard, Work Smart As Well

So, with that in mind, I immediately readjusted my timeframe for achieving my goals. Now I thought, if I took a bit more time out, it would take me, say, six years, instead of five years to become financially secure. Besides, all these goals were pie in the sky because, after setting them, along the way I would have moments when jobs went wrong and we lost money. I would think, "What a dick I am," thinking that one day I could be financially stable with a million quid in the bank; I must be bonkers. At that point I was cleaning fcuking windows at 30p a house and putting three ridge tiles on roofs for £4.50; where did I get my sums from, or the five years? Uh - dreamer!

The next day, I didn't rush out the door; I took Elaine to school before I went to work. I think Marilyn just wanted to know it was about us, and not just me. The day after that I made up for the time lost, then everything was back to normal and, just a few weeks later, we got our first two big jobs from both lots of parents. After that we never stopped, so maybe not such a dick after all!

## Goals

Goals are a normal part of life, aren't they? If anybody said no, I would be lost for words; my goals may be different from yours, but the categories should be the same - goals relating to: personal, family, friends, work, money, lifestyle, home, location, hobbies, leisure, fitness, food, education, etc., etc., etc., etc. Then there are sub-categories in all of these, and then the detail that goes along with achieving your goals.

Goals are like juggling balls - you have to keep practising; and just because you drop some, it doesn't mean that you're no good at it. Don't give up, just do it again. If you have a goal, it means you will have already made an effort. To achieve a goal, you have to give something of yourself - effort - and the more you give to the world in the way of effort, the more the world gives back to you in the form of abundance. But, most of the time, the world tries you! So it often takes a bit longer than expected.

One of my goals was to have a home in Switzerland, as my sister, Carol, lives there. I achieved that in 2004, thirty years after setting that goal. I bought a piece of land that had permission to build five terraced chalets; I put only one chalet on the whole plot as, at the time, I was thinking that maybe we would be tax exiles. Marilyn said no, she would not leave the UK, because she was not leaving the grandchildren and the girls, so I just paid the taxes as normal. I wouldn't have left anyway; Marilyn has said a thousand times that I was just letting my tongue wag in the wind.

I do know now that, if I were to do this again, I would have built the five smaller chalets, keeping one for us and selling the other four. I saw an advert in the *Sunday Times* advertising 17 plots for sale. We arranged to go and, as usual, I made full use of the trip by taking Dad to see Carol. It was February 2004 and, as we went up the mountain, it got horrible, raining and foggy; then the sun came out - what a contrast.

**2005. Dad outside our completed chalet, named after our daughters Joanne (Jo) and Elaine (Elle) "Chalet Joelle"**

**The view from our lounge window is spectacular all year round**

# 8 Years of History

## *Some background information before we get any further*

Bringing you up-to-date from the beginning in 1966, and going fast forward up to where our business started in the autumn of 1974.

In 1966, I met Marilyn. She was 15 years old and I was 16. We instantly fell in love and decided to get married, have some children and buy a house; the first step was to buy the house, which we did two years later after saving every penny we earned working for other people, a total of £650.

In 1968, after looking at probably one hundred houses over the previous two years, an offer of £650 was accepted for a dilapidated terraced house, 72 St Martin's Street, Peterborough. The asking price for that house at the time was £1,075 so, without knowing it, or even thinking about it at the time, we got a 40% discount.

SIDETRACKED

Just something that I feel is a very important point. The £650 wasn't what we thought the house was worth; it was the amount of money we had at the time. When we had saved up £250, I was making offers of £250. I feel people should not be afraid to try and make a deal with what they have available to them at the time. They don't know what the seller's circumstances are, so should not try and guess.

BACK

I say I was putting in offers, but that was a matter of speech; in fact, I would say what amount of money we had got, and my future father-in-law would put the offer in to the estate agents for us, as we were too young to make offers, and to be taken seriously.

For a start, in the 60s you weren't allowed to own property unless you were over 21 years old. Estate agents hadn't got any experience of dealing with anybody under that age, especially 15, 16, or 17-year-olds. Come to think of it, they probably still don't, so how could two kids of 16 and 17 go into an estate agency and offer £250 for an £800 house? They were not going to take us seriously.

# My Father-In-Law Didn't Care

I had a father-in-law-to-be, whom I thought at the time was a bit crazy. He didn't care what the estate agent said; he had no problem in going in to any estate agent and giving them a silly offer. If they refused it, he would have no problem; he would just walk out. I would have just been a bag of nerves, and felt so embarrassed. If that had happened to me at that time I probably would have been too embarrassed to go back into that estate agents ever again, which would have ended up as a lose-lose situation. I learned, there and then, that you can't do everything yourself; so recruit people with different strengths to carry forward your vision, knowing what their task is and how they fit in to make the project a success.

## *"We are all just cogs in the big wheel of life; no one better than another"*
Neville Wright

So, without him having the strength of character to do that, we probably wouldn't have got on to the property ladder in the first place. The house was bought with our cash, but my father and Marilyn's father had to own the house until we were 21 or, like the solicitor said, "Until you are 21 and responsible people." I suppose it depends what you call responsible. I am 64 now, and I don't feel any different from when I was 18. Thinking about most things has not really changed, so obviously the government of the day got something wrong, or maybe I am still irresponsible.

*We were married at New England Methodist Chapel on 4th July 1970 and, on 26th April 1971 our beautiful baby girl Elaine arrives, making a start to our own family.*

I remember one night in March 1971, when I got home from work around 7pm. It was cold and dark, Marilyn was 8 months pregnant with Elaine and was fed up; she wanted to go to the seaside. Obviously I thought that would be nice in the summer, but she wanted to go there and then; and sometimes you don't argue, you just do it so, an hour and a half later, we were outside a fish-and-chip shop in Hunstanton, Norfolk.

It was too dark to see the sea. I went into the fish-and-chip shop, bought a small bag of chips and asked them if I could have some scraps as they were free, and a very small bottle of pop. I got back into the car and showed Marilyn what we had left in the world in the way of money - one and a half pence.

It was a good job I had enough petrol to get us home. On the way back, we stopped in a lay-by because the Council had piled up some sand they had swept off the roads that had drifted off the beach. I needed some to finish off a path in the garden. I thought it was nobody's, so there would be no harm in having some.

I started to scoop the sand with my hands into the three-wheeler (Del Boy) van, throwing it as quickly as I could. When the van had about 4 barrow–loads in, it suddenly dawned on me what I was doing and what I could be letting myself in for if I were caught doing this. I went all the way home worrying. I used that sand on the path but, when the winter frosts came, the path disintegrated because of the salt in the sand. I could hear my mum saying,

## *"It's the Lord Jesus punishing you, Neville."*

Elaine arrived 9 months after we were married; it was the best thing ever for us. At that time Marilyn was very shy, having been brought up with the thought that children should be seen and definitely not heard. Now she was a mother, a dream come true for her; as for me, I think it's the proudest moment of any man's life to become a father. Well, it certainly was for me.

Marilyn couldn't go back to work as, in those days, people looked after their baby and there was no right to a job, so we just had to get on with it. But it made us a family and that's what we wanted; we were happy. In life there are things that money can't buy: one is pure happiness, and the other is pure love, and we had them both for a while. On the other hand, life was shit without money to spare.

Over the next 3 years, we moved 4 times. Marilyn would spend her time looking after Elaine, doing some decorating and gardening while I went to work although, with no money spare to spend on herself and Elaine, and being alone every day while I was out at work made it difficult for her. I thought that she had depression, which would have been the worst thing ever, but it wasn't; it was her life at that moment in time and I couldn't do a thing about it until 1974, when I was fired.

BACK

In the spring of 1972 we sold our first house for £2,100 and moved to 13 Northfield Road, Millfield, Peterborough, a semi-detached house, this time with a front garden and garage space. For £2,000 it was a bargain, and again in need of modernisation. We thought we would stay there forever, but unforeseen circumstances took us down paths that we just couldn't have ever imagined.

**13 is now our lucky number, on the right; it cost £2,000 in 1972.**

SIDETRACKED

This house was a few doors away from one of Marilyn's aunties and about fifteen houses away from my mum and dad. The lady who owned it was a friend of my mum and dad. When I was 12 her husband died, and I had his sit-up-and-beg bike; if you don't know what that is, it's just an old man's bike from the 1930s.

This was my first bike, a Christmas present from Mum and Dad. My dad put racing handlebars on, and then he put bright yellow tape on them, and a bell. I loved that bike, no matter what the other shitty kids said about it; it cost £2, all that my parents could afford, and I was just so excited and grateful to have it.

# Which Fork Will You Take?

BACK

The son of the deceased lady was, I believe, the chief inspector of Peterborough Police at the time. The house was on the market for £2,300 because they were friends of Mum and Dad. We got it for £2,000 as we had sold our house but, no sooner had we agreed to buy the house when our house sale fell through; the buyers could not get a mortgage on it.

We put it back on the market and luckily it sold again for cash to a man who was getting a divorce. This time it took about twelve weeks to get the money. This was about ten weeks longer than we told my dad's friend, by which time he was getting very frustrated with us. If he had pulled out of the deal, our life could have been completely different. I hear of people who have had similar experiences and have been put off moving for life. In that case we would now be worth £150,000, instead of £100 million; it's as easy as that, deciding which path in life you will take, and then just doing it.

At the same time as buying this, we also looked at a similar type of house just around the corner for the same price. I wanted to buy both of them by getting a mortgage; I would renovate them both, and sell one, with no thought of where the money was coming from or how I would do the work. I told my mother what I wanted to do; she couldn't understand what I was telling her. All she could think about was that, when the winter came, I would have to light fires in the empty house to stop it from getting damp and, as I was working, how would I have the time to renovate it?

The majority of houses didn't have any form of central heating in those days, only coal fires and, as I was working, it would be hard for me to find the time. Mum was thinking as a homeowner, I was trying to think as a businessperson. I didn't realise that at the time; also, I could have rented it out, but that never crossed my mind.

My mum was right; obviously she was, because I couldn't get the money. I was dreaming. Mum was concerned that I would be taking on more than I could handle although, if I had been able to get a mortgage to do it, both properties went up from £2,000 to £6,500 in only nine months.

Easy to say after and, of course, you have to be able to get the money; and what if they went down in price? I had nothing to back it up. There are some things that happen in life that you just remember; that was one of them, because I believe we could have spent £500 on the renovation and the mortgage for nine months, making a gain of £3,000.

I wasn't ready to do it because, if I were, I would have done it. That said, there was a respect for my mother, something that money can't buy and, at this point, if I had thought it would turn into a business, this decision would have doubled the business in one go. A lesson I learned for the future, or so I thought.

## Mum Was Right; it's Too Late to Tell Her

My mum was right after all, because we didn't have the money to renovate one house, let alone two. My mind went into chess mode; I figured out that if I were to take redundancy I would have the money to renovate the house, leaving my really good job with the shift pattern that allowed me to do part-time work. I don't know whether things just fell into my lap throughout the years, or whether I took opportunities that appeared in front of other people as well as me. The company where I was working had just done a time-and-motion study which identified that they were overstaffed, one member of staff in every twelve.

At the same time I overheard a conversation that two people on my shift were having; one was saying he was thinking of applying for a civilian job that was going at an aircraft fuel base where his brother worked, as he preferred a day job. He was having trouble making up his mind what to do.

I applied for that job and got it, so I immediately applied for the redundancy. There were only twelve staff per shift, and the other men on my shift seemed to be relieved that someone had volunteered for the redundancy, because they all wanted to stay; or so I thought. If no one had volunteered, there would have had to be compulsory job losses.

I was thinking of only one thing, and that was to get the money to renovate the house we had just bought. It really did not occur to me that I was giving up a good job that gave me literally two weeks off a month, and spare daytime on the other two weeks; but I was blinkered, I was focused only on my goal at that time. I received £350, including my accumulated holidays, enough to renovate the house.

# My World Fell Apart

I was so happy to get the money for the house renovations and a job as well. It was the third week of March 1972, we had moved only four streets away, but it was worlds apart; a front garden, a garage space, money to do the works, and a new job starting on 1<sup>st</sup> April. Life was great, with everything falling into our laps.

Then I got a letter saying that the job had been given to another person. My world fell apart - what was going on? I phoned Charlie, the boss, the one who interviewed me, the one who said I had the job; he intimated that he had been told that I was no good for the job. Apparently it was the man that I overheard talking about the job; he couldn't make up his own mind about leaving and he didn't like me doing what he lacked the courage to do himself, so he told his brother that I was lazy and, of course, he was right. At that time, in that job, I could have shown a bit more enthusiasm.

The new job was only waiting for the next war to start; how hard could that be? I should have proved myself in one job to be able to get another, but I could not see the big picture, as everything centred on me as far as I was concerned, at that time.

SIDETRACKED

I then seemed to go into a depression; I stayed in bed most of the day, not wanting to do anything. I thought that because I had volunteered to leave my job I wasn't entitled to any benefits, so I did not apply. I did not know that I could have claimed unemployment benefit. Also, the tax ran out on our van so I could not drive. Things went from bad to worse, life wasn't fair; I stopped renovating the house and did nothing for three or four weeks.

My brother and his wife, Judy, came around one day to look at the house. I was telling him about all of our troubles, when he looked at the tax disc on the van. He said, "This does not run out until the end of May." I thought it ran out at the beginning of the month that was on the disc, not at the end; what a plonker.

Then, about a week later, after four weeks of despair, my dad got me a job, again with the Electricity Generating Board, but this time working on the overhead lines. In those days some farms still did not have electricity connected to them, so my job was in a gang of six men erecting poles and then climbing up them on one-inch spikes attached to my boots, to connect the electricity cables across fields.

It was brilliant; my faith was restored, my energy returned, and I resumed renovating the house with enthusiasm and pride. Unfortunately, I could do the renovations only in the evenings and at weekends. I should have made the effort and done this when I had the time, instead of lying in bed. I was so mad about not getting that job - it had played on my mind every day. My next door neighbour just happened to work as a linesman; he said that I would never stop there as you have to be a certain type of person and he said that I wasn't that type. Whatever did he mean?

## Minds Are Powerful, and Underrated.

### *"A roller-coaster ride of a lifetime, full of ups and downs, had just begun. If only we had known; no wonder I love roller coasters."*

BACK

In June, I received a letter saying that the new person that had been employed was not fit enough for the job, and would I like to have another interview? Yes, I thought, that would be great, just to wind that bloke up who said I was lazy. I got the job and started in the July but my dad was not pleased, as that was the third job he had got me that I had left. "Sorry Dad."

## Isolated

*Greystones, 1972... £7,500 ... and now, 2015 price around £400,000.*

# *"Ignorance is not bliss, it's just Ignorance."*

Rob Moore

In the autumn of 1972 we sold the second house that we had renovated, for £6,500, and then bought a detached bungalow on the outskirts of the village of Northborough for £7,500. Surrounded by farmland that looked so bleak in the winter, we just hated the isolation of it. We had got a mortgage of £3,000, leveraging cash for the first time by £2,000, enabling us to purchase an investment property for £1,250, leaving £750 in cash.

They say ignorance is bliss and he who dares wins but, as my friend Rob Moore, who co-owns Progressive Properties, says, Ignorance is just Ignorance. That's what it felt like in the spring of 1973, when we naïvely bought a detached, derelict bungalow, 26 Alexandra Road, in an auction for £7,500. We wanted to get back to Peterborough and live near our parents, not realising that the money was payable within 28 days on the auctioneer's hammer falling, with 10% deposit payable immediately.

### *26 Alexandra Road Peterborough 1973 £7,500*

It was a good job we knew Langford Smith, the auctioneer; we said we would pay the 10% the next day with the £750 leveraged from the existing property that we had bought about 6 months earlier. That's one thing in the property world - if you say something and then do it, you are the exception, and that will get you so far in any situation.

Payment for the balance on Alexandra Road was due within 28 days, or we risked losing the deposit; £6,750 was needed.

In our naïveté, I suppose, we thought we could sell our own house quickly, but a recession had already started; a sale and completion were not going to happen in 28 days. There was only one thing to do and that was to find some money, and quickly. In 1973, £7,500 was a lot of money; forty years on, it's a job to understand how crazy we were.

SIDETRACKED

The next morning I took Marilyn to my father's house in Peterborough as I was going to work; she had to come with me because she couldn't drive. I was telling her to go and see a bank manager, any bank manager, and ask for a shed-load of money. I am saying this to a girl whom I thought had just gone through 2½ years of postnatal depression; well, that's what it seemed to me.

It seemed a big deal for her to get up at 5.30 am, as this wasn't normal for her. She had nothing to get up for; normally, her day consisted of looking after the baby and watching TV. She told me that it was probably the most mind-destroying six months she has ever had in her life.  It was in the winter; it was so cold and dark for so long; we never went out, we never saw anybody, and we thought we would like living in the country, but we didn't, so we were going back to town.

I can't imagine how she was feeling going to a bank. I never asked; it never crossed my mind to do so. I just needed to get to work and, as for Marilyn, being alone for twelve hours a day watching TV must have been soul-destroying. No wonder she was feeling depressed. She said that it wasn't depression; it was shyness, insecurity, and not getting out of the house. It would affect anyone and, well, I know it would have affected me. If it were now I would know what to look for, what to say and do; I was aged 22 then, knowing nothing, yet knowing it all.

BACK

There were definitely two different worlds for us at that time; we didn't know which one we were in, but you could say we were in the chrysalis state, waiting to become a butterfly. I was employed, but my mind was becoming self-employed whilst still being employed. I got into a rut, doing things like a zombie, getting up at the same time, going to work at the same time, going to bed at the same time, even eating the same food on the same day.

Whereas, when I went into the self-employed mode, the 24 hours in the day were 24 hours self-employment. The day was not broken up into work, rest and play. When you start a business it is work, work and work from an outsider's perspective but, in our minds, it was play, play, play; well, I had to tell myself that business is like playing your favourite game. It worked because I didn't have any games.

## Off To Get Some Money

Barclays Bank was only one street from my fathers' house, so we decided Marilyn should go there; she would go and get the money from there so we could purchase the new property; easy as that - no problem.

Marilyn went to Barclays on Lincoln Road, Millfield. She asked at the counter if she could see the manager for a loan, and he duly saw her. The first thing he asked for was her account number, to which she said she didn't have a bank account with Barclays. His name was Myers Tennyson. She explained the situation to him of what had happened; he said he was curious to know why she had chosen his bank - could she tell him the reason for that? Marilyn said, "Well, I don't drive, and this bank is the nearest bank to my father-in-law's house, which is where I have just walked from." Bank managers were the decision-makers in the 1970s.

She came out of the bank that day having opened a bank account. That's what you would probably have expected, but the difference in those days was that you were speaking to the decision-maker, and in that new bank account was £6,750. Sometimes in life, the harder you work the luckier you become.

I honestly think that, in this instance, Marilyn had gone in and told our life story to Mr Tennyson, and he could see that she was a sincere and genuine person with so much passion and conviction for what we had done in the past, and what we were doing then. I am sure he could see that we were worth lending to, although he had never seen me; it was all due to Marilyn.

*A journey of thousands of miles starts in your mind; don't just leave it there. As Zig Ziglar says, "If you were to wait until all the lights were on green before setting off for town, you would never get there."*

# We Lived In a Caravan

## *"We all adapt to our surroundings, rich or poor alike"*

There are always strings attached when it comes to borrowing money with little understanding and, of course, there was nothing else we could have done; we had taken out a bridging loan, not really with any understanding of the implications involved when buying that bungalow. Barclays held the deeds for that, plus they held a charge over our existing home, which we had put on the market.

Sales at that time in general took a nosedive; the market was dead. Three months on, nothing had happened; then we received a letter from the bank to say we had another three months left on the agreement - what agreement? To sell our house and, if we didn't find a buyer, they could put both houses up for auction. To be quite honest, that scared the shit out of us; we didn't know, or understand, about the agreement we had obviously signed.

I went to the agents and said we needed to sell the property quickly. As luck would have it, we managed to sell our house, just in time, for £10,500. We paid the £3,000 back that we owed on the mortgage, leaving us with £7,500 to pay off the bank. There is a saying "By the skin of your teeth," and that's what had happened; our life seemed to be a series of skin-of-the-teeth scenarios. I don't know whether it was an adrenaline rush or just stupidity that made us do these things; maybe it was the overwhelming desire to be financially free at some time in the future. Thinking about it now, I believe it was a combination of all of them.

I do think a lot of people in business do the same thing; they push everything to the limits, just as we did ourselves, all of the time playing a game of dare but not really knowing it. We then needed to renovate this large, 4-bedroomed derelict property. We could get only a £3,000 mortgage on the property because of its condition and, out of that, they would give us only £2,000. The other £1,000 they would keep back until the structural work had been completed. We ended up with £2,000 to refurbish it, which was clearly not enough; we needed £3,500 to £4,500. The place was uninhabitable, so we had to find somewhere to live.

So we lived in this 10ft. caravan in the back garden, in the snow, through the winter of 1973/74.

This picture was taken September 1973, at Billing Aquadrome Park. We went there for a weekend with my cousin Rodney and his wife Pauline, one of the happier days because it was warm; when it snowed it was a different matter. I was away working twelve hours a day, leaving Marilyn to look after Elaine, trying to do whatever she could to renovate the house so we could move in. Some days, when I got home in the cold and dark, I could see that she had been crying. I just felt helpless and stuck in a rut with nowhere to go; I could not see any way out of this dreadful situation that I had got us into.

## Stuck With Nowhere to Turn

That was just the tip of the iceberg. I went to work for twelve hours a day and I left Marilyn crying. She tried her hardest to renovate the house, with no money to buy proper tools, equipment and materials to do a proper job, and a child who needed entertaining in the snow, slush and mud. I hated going; the thought of leaving her in that shithole was unbearable. I felt so ill right in the pit of my stomach with the thought of not being there to help, but what could I do? I knew that I had made a terrible mistake in buying that property, and with no way out, or that's what I thought at the time.

We used to boast about the mod cons we had in the van, when people asked how we were getting on. We would say we do actually have running water; yes, it's the condensation each morning that runs down the inside of the van. It was gruesome; temperatures went down to freezing, but that was an exception; most nights were only really cold. It wouldn't have been so bad if there were just the two of us, but having a 2½-year-old wanting to play in the snow on a building site was a different matter; it didn't bother Elaine, as she didn't know any different, but for Marilyn it wasn't ideal dealing with wet clothes, with no washing machine.

# Do nothing for £600,000

Turn £1,000 pounds into £600,000 pounds without doing anything. £1,000 pounds in 1945 invested in property is worth £600,000 today in 2014, with 69 years of rent making another £40,000.

One day I asked Charlie, my boss, if I could borrow the works ladder, something that I would never normally do, but I was desperate, as our tenant's house had a slipped slate and was letting in water. He agreed, something that I did not expect, as he was such a grumpy person, always sticking to the rules, a real jobsworth.

He said that he really admired me for doing what I was doing, investing in property, and wished he had got the courage to give me his £1,000 to invest for him, savings that he had had in the bank since 1945. He told me that when he was my age, he not only worked on the same aircraft fuel depot that we were working in but also, on top of that, he also kept pigs throughout the war, and that's how he made this money. He said that at that time, although he could have bought four houses in the village where he lived for £250 each, he could not bring himself to part with the money; the houses by this time, in 1973, were worth £1,500 each. Just in that five minutes I knew we were on the right track; it boosted my spirit and renewed my conviction that I was right. Now, in 2014, those properties are worth at least £150,000 each.

SIDETRACKED

We jumped into things at that time, by the look of it to other people anyway, with no consideration for what we were doing, as it wasn't normal to keep moving house in those days, especially if you owned them. We haven't changed; we have just bought a 60,000 sq ft empty office block. The agent rang at 5pm, we went by it in the dark at 7pm, and then rang the agent and bought it.

Talk about jumping out of the frying pan into the fire; very soon again we ran out of money. This seemed to be the story of our lives. We moved into the property with no floor coverings, no heating and still masses of work to do, although it was marginally better than living in the caravan, in our minds anyway.

I remember one day, soon after we had moved into the house, Elaine, our daughter, who was nearly three, had gone to the bathroom. There was an almighty crash and we went to see what had happened. The problem was that there was some loose plaster; she had got her hands behind it and pulled about a metre of thick plaster off the wall. We laughed about it, but hated living in those conditions; still, it couldn't get any worse than it had been over the previous year, could it?!

The terraced house we had bought for an investment of £1,250 the year before was yielding 50p per week in rent. We had hoped that the tenant would move out so we could sell it for a profit, but the lady said we were the best landlords that she had ever had in over forty years; she said she would never leave us. As nice as it was, it was no good for us and, when we tried to sell the property with her as a sitting tenant, there were no bidders.

Why would she leave? We had the wrong mindset regarding business; every month when we collected the £2 rent she would tell us there were problems with the house - the latch on the gate was broken, the gutter needed cleaning out. I did the jobs for her at the weekends; it took so much time and I blamed her in my mind, feeling I was not responsible for the problems, even though it was our property that we had bought to make money on. I was thinking about me and, with that attitude, I was never going to make it in a property business or, for that matter, in any business. I was thinking stupid - I was thinking that everything should be easy.

In 1973 the recession really started to bite, the miners were on strike and then, on 1st January 1974, the government announced a three-day week. Industry was allowed electricity for only three days a week, so people were being laid off. The country was grinding to a standstill, the unions were encouraging everybody to go on strike, inflation was 20%, people were made redundant and garbage piled up 5 metres high in the churchyards, spilling over into the streets.

Britain was coming to a standstill. The miners wanted a 26% rise and rejected 13%; Britain was facing the worst economic crisis since the Second World War. The UK stock market crashed, followed by what began to be a worldwide crisis. A General Election was called in February 1974; Edward Heath, the leader of the Conservative Party, lost to Harold Wilson, the leader of the Labour Party.

With this going on, my job abruptly came to an end. I was working on an aircraft fuel depot at the time. This was the one that had rejected me in the April of 1972. I had worked for the Electricity Board for only eight weeks before I took that job. I was thinking I should have stayed there; I found myself repeating what I always said I wouldn't say, which is, "I should have."

My job was in depots that were in strategic parts of the country, and which were hidden underground; they had been in place since the Second World War. These were emergency fuel supplies for aircraft bases, in case of national emergencies. I hated this job; it was boring and a total waste of my time and my life, and we were there in case of war. Charlie, who was the supervisor, had been sitting at his desk since the last World War for some thirty odd years. It was like God's waiting room. I was getting paid for it, and that made all the difference; that is what had kept me there.

## Be Careful, Wishes Can Come True

I knew I was wasting my life and, of course, I now know that if you think and wish about something often enough you will get your wish and, of course, I got my wish - I got fired. More government cuts. I'd been there for twenty-three months; I was told to go immediately as, if I had stayed a month longer, they would have had to pay me redundancy.

## Don't Just Talk About It, Do It

Although Marilyn and I had always wanted to work together to create a business, it was one thing talking about it and another thing actually doing it. When I got fired it was a great time to do something that we wanted to do without risking our job - in these circumstances, we hadn't got one to risk. I thought that we couldn't lose anything, as we hadn't got anything.

# Three Months on the Dole

## *"A feeling of despair"*

After being made redundant we spent the next three months finishing off the renovation work on the house; we managed to do the bare minimum that was required by the mortgage company to receive the last £1,000, and then promptly paid off our bills. We had done the main structural work, roof, windows, most of the plastering, electrics, and carpentry; it still looked a mess, as we needed to decorate but, once again, we were out of money.

I can hardly describe the feeling of not having any money; hunger, I suppose, is the first, an ever-present feeling, and there would be no need for a waste-food bin in our house like there is today. Time on my hands was another, but with that time we learned that dandelions are salad and stinging nettles make soup, along with any other trimmings of veg that just get thrown away now.

Another thing that a lack of money does to you is sharpen up your eyes and ears to every opportunity around you. Waste is everywhere. I learned so much during that time that stood us in good stead when we started the business. To waste anything is bad enough, but to waste time is criminal. All waste comes down to money, and this can easily be the difference between going bankrupt and surviving.

# Who Did I Think I Was?

After being fired, I went to the employment office for an interview. The lady said to go to the dole office now, and then every Thursday morning. I said that there was no way that I was going to stand there with those skiving layabouts. She got so angry and told me that they were good, hard-working people who had lost their jobs in the recession, just like me and, if I wanted any money, I had to queue with the others. That sorted me out and brought me down to earth; what a twat to even think that I was any better than anyone else.

I still felt bad queuing up every Thursday each week to present myself; the first time that I went I felt so embarrassed because, up to that time, if I had finished a job I would have had an offer of another job the same day. It was so easy then. My thoughts at that time were that if you were on the dole you were a no-good, layabout scrounger, living off decent working people just like me.

## A Cup Of Tea Would Be Nice

That day I went begging to the government for a handout, I felt that I did not want to be in the same line as the others. I wanted to be treated differently, better. "Maybe they should give me a cup of tea and a biscuit and some sympathy." I cycled to the dole office from where I had just had my interview, at the Job Centre.

There was no way that I was going into that place when anybody else was in there, so I waited outside around the corner. I watched and counted twenty people going in and twenty people coming out. There was no one around, so I quickly ran through the first set of double doors, through the second, swinging set of doors, thinking that I would be in and out before anybody came in and saw me. (Shit). I hit a wall of people who were in two rows standing from the counter stretching back to the bloody doors. Lesson learned; I should have taken more notice of the people going in and out, and the clothes they were wearing.

Now I felt just like the people that I had despised. I felt like the lowest of the low, scum. I felt embarrassed and humiliated that I had turned into a beggar to feed my family. I was caught in a destructive spiral of despair.

They would ask a question, "Have you done any work this week?" I wanted to say, "Do you think I'd be in this f*****g place if I'd got a f*****g job?" But I didn't, because I was too embarrassed just being there and, obviously, I didn't want to draw attention to myself in case someone recognised me. I wouldn't have really sworn - the dots are just to emphasise a point.

With no hope of getting a job, it was a job in itself to keep positive and motivated, especially with not having any money, so I devised a plan that wasn't to make me rich (although it did), but just to try and get out of the dreadful situation that I was in; just like millions of others who were in the same situation at that time.

I had lost contact with Albert, as I had not worked with him since leaving the land reclamation some two years before. I did not have the courage to go back and ask him for work, and besides, he had rejected my offer of working together painting and decorating, and also renovating houses to sell on once renovated. I had talked about eventually keeping some of the houses to rent out so that Albert would have an income for when he got older and stopped working.

A rejection of an offer was one thing when I had a job; to get another rejection when I was on the fcuking dole was an entirely different matter, and besides, I wanted to look after my family and anybody that worked alongside of me as a partner. I knew Albert would not come along for the ride, something I regret as he had taught me so much and I believed that I owed him. This has still not changed in my mind, as I would have looked after him for the rest of his days. You can take a horse to water, but Albert wasn't interested.

## I Thought At Least I Deserved a Medal

One week, I went to the dole office with a bright idea; I thought they would greet me with open arms. I said:

***"I'm finding it extremely difficult to make ends meet, so I would like to start doing some window-cleaning. If I could tell you each week how much I've earned, then perhaps you could make the money up to what I'm getting now, and then, when I have exceeded that, I can stop coming here."***

Behind the counter was this ginger-haired, stuck-up, pompous arse with a plum in his mouth; he was about the same age as me. He said that I couldn't do that; "You are either on the dole or off of the dole," with a few more words to wind me up, as he could see that I was on the edge of despair.

I said, "How do I get more money staying on the dole, then?" I was in a Catch 22 situation; I thought there must be a way because, by the look of some people that were queuing up with me, these people were dressed as though they were going to their office. Looking back, I'm sure they dressed like that so people wouldn't realise their circumstances. These people had a standard to keep up in front of their friends and the community. Fortunately, the one thing we didn't yet have was a standard; well, not above a 10 ft caravan, anyway.

If I could get a job sweeping the roads, I would. Unfortunately, some people there couldn't do that because they had too much pride and status; it would be near impossible for them to lower their standards but, from where I was, sweeping gutters would have been a step up. The man behind the counter looked at my file and said, "You have one child." I said yes.

He said, "If you want more money then you should have another child; that will increase your benefits."

I said, "Are you having a laugh? You are saying I should have another child when, actually, I haven't got enough money to feed the one I've got."

My mother and Marilyn's Auntie Flo used to bring food round for Elaine; pity they didn't look at us, they didn't realise we needed food as well.

That idiot in the dole office made me feel both angry and sad at the same time, but he couldn't alter the system just for me. With that, I told him that my employers could not look after me, and the government certainly couldn't look after me, so I would look after my family myself. He said, "Are you saying you want to sign yourself off?" I said, "Yes, I am." He gave me a yellow card and a pen, and said, "Sign here." I signed the card then stood there and stared; I thought that he would offer me more money. He looked up and asked if he could help me; I asked him what I should do now. He replied, "Do what you like; you don't have to come here any more." With a smirk, he looked past me and said, "Next."

## A Clearer Vision

My anger and frustration for those few minutes had backed me into a corner, when I made a stand against bureaucracy and lost (or, as I know now, really I had won), and so I walked out of the dole office thinking, "Sod 'em, that's told them." Then I thought that, unfortunately, my mouth had got the better of me once more; I'd shot myself in the foot. I got on my bike and thought, "What the hell have I done?"

I cried on the way back home, thinking I'd let Marilyn down. I hadn't got enough money beforehand, now I'd got nothing and, as the saying goes, "I hadn't got a pot to piss in." Remarkably, this gave me a clearer vision on the whole situation; or was it the kick up the arse that I had needed?

It took me about twenty-five minutes to get home; it would normally have taken ten, but I had got to compose myself and think what I was going to tell Marilyn. When I finally got home, I told her that I had told the man at the dole office what they could do with the dole money, and that we were now fortunate enough to be able to choose our own way in life. I was going to start the business myself, without any help from the government.

She just accepted that I was right. Obviously I didn't tell her that I had backed myself into a corner, or that I cried; I acted very positive, considering what I had done. She will find out only when, or if, she reads this.

SIDETRACKED

Some advice for anyone who is thinking about looking after themselves: focus in any type of business; it doesn't matter, it's all the same if you want to eventually be financially independent; focus any time that you want something in your life. You have to give everything else up, or put it on hold, so that you can focus on what you want; just note that everyone involved with you must be in the same frame of mind, or it won't work.

***"Focus on your goals; do not deviate, don't get side-tracked. Work, work, work, but remember: if you only 'work' you will do it forevermore and, in the process, will end up poor."***

Neville Wright

# Just Keep Pumping

BACK

Motivational speaker Zig Ziglar tells a very interesting story; it's called *Prime the Pump*. If you had a well and the pump was dry, you would have no choice other than to prime the pump; that's if you wanted that fresh, cool water that is down there. One person would have to pump like crazy, and another person would have to get some water and pour it into the pump.

Now, if the nearest water was in a dyke 50 metres away and you had only one bucket, what would you do? Yes, that's right - run, and run very fast, there and back, over and over, never stopping because, if you stopped pouring the water or pumping the pump before the pump was primed, the water would just go down the well, and then you would have to start all over again. Yes, I know now; I should have got two buckets.

# Business Is No Different

That is what happens in all businesses, and ours was no exception. Marilyn ran with that water, and I pumped that bloody pump until we were shattered; then we changed over and carried on some more, every day and every night. When onlookers were sleeping, or watching TV, or on holiday, they didn't notice we were working, keeping under the radar and afraid to shout about ourselves, just in case we failed; until eight years later when, in 1982, we bought what was probably the best and most expensive house on the market at the time in Stamford, Lincolnshire. It was new, it was magnificent, and nobody whom we knew could believe it was ours. In fact we couldn't either, and we had bought it for cash without any mortgage.

# Thanks for the Support

Then, when some people saw the rewards we were getting, they sadly and indirectly questioned how we got them; some even said, behind our backs of course, that it was impossible to have got these things lawfully. Only we know the true story of how we did it, and I will tell you over the following pages.

*Park House, Stamford in 1982; it looked magnificent standing in its parkland setting. Just a little different from the 10ft caravan we were living in only eight years before.*

So that's caught up to where we started; something that, for us, was an incredible journey from literally rags to riches.

# Back to 26<sup>th</sup> September 1974

## *"The day I stopped blaming other people"*

I knew that with no hope of getting a job, it was the right thing to do, so we opted for self-employment. That was on 26<sup>th</sup> September 1974. That afternoon we walked to Pridmores, the haberdashery shop next to the bus station on Millfield to buy a yard of scrim, the cloth for cleaning windows, and then went on to my dad's to ask if I could borrow his wooden ladder.

## From a Beggar to the Chairman of the Board

In the morning I considered myself a beggar, yet in the afternoon I became my boss, the Chairman of the Board. That afternoon I made my first investment, a 37p piece of scrim and, at the same time, I leveraged one of my father's assets, his ladder.

The next day was Friday. I walked out of our house with his ladder on my shoulder, my bucket in my hand and, of course, my 37p piece of scrim. I went to the next-door neighbours and asked if they would like their windows cleaning; they told me to go away and then shut the door in my face. Feeling like a real dickhead, I knocked on the next, then the next, and so on. I couldn't wait to get out of my road; I thought, "What if people see me?" I was getting hot with embarrassment. I earned £3 that day and, when I say day, I mean 12 hours. I could have got more on the sodding dole.

It made me more determined to succeed. I went out the next day, which was a bit better and, as the days went by, I became more confident in myself. I thought, after the first few days, that business must be like climbing a mountain; just a pity I was at the base in the shade, in the bloody cold.

## I Was Proud of Myself

Then, for the first time in my life, I was happy with myself; I was proud of me, and there was no way I was going to pack this in like I had the previous 17 jobs that I'd had. The next-door neighbours had never spoken to us; they gave me the impression that they looked down on us; maybe they could see us from their house, living in our caravan in the back garden.

I knew that, yet I still knocked on their door; why? Maybe I should have gone to another street to start the business. I thought that if I kept it local my overheads would be low; also, I would have more time working, instead of travelling. Nothing has changed after all these years - we still keep work within a sensible radius of any of our businesses unless, of course, it is web-based.

Now, I would still knock on their door and explain what my situation was. If they shut the door in my face, I wouldn't feel bad like I did 40 years ago; I would think they have just lost an opportunity. Thank goodness for Mr Preston, who lived on the opposite side of the road from us. He let me clean his windows and restored my confidence. He was a chiropractor; I believe his daughter still runs the business from there today.

## My Bird

I say it was the first time in my life that I was happy and proud of myself; I think I should say in a commercial sense. There was a time before that when I was proud of myself and the happiest boy alive - in 1966, when I picked this 15-year-old girl named Marilyn Todd to be my bird. That's what boys called girls in those days. Or did she really pick me? Anyway, Marilyn has been my lifelong bird and soul-mate for 48 years; she has always had the chance to fly away and, sometimes, I wonder why she didn't.

I know whatever you do in life is not always going to be easy. In fact, when life is really hard you become immune to a lot of things; the pain threshold is much higher than normal, but the results can be spectacular. The first week, I earned £12; it was £7 less than I had been getting from the dole, but I thought it could go only one way from there and, I am pleased to say, it did.

## Don't Take Things Personally

Some days I thought people were a bit strange. I didn't like the thought that I was being taken advantage of in the way that, when I asked potential customers if they wanted their windows cleaning, all of them would ask how much. "I charge 30p," I would say. Some would then say, "I will just have the upstairs cleaned for 15p, thanks; I can get my husband to do the downstairs." Fifteen pence for the upstairs? "Sod off," I would mutter under my breath to myself. You see, they controlled my business at that time, not me.

Then they would bring out some type of window cleaner and they would expect me to go over their windows with this stuff after I had washed them. It did teach me to avoid those houses when going down the street the next time; I thought, "That's taught them."

Then I realised that the customer wasn't taking advantage of me; I was offering a service and they would just renegotiate my offer to one that suited them better. I didn't realise at the time that this was happening. I could have said to them, "No; I will do the whole of your house for 30p, or just do the upstairs for 20p."

When they brought out the cleaning stuff I could have said that would be an extra 50p, to stop them doing that; but I didn't, because the fear of loss got to me. I accepted what they offered, but then both of us lost out after that because, the next week, I would avoid them when I walked down the road cleaning other people's windows. It took me a long time to understand about negotiations.

Of course they weren't strange at all; they were just doing what I did with the estate agents. I was offering an amount of money for a house, and that's exactly what they were doing with me for my services; but I took it personally. Once I stopped taking things personally, I could say no to their offer without getting upset. It took me years to realise this. I still think back to those days when I was cleaning their next-door neighbour's windows; I could see them looking out of their window, expecting me to knock on their door.

I think how stupid I was; they were potential customers, not just for their windows, but for the whole of their house if they needed any work doing. Also, they were my advert for their friends and family. I think sometimes I was so screwed up, having never been in this position before, too proud to ask for advice on how I was doing and thinking that, if I did ask anyone, they would think that I was a failure for asking.

When people tell me now about their experiences in their businesses, similar to what I've just described, I say to them, "Stand still; take a moment to think of positive possibilities that could materialize out of this situation. Could it be leading to greater things?" I needed money to buy food and I guess everyone knows that, when you're hungry, you tend to be tough on yourself and everyone around, including some of your customers, as I did. The lady who wanted to get the best value for money out of her window-cleaner was doing nothing wrong; it was me that wasn't very clever. Then, gradually, while I was still cleaning windows I started to think differently, as I had never had to fend for myself before.

# I Had To Become a Salesman

I sold my motor scooter, which I had used to go to work on, and then I realised we had a greenhouse in the garden, so I sold that. We sold the caravan that we had lived in, and then I started selling our furniture that Marilyn's parents had given us, as we didn't need it.

We needed the space in the house, as we had started to make cushions and toys out of fabric for my brother who, at that time, sold toys from his father-in-law's market stall. Our house became full of rolls of fur fabric for cushions and shag-pile carpet, which we used to make the toys out of.

## Remember You're a Womble

Wombles were the favourite out of all the toys in those days. We made all kinds of toys, mainly in the evenings and at night when there was no other opportunity to make money. The Wombles were furry creatures, children's characters on television. There was also a book and a pop group with the name. These creatures had long hair, and the only thing that resembled them that we could make the toys out of was carpet.

We used shag-pile carpet; it was all the rage in houses. It looked good in some people's eyes when it was new, but you couldn't clean it. The drawback for making toys was that the backing was very thick and, to sew the pieces together, you needed an industrial sewing-machine, something we hadn't got, so obviously my mind went into problem-solving; I came up with this brilliant idea of filing the back of the carpet.

I borrowed a heavy-duty triangular file from my father; then, in the evenings, I would take lengths of material into the workshop and pull the strips of carpet backwards and forwards over this file, which I'd placed in the vice. I would do this until the backing was just thin enough to go through Marilyn's sewing-machine, but not so thin as to make the Wombles shed their fur.

This would go on until my hands were red raw and I couldn't hold the carpet, as the rough carpet would be like holding sandpaper the wrong way. Another thing we made were cushions, hundreds of them. I used to roll out the fabric on the floor of our lounge, and then put templates of hardboard over the top, mark the fabric, and then cut it all up again until I couldn't cut any longer as the scissor handles would chafe my hands to the point where they would bleed.

Looking back now, I can't imagine why I did it. When people saw my hands they would ask what on earth had happened to my hands; when I told them what I was doing, they said I must stop doing it before I get an infection in them. While I was doing this job I would go around with plasters on my hands for months; unfortunately I contracted dermatitis, which took years to eradicate.

Marilyn would then sew the fabric for the cushions and animals inside out, and then I reversed them and filled them with stuffing. This microfibre would not only fill the cushions and animals, it would also fill the whole of the house, so we had to have the windows and doors open to let it out so we could breathe. Because of that, we had to wear our coats as it was cold, a knock-on effect.

We made all types of animals and then went on to make pictures and frames. It seemed to be going all right and we were making a few pounds each week, working at night until the early hours of the morning. I don't know what happened, but I believe my brother and his father-in-law had a disagreement. His father-in-law came round to our house and picked up all of his finished stock, then asked for all of the material we had; he said he needed it for a rush job that night.

I didn't believe him, but I gave it to him. He owed us £8, which he said he would bring round another day. That's 40 years ago; I'm still waiting. I just put the £8 into an inflation calculator - it comes out at £70.66 in today's money that he owes me.

We desperately needed to be making money then; it was such a shame he did that to us when we trusted him. What did he get out of it? £8. Marilyn was devastated - it was a week's work to her and nothing to him. He acted so bloody posh; he had been in the RAF and, the way he acted, people would think he was a senior-ranking officer, and we respected him until that day. Then, to us, he was just a shit.

He would give us 10p for making each cushion. It wasn't a lot, but we were happy for any amount we could get, especially when you could earn money in the middle of the night when no one else would give you a job. I never did find out why he didn't pay; he never said he wouldn't - he just didn't.

## A Million in Tax? You Must Be Joking

Early on in the business I decided that I wanted to pay a million pounds in tax each year. When I told people this, they thought that I was crackers; people still do, 40 years on. My thinking is that if I am paying a million in taxes; just think what I am earning. The most that we have given personally is £11 million in one year; I just wish it were every year.

A couple of years into the business, when we were getting ourselves established, our accountant had a letter from the taxman asking us to explain how we accumulated the money to start our first shop and build the two businesses we had established. He couldn't understand that it started with 37p. I think the taxman's motto is that there are no honest people in the world; well, I wonder if he is saying that as he looks in the mirror each day. It's a sad world for some.

The taxman tried to say we had planned through a series of property transactions from the time we got our first property up to creating a property company and, therefore, that we should have paid tax on any gains. Although we were living in the properties ourselves, the taxman thought we should pay tax on any increase in the value when we sold them; but the Government made the rules, so the government should not break them.

When you live in a property for more than 6 months, and it is your only residence, you do not pay tax on the increase in value. The taxman was saying that we planned all of this from the age of 16, which is obviously not right. If we had the brains to plan this, I would also have had the brains to do it a lot more quickly and easily. He also couldn't see that money to start the shop was just a few pounds accumulated from the window-cleaning business, paying for the second-hand prams.

We did buy the building with the money that we leveraged from our house sale in the way of a mortgage; maybe the taxman would rather we had bought the house outright and not bothered about business. Taxmen don't seem to understand that business people are the country's biggest and best unpaid tax collectors for the government.

However, we had to explain to them the reasons we moved the amount of times we did, how we got the money and where from, how much was spent on furniture and, basically, our life history. I do wish now I had a copy so I could print it off here. The investigation went on for a few months; when it was over we were presented with a bill for £2.30 for non-payment of VAT on a second-hand lawnmower which I'd bought, cleaned up and sold through the business to try and make a bit of extra money.

We could not get a mortgage, so we bought our first house for cash, £650; yes, £650.

Then, from a terraced to a semi detached
**Because Marilyn wanted more space**

Then, to a detached in the country
**Because Marilyn wanted to live in the country**

Then, to a detached in the town
**Because Marilyn didn't like the country**

Then, a new semi detached
**Because the other was too big and costly**

Then, a new detached house
**Because of a fantastic deal**

I can't believe how the taxman and the government have a policy of pursuing things like this to kill business off before it starts, instead of encouraging people to get started in business knowing that, if they are successful, taxes will naturally come along in much larger quantities when businesses are established.

Our business has probably raised in the region of £50 million for the government in taxes over the last 40 years; and to think that being pursued for being creative very often makes people think that it's too much aggravation to be self-employed; yet the dole office were willing to tell me that, when I was claiming, if I had another child they would give us more benefits. Uh!

This is another example of greedy people, the government, cutting their noses off to spite their faces. The tax people said we planned a series of transactions to accumulate wealth. What actually happened was, because I was besotted with Marilyn, if she wanted the sky I would have worked my hardest to get it for her; so I tried my best.

SIDETRACKED

Ironically, if we could have got the mortgage on a £3,000 new house in 1966, we probably would not have moved or gone into business. In fact, we might still have been there, with the taxman getting nothing, instead of £50 million in all kinds of taxes from our businesses over the last 40 years. I am so pleased that I didn't earn enough to get that £3,000 mortgage, and so should the taxman!!

We aimed to pay an enormous amount of tax each year, that becoming a subliminal priority goal in life. On the other hand, the accountants use every legal loophole that they can to save us tax, as we think that we can make a better contribution to society with the money that we save - more than any bureaucracy can.

BACK

Money is to be used, not hoarded, and we have spent only a fraction of our income on ourselves and the rest always on the business. It makes me laugh when I see the prime minister accusing well-known people of evading tax; no, they're not, they are using a system that the government have approved. If they don't think people will use the rules, they should not make them.

I also think that people shouldn't be proud of not paying tax. If you don't pay you shouldn't have a say, and I class do-gooders as the ones who pay the most, not the arseholes who live off the taxpayers full-time, then whine all the time. At the other end of the scale, companies like Starbucks and Google are making millions in the UK, then they pay very little tax because of the incompetence of the government in not making the right rules; or is there another reason?

## You Can Have Money for Nothing

I talk to many people who want to make money, but some have a real problem with this thinking, as their minds think debt instead of investment. At the moment, in 2014, there is a window of opportunity in the UK; the banks are paying maybe ½% or 1% interest on your money and lend at between 3% and 5%, which people can then invest into things that make between 6% and 30%, sometimes a lot more. It's just a matter of seeing opportunities.

# We All Struggle in life With Something

## *"What pushes you?"*

Marilyn wanted financial security, because when her mother and father were young they had a terrible struggle working in, and trying to save the family bakery business from going bankrupt and then, when it consequently failed, they closed it down.

The other thing she craved for was stability, after the experience of her father having a nervous breakdown from losing the business, seeing the long struggle to overcome his illness, although she didn't realise it was an illness at the time - she just thought her father was permanently awkward with her.

Marilyn's thoughts on this at the time when I met her in 1966 were that her father hated her because her mum was expecting her when they got married. Somehow, Marilyn thought that her dad blamed her for having to get married, but that was not true. Her parents never explained the illness to her or, if they did, she couldn't understand it, and, of course, the mind plays games with you if you don't ask questions; but she wouldn't dare, and what questions could a child ask?

SIDETRACKED

She certainly can't ever remember being praised, or told by her parents that she was good and that they adored her. Marilyn's mother was wrapped up in keeping her father calm because of his breakdown, as he was likely to go off on one at the slightest thing. Having said that, Marilyn doesn't remember much about her childhood, as she seems to have blanked it out; until, that is, I came along and, like everyone else, we said we would bring up our kids differently.

It would be great to know what your kids think of you when they are growing up; you then could explain why you were doing what you were doing, or it could give you a chance to alter what you are doing as a parent. When I was a kid I just knew I was loved, even though I was beaten most days. Funny!

If I had my time again I would tell my kids every day that I love them. It's easier from the start and, if I had done that, it would have banished all of the negative things because you can't be negative when you are talking positively.

# "There are no bad children in this world, only bad parents."

Neville Wright

I have always told my four grandchildren that there are no naughty children in this world, only naughty mummies and daddies and, oh yes, of course, naughty nannies and pops; that's Marilyn and me. It works; it's reverse psychology - I have four wonderful grandchildren from 18 months to 20 years old.

## It Was a Difficult Time for Everyone

BACK

Just to put things into perspective about Marilyn's father; when he came out of hospital he got a job straight away, but he could only hold it down for a couple of weeks because of his health. Then he got another, and another. He had lots and lots of jobs and gradually, over the years, he managed to hold each one just a bit longer. One of the jobs he got was as a milkman; he has said he doesn't know how he controlled the horse and cart because he was so ill. It was in the winter of 1963. One day, in the ice and fog, a coal lorry ran into the back of the cart and the horse bolted without David.

## I Just Thought He Was Bonkers

I can't imagine what state he was in when that happened. I feel for him, being in the situation he was in throughout all of those years. He has always worked, not just one job, but also sometimes two and three jobs he had going at the same time. When I met him in 1966 he had three jobs - one full-time job as a computer operator on shift work; in between his shifts he would man a kiosk in a petrol station and, at the same time, he would have a football coupon round.

This is a man who was so ill that for ten years he had to hold onto the railings as he went to work so he didn't fall over. The government nowadays should use people like him as a benchmark for giving out social security payments to people who say they are incapable of working.

Marilyn used to say he would go for weeks and weeks without talking to her which, to her, was mental torture and unacceptable. He clearly needed help from the doctors, who let him down.

It didn't help when I came along in 1966, a very good-looking young man if I do say so myself, seeing his daughter and sweeping her off of her feet. I thought obviously he was frightened that I would make her pregnant and then run away; well, he would have been right about the first bit, if I had got the chance, but not the second.

I just thought he was bonkers; I didn't understand what was going on, although I was told; it really did not register with me. He would make life so difficult for us at every touch and turn which, in hindsight, was the best thing that could have happened as it strengthened our relationship.

On the other hand, our relationship could have ended so many times because of that. He wouldn't let Marilyn go to a pub, so I didn't; he wouldn't let her go to a dance, so I didn't; she had to be in by 10 pm so, consequently, we never saw any film endings. We had to leave the cinema 15 minutes before the end to catch a bus because, if we were late home, life for Marilyn would not be worth living. This went on until we got married.

All of this was in the most difficult of times and circumstances of trying to get a better life, dealing with so many jobs, the lack of money and the lack of experience. Of course I now know we were doing all of this while our brains were still developing from children to adulthood; scientists say brains are still developing up until the age of 24.

I have my doubts about that, because Marilyn says mine very often is still like that of a child. She says to me, "You're worse than Charlie and he is 10 years old." He's our eldest grandson. By this time my father was a changed man with me. I am convinced it was because of Marilyn - I think it would have been a bit embarrassing for him if he hit me in front of her.

## Dropping Below Our Standards

When we were buying the first house, my dad said that I was dropping below my standards because we lived in a very nice area of Peterborough, even though the house that we were buying was only five minutes away and both of our streets were two minutes from Millfield, where the shops are. However, the street that we were going to had all terraced houses that were on the road, whereas Dad's street contained detached houses that had front gardens and garages. I said to him, "Dad, you have a standard, but I haven't found mine yet."

## We Were Before Our Time

At that time it was normal, when people got married, to rent rooms or a house before they bought their own. I wanted to put my money into a property instead of renting, even if it was in an area that Dad thought was not so good as the area that we had been brought up in.

The house we bought had no front garden, and most houses down that street had back passages where you had to go over your next-door neighbour's property every day. I found the people were more caring and friendly than any others we have known in the places we have lived in; I think it was because they were all older and from the war era, when people shared what they had with each other. Also, women didn't go out to work before the war and, consequently, there were closer communities.

Dad soon got over his problems. He probably told his friends that I had bought a house but omitted to tell them where it was. When he saw what we were doing, he spent a considerable amount of time and effort helping us to renovate the house. I really think he was just trying to protect us because we were very young, and it was very unusual, really unheard of, what we were doing.

There was no benchmark for him to compare us to but, after all, it was him who continually said to me, "I should have," when I was young, so what could he have expected from me? All those years of subliminal teachings, and I needed to prove to him that I was in fact taking in what he was trying to teach, and that was to be a good person.

## I Worked For a Madman

I went from working for idiots to working for a boss who was a madman; yes, that was me!! When your back is against the wall you work like hell to survive; it's just not like working for someone else; it's all down to you; the buck stops with you. There is an Italian saying which I like, that goes something like this:

## *"The fish stinks from the head down."*

*In other words, I am responsible for everything in my life; my marriage, my finances, my family, my business, my friends, my troubles and my triumphs. I am where I am right now because of an accumulation of what I have done throughout my entire life up to this point in time.*

## I Am Responsible for My Life

I am responsible for everything that's happened in my life. Now I cannot blame anyone for anything, that's just great!! Now that gives me a clean sheet of paper every day, with nothing to stop me writing whatever I like, and to do whatever I want to do. List the things that you want to do, have and to be, the people that you want to be with and share your life with.

Just remember that, unfortunately, it doesn't mean that each one of these people is thinking and wanting the same things as you are.

## We all Struggle

Well, I suppose we do all struggle all of our lives with something or other and, if that's the case, I think it's all right as long as those things keep on changing. I just used to think that we would continually struggle with the same thing; then we found out that, with perseverance and need, we could get over the "problem". This in turn led to more problems and different struggles.

At this point we realised that this is just life and also realised that, the more struggles we got over, the more we could do and the more money we made. So, with that in mind, we actually started to look out for problems, in whatever we were doing, before they occurred.

Nowadays you would call it risk assessment; that encapsulates everything in the journey from why a product is being made, through the design and the manufacture, to the ease of use by the end user, and on and on it goes. A tiny example: because I am dyslexic and could never write a cheque out, we taught our till staff to recognise the telltale signs; when customers were struggling, we would immediately say, "Shall I do the cheque for you, as we have a name stamp?" And invariably we would write the whole cheque for them - another happy customer.

# Focus

## *"Follow one course until success"*

SIDETRACKED

This is what it was like when I first started. Imagine it's just becoming dusk; at the end of your street appears a boy with a ladder over his shoulder, and a bucket in the other hand. You're saying, "What's strange about that?"

The strange thing is that this boy is trying to run, well, trying to go as fast as he can with a ladder and a bucket of water. He runs down the street until he gets to a house about halfway; his bucket goes over the top of the gate. With one finger he unlatches the gate and he races through it.

You look up the street expecting to see someone in pursuit, but there is no one; as soon as he gets through the gate he's got his ladder up against an upstairs window. He has already knocked on the door. He goes up the ladder and starts to clean the windows; the owner of the house comes out and looks up at the boy on the ladder, and the boy shouts down, "Could I have some clean water, please?" It's getting quite dark and eventually he can hardly see.

He finishes off the house and a smile comes over his face when he receives the last 30p of the day. This one's a bonus because it's an extra he's got in before the light faded completely on his minute-to-minute goals that have been set and re-set over the day. He now starts to walk home, smiling to himself, thinking about the extra 30p and what he can do with it; it's a bag of cement or a wheelbarrow-full of sand, which is 14 heaped shovels.

He then looks at his hands. They've been in a bucket of water all day and they're frozen cold and wrinkled; the plasters from the morning have fallen off hours ago, the raw skin is there from the night before when he had been cutting up the rolls of material for his wife to make products for his brother's market stall. Then they start to hurt.

BACK

Well, that was me. If I was painting or renewing guttering or something like that, I would carry on working on that ladder until

---

my legs shook uncontrollably through tiredness and standing on the ladder in the freezing cold or rain. I would be in such pain that my fingers locked together, being so cold - I would get cramp and have to pull them apart with my other hand to release the tools.

I was driven through the fear of failure. I just couldn't fail; you see, I had burnt my bridges the minute that I told the pompous ginger in the dole office that I would look after my family myself. I could only imagine what he would have said to me, turning up cap in hand. That, and many other thoughts, drove me on no matter how difficult things were. I am saying me, but Marilyn had exactly the same attitude.

## A Goal Within a Goal

If my goal for a day was to paint for eight hours, I had an inner goal that wanted to achieve 12 hours of normal painting by working faster and not taking breaks. I used to repeat to myself, "This is easy, this is easy, this is easy." I would start off painting windows, which needed a steady hand for the straight lines and, as the day progressed and I got more and more exhausted, I would shake.

So, in my minute-to-minute goals, I would go on to things like painting the garage doors. I could still paint, but with a roller instead of a brush, where it wasn't so obvious that I was shaking, as there were no defined lines like on windows. I realised after a while that I was only painting with one hand, whereas I had two, so I was only working at 50% capacity.

## Ambidextrous

I became ambidextrous; I ended up with two paintbrushes, usually a large one and a small one, the large one for the main work, the small one for cutting-in, plus a roller and, where I could, they would both be going, but that's a lot easier said than done. One customer said to me, "You're ambidextrous, aren't you?" Not understanding, I said, "No; I'm married." He then explained, and that was embarrassing.

SIDETRACKED

At this point I should tell you my star sign is Gemini. Marilyn always says she got two for the price of one when she got me. To top it all, I had problems with my back; some days it was like being stabbed repeatedly. I remember on many occasions falling onto my knees with pain and having to roll on to my back, pulling my knees up to my chest, rolling from side to side to put my spine back into a straight line after the discs had come out. If people had seen me they probably would have thought that I was mentally insane.

I was in such excruciating pain I could not do anything else to get my back aligned. This went on for the next twenty years before I had an operation and, thank goodness, for the last twenty-two years I've been able to do anything without pain. Another thing I did, which people would think a bit peculiar but I thought it was quite normal, was to paint houses by torchlight. Mind you, I would only put the undercoat on in the dark.

I would work in torrential rain, digging holes and putting fences up as, once you are wet, you are wet, and one advantage is that you can put your concrete in the hole dry, because the hole is full with water.

I used to clean second-hand bike-frames, and put six at a time on Marilyn's washing line and spray them. The neighbours thought I was crazy as, invariably, the wind would blow the spray in my face and I would turn blue; people now pay to see the Blue Man group - maybe they saw me first and got the idea.

I did this for my brother; you could have any colour bike in his shop that you wanted, as long as you wanted blue. I think blue was cheap at the time. I would take on any job going as long as it would not bring shame on to my mum and dad by being immoral or illegal; also, anything that did not involve reading, writing, or spelling.

BACK

I would be mending roofs in the morning, cleaning blocked drains in the afternoon and then, in the evening, I would be putting up "For Sale" boards for a property agent and, all of the time, keeping my eyes and ears open, asking people if they knew anyone who needed anything doing; nothing was too small to do. If I ever faltered in my positive thinking, I would repeat to myself what Muhammad Ali, the world boxing champion who taught me so much, said:

**"Neville;**
**"If I were a garbage collector I would collect more bins than anyone else; I would have the title 'Champion Bin Collector of the World,' and I would do it before any of my opponents got out of bed."**

Although Ali never actually spoke to me directly, I imagined he had, because that's how he came over when speaking on the TV. I knew that, once Marilyn started to work with me, everything would be all right. I had the idea that she would be safe; I would be able to look after her and she would be able to help me with my dyslexia - a goal within a goal. We would be stronger together than apart.

At that time Marilyn couldn't drive and was nervous about getting a licence. She needed to be pushed into getting one, and the only way I could push her was to say that, if she wanted security and money to spend in the future, this was the one thing that stood in her way.

# No Sympathy, Just Lots of Empathy

If you can imagine, this was a massive leap for her. She had just been through four years of staying at home by herself, and I wasn't just asking her to get a driving licence. She was going to drive a truck full of bricks, sand, cement and roof tiles; she was going to mix concrete, go on roofs and dig trenches. But I forgot to tell her all that; what I actually said was, "You could make it easy for us by getting bits from the builders' merchants and doing the invoices in the truck to make things quicker."

Quite a big difference between a nervous housewife worried about getting a driving licence and what Marilyn was embarking on - being a truck driver, loading and unloading building materials all day.

If I had told Marilyn what I wanted her to do she may have been scared off, although I doubt it, but using the Kaizen method of one small step at a time builds confidence, and it works. I have used this method of thinking and doing all of my life, even long before I heard of it when I got the CDs and, like so many things you do, you have a feeling that you are doing it right, but to have someone else say the same thing confirms that you are on the right track.

SIDETRACKED

Early on in my life I knew there was knowledge in books that would tell me how to think, act, and do things to make me successful, but I didn't know how to unlock those jumbled-up letters. I started with vinyl records, then tapes, then CDs. Gradually over the years I would learn how to recognise words. Maybe I could read one in five words. Some of the books contradicted what I thought business logic was, so I didn't take any notice of them but, when I re-read them twenty years later, at the age of 45 (by then I could read one in two words), they made complete sense. Now, at 64, normal books are OK, although I am doing university courses on the mind, and some of those words are challenging.

## My Eyes Just Couldn't Focus

When I was at school, focus was an entirely different matter; every time I blinked my eyes the letters would change. Below is a chart that the teacher would put on the blackboard with one word in each box, and then tell the kids to come up to the front of the class and point to a word and read it. I would watch the other kids to see where they pointed and what they said. I then could remember, 3 across 2 down is "ran", 4 across 4 down is "trap", and so on. The first time, I only remembered one word; unfortunately, the kid before me said the same word. That stuffed me that day.

| COW | PIG | HEN | DOG |
| CWO | GPI | EHN | GDO |
| CAT | MUD | RAN | MAM |
| ATC | UDM | ARN | MNA |
| DAD | NUT | ANT | TAP |
| ADD | UNT | TNA | PTA |
| CLAP | MILK | SNAP | TRAP |
| PLAC | MKIL | ASPN | PRAT |

I could see that the box had only one word but, every time I blinked the letters changed places, so all I could do was to copy others and, when the class started reading from books, I then became a truant because I was so scared of the punishment. The teachers didn't seem to have any time for me and there wasn't any helper like there is now, and I wouldn't tell my mum and dad.

## Focus On the Things That You Can Do

BACK

I would do whatever I was capable of doing, while looking out all of the time for better paying jobs. There are only 24 hours in a day, and I knew that I shouldn't waste one of them. I knew that, if I hadn't got enough money to live the life that I wanted, I would just have to work more.

I have now read hundreds of books and, in some way, have made money out of every one, some within minutes of reading them. The first book I had when I was 13 was on yoga; I still have it. I have practised this for mental and physical wellbeing. The next two books, which I read at 17, were on pig farming; I still have them.

Pigs are like humans - curious, mischievous, funny, lazy, and don't know when to stop eating.

## I Don't Understand

I have people say to me that they've read this or that book, but they don't understand most of it. Well, don't worry about what you don't understand, but concentrate on the bits you do.

In 1975 I was painting the outside of some flats along Lincoln Road. It was a few doors away from the school that I sometimes attended. The flats belonged to Mrs Preston, the lady who lived opposite to us; her husband gave me the window-cleaning job on the first week I started the business.

One of the tenants looked like a hippy; he certainly didn't do anything in the days when I was there. Perhaps he was on his holiday, or worked at night, but not in my mind. I asked him if he could open the window so I could paint it. There was a book on the windowsill; the title was *The Lazy Man's Way to Riches*, and I thought, "He's lazy and seems to survive, so it must be a good book," so I bought it.

Although I struggled to read a lot of the words, these gaps naturally got filled in by the words that I could understand which surrounded them. In short, it quite clearly said that I was responsible for my life, I couldn't use failure as a crutch to stop me doing things, and my mind was mine and would make me rich. I think the word "lazy" was reverse psychology.

Another book was called *Grow Rich While You Sleep*; it reinforced what we could achieve and the power of my mind. I say "we" because we were a team, but Marilyn hadn't got the interest for all this rubbish as she had got so much more to think about and at the end of the day she was just shattered. I, on the other hand, thought, "*Grow Rich While You Sleep*; I want some of that."

Napoleon Hill's book was *Think and Grow Rich*, a huge book that came with eight tapes. It took weeks to study, and the only thing I really got from it was to focus; simple, brilliant, and worth every minute spent on it.

## Nothing in the Books Is Any Good

I have read 100s of non-fiction books over the last fifty years and continue to do so, on a daily basis. Every one of them has held lots of information that has told me what to do and how to do it. They explain how to have, be, and do everything that you want in life, but none of this stuff is any good at all, and will not work for you unless you do. I would say that I've had to focus 90% on whatever I am doing, and the other 10% on what's going on around me, looking all of the time for new ways to go.

Unfortunately, from time to time I have forgotten, ignored or thought that I could bypass the principles in these books and CDs and, to my amazement, I have come unstuck.

## LOST BOOK

I have lent many books out over the years, most never finding their way back. One that I lent was my 1973 edition of *The Lazy Man's Way to Riches*, by Joe Karbo; if you are the person reading this, can I have it back please, as I don't want to spend £53 on an old original one that cost me around £6.50? Mind you, I have probably made millions from it, but I am also sentimental.

## *The 7 Habits of Highly Effective People*

In 1989 I bought *The 7 Habits of Highly Effective People* by Stephen Covey. I still have the six cassettes and work book; the work book didn't get filled in, but I listened to the cassettes a hundred times. I reckon I made a million pounds from them. I think they cost £39.99 in the 80s, but now the price for used ones is £4.90; can you imagine, less than a beer?! £5 for a million pounds' worth of information!

## *The Psychology of Achievement* by Brian Tracy

This is another one that I would recommend; there is a lot of good stuff that will help to trigger your own ideas. It's so easy today, with all of the information about, but there is always a but - too much information before you get started can freeze your brain into procrastination.

These things will teach you how to develop and run a successful business for the long run. Technology, on the other hand, is here; it can attract customers away from your business easily, all other things being equal. In the future technology, combined with awesome products and instant customer gratification, will make business practices as we know them, a thing of the past. You don't need to know how to program or even turn on a computer to be an

Internet success; all you need is to employ technicians to turn your ideas, thoughts and dreams into reality. ***"Just look at Jack, Ma"***

One of our tenants asked me today how much my Range Rover cost. I told him £107,000, and he said it was all right for me! He could get one for less than a fiver if he knew where to go but, of course, he would want it now, not in a few years' time and, in doing nothing about it now, he will still be in the exact same position in a few years' time, when the price will be £170,000.

***This picture was taken on 15<sup>th</sup> November 2011***

I initially was going to write a book on dyslexia, so I thought that this picture would be good to have on the front cover. I shelved that idea because I only had my own experience, and thought it wasn't enough to help other people on this subject. That's fear for you.

Then I wanted to write a book on our nursery business for our grandchildren, as Marilyn and I really didn't know anything about our grandparents, let alone our great grandparents; but I couldn't get started, as there were always other more pressing or existing things to do. I was then asked to do a history of Marville Properties, so I did that, as we still had the business and there was no emotion stopping me; this was slow but easy to do. The book on the shop was an entirely different situation and immediately I started, well, within the first day, I realised that the two subjects were actually one; it's our lives that count, so that is what this book is about.

For 30 years my car has been my classroom. I have bored my kids silly listening to the motivational stories from countless people on tape, then CDs. I have already mentioned a couple, but the principles and philosophy are timeless; readers who want to improve their business might take time to explore some of this other stuff.

## My Favourite: *See You at the Top* by Zig Ziglar

It is just amazing what you can learn; I started with Zig's stuff in the early 80s and it's still as powerful today as it was then, with his motivational story-telling that you can relate to your own life.

## *Ageless Body, Timeless Mind* by Deepak Chopra

You are only as old as you think you are. This is fascinating; he explores the mind and body, meditation and philosophy among so many other things; everyone should at least give this some time.

## *Think and Grow Rich* by Napoleon Hill

I would say this teaches people to discipline themselves to achieve whatever they set out to do in life, and how you have to think to build an organisation that you desire.

## *The Lazy Man's Way to Riches*; my book is back

I've added this in after I had finished the book as, in December 2015, the book that I lost years ago found its way back; that's the power of Joe Karbo's book, or my subconscious mind willing it to appear.

# Face The Fear

## *"If I didn't, I would always be running away forever"*

There was absolutely no hesitation on Marilyn's part about being in business together. We had always wanted this but, nevertheless, it was still so exciting; every day we pushed ourselves, not really knowing where we were going. Every now and then there would be a moment of triumph when we bought or sold another property or made a bit more profit on a job that went well. That made it all worthwhile, making up for the jobs that took twice as long to do, and not only wiping out all of the profit in the job but actually costing us money. With hindsight, the more quickly you make mistakes in business, the fewer mistakes you will make when the business gets bigger; but we didn't want too many - well none, really.

## I Was Left High and Wet

In life there are hurdles you have to jump if you want to succeed; they are an everyday occurrence. You can keep putting things off, like getting a driving licence but, one day, you have to make that leap, usually when the rewards outstrip the fear of doing it, or the lack of rewards. In other words, if I'm not getting what I want out of this, then I might as well face the fear and do something else and, if I get nothing for my effort, then I'm no worse off.

Sometimes you have to be pushed - we pushed each other to the brink; and as for the rewards, they were always there, by having the challenges of working with each other every day. The first week that Marilyn joined me I had an emergency call from Pete the estate agent. He asked if I could mend a roof damaged in the high winds. The wind had blown some tiles off and the rain was getting in, so I went with my new aluminium ladder that my mum had bought me for Christmas 1974. I've still got it somewhere; it cost £53, which was a lot of money then. The wooden ones were just being replaced by lighter, stronger aluminium.

I put the ladder up, resting on the cast-iron gutter and went up. Unfortunately, there was nowhere to tie it to but, luckily, the house next door had a bit higher roof that meant I could push my homemade roof ladder up the roof and against the protruding wall of the next house. This ladder that I had made had got supermarket trolley wheels off an old cart and shelf brackets held on by one-inch screws to hold it over the ridge. It had a mind of its own and, with the swivel wheels, it was lethal. A proper roof ladder would cost £34.

I managed to get on the roof just as a big gust of wind blew the ladder; Marilyn was trying to hold on to it but it was too heavy and over it went, crashing to the floor. I was stuck on the roof; the wind was howling and it was raining, and now I was shitting myself. The ladder had gone over and taken all the skin off her leg, landing across her foot. She was lying on the pavement, thinking her foot had been broken; I felt helpless - I was stuck. Before I went up to do the job I told the tenant what we were doing. He stood at his door throughout this, just watching us and, after what seemed to be an age of Marilyn trying to pick the ladder up, a man who was passing by helped her with it. That was Marilyn's initiation into the business.

SIDETRACKED

We soon realised that two minds working together are better than three separate ones doing their own thing. Years later, when we had five heads in Kiddicare all going in one direction totally in the zone 24/7, there was no limit to what we could do. Those five minds infected probably fifty more around us, all working together and knowing what part they played in the success of the company. It's all a matter of transference of feelings. If I can transfer my thoughts, feelings and desires to someone who has ambition, wants and needs, but doesn't have a vocation, if they are really willing to learn then there is success. Everyone has a slightly different opinion of what to do once their success has been achieved, and not everyone achieves their own success on the same project at the same time, even though the outside world looking on may think so.

# We Wanted To Help Each Other

BACK

Marilyn got a licence and drove the VW pickup truck with no problems. In the 1960s and early 1970s, lots of things were new to us; we were nervous about using the phone, and the thought of going on a plane was just scary and out of this world. I am sure that nowadays people would not understand this, as this is normal now. We had no time to hesitate after going into business; we had just got to do it, and we helped and encouraged each other through these things. When I was young I didn't know that I had dyslexia; I just thought that I was dumb because, in the 1950s, if you couldn't read you got put into the corner of the classroom with your face touching the two walls. This just taught me to be afraid of the teachers and to hate school.

In 1955 the school doctor gave me a pair of glasses, as that was the cure for not being able to read; either glasses or a good slapping. Of course neither solved the problem but only succeeded in teaching truancy. I thought that having Marilyn on board would give us far more scope with the business, which proved to be right. Not only could she read, write and spell, which I thought was marvellous, she could also help me, as I could never understand why the letters moved around. I didn't know how people deciphered all of those jumbled-up letters, but Marilyn could, and she could work with me.

I knew that Marilyn was more educated than me, but it was only at the age of 40 that I finally admitted that I couldn't spell. She has told me how to spell the same freaking words, three letters at a time and, although sometimes she has shouted at me to listen, she still has the patience, the perseverance and the understanding to help me with whatever I am doing; but I know now that I couldn't have been educated any differently in the 50s and 60s.

Just to give you an idea: the other day I was writing the word "minute" On the next line I spelled it "mniute," and further down the page was "mintue." When I signed myself off the dole, I think my signature was something like "n.d.wirhtg." I have had to go back over this book many times, as things like all the "nos" were written as "ons." It's not until someone reads a page that I know. Maybe I didn't legally sign off the dole, and they owe me 40 years back money, Ha-Ha-Ha, considering I have never had a proper job since then.

Marilyn did her homework, whereas I made bonfires, climbed trees and looked after my animals. She took her exams, although on the day of her 11 Plus she failed; two hours of nerves can alter a child's life forever, even when their course work is up to the high school grade. Dyslexics picked stones off the playing field because that's all they were good for, while normal kids took the lessons.

Marilyn wanted to learn. As for me, when a teacher put me down, or said that I was stupid, I obviously wanted to adhere to their expectations and prove that I was taking notice of them. So, in a way, I didn't fail my teachers; well, I mean,

## *"I did not fail my teachers' expectations of me."*

## Keep Up With Inflation

The day we sold our house on wheels was a happy day; the snow had gone, we moved into the house, we had sold the caravan for £630 to keep us going; and to think that seven years earlier we had bought our first house for £650. This showed us where property prices were going to go in the future; in fact, all prices. Ten years later Marilyn bought me a watch for £650; then, two years after that, we bought a patio table and chairs for £650. By that time the £650 house was worth £14,000.

## The Flea That Jumped Higher

Tiny things can make a big difference. I heard a story on one of Zig Ziglar's tapes about a circus that trained fleas. It was simple how they did it; all they did was to put the fleas into a jar and put the lid on. The fleas would hit the lid every time they jumped. Eventually the fleas jumped just short of the lid then, once the lid was taken off, the fleas could not jump out. They had been conditioned not to jump any higher. It's the same as kids who are told that they won't amount to anything; they are conditioned not to jump too high.

Fortunately, I never listened; I think I was a bit deaf as well as thick, and I just kept jumping.

Shortly after Marilyn joined me in the business working on the building sites, we found that our income was increasing and, within literally a few weeks, we had got enough money to finish off the decorating in the house and make the garden look respectable by clearing the building rubbish away, laying new grass, and planting the borders. In this way, any buyers would not be put off by what looked like a builder's yard or, as most people would say, a shit hole.

We needed to sell the house because the property was too big with its four bedrooms, and it had an insatiable appetite for electricity for the storage heaters. When I say we earned more money in a few weeks, I was talking about only a few pounds really, a tiny amount to finish off the job; a few pounds make all the difference when you haven't got any.

## Present Your House as a Picture

SIDETRACKED

When I was working on the Land Reclamation Project, a man came to work on the same shift as myself. His name was Bill something; he was a cocky Londoner who knew everything. He had travelled, working in lots of power stations amongst other things; that's if he was to be believed. He was in his 40s, with lots of experience that I could listen to. I worked it out that if he had stayed at each of the jobs that he said he had had for three months, he would have been at least 120 years old. Having said all of that, he did tell me one thing that has stuck with me, and I have acted on ever since. He said, "Neville, when selling a property present your house as a picture, and the garden as the frame;" those few words compensated for all of the shit that I had to listen to from him over that year. When I look back I can see why the neighbours did not talk to us, seeing a garden looking like a rubbish dump.

BACK

No sooner had we put the house on the market than we sold it for £12,500. The couple who bought it only looked at the inside together for a few minutes and then went; then the lady came back a minute later, and spent about 30 minutes looking around. The man sat outside in his Rolls-Royce, listening to *The Archers* on his car radio. It was 7 o'clock in the evening, and that's what millions of people used to do at 7 o'clock in those days, but not all of them sat in a Rolls-Royce. I think that if I hadn't taken notice of Bill about the garden we would have not sold the house so quickly and for so much. **(Thanks Bill)**

## We Now Had a Choice Which Way to Go

Suddenly, the sale gave us £9,500 in cash after we had paid off the mortgage. It was incredible to think that when we were 16 years old we had an ambition to have our own house. I thought I was going to struggle paying a mortgage for 25 years before owning it. Here we were, nine years after we had first met, with enough money in cash to buy a really super detached house or, probably, six terraced houses. We knew we did not want to end up living back in a caravan; one thought of that, even on the hottest summer day, would make us shiver.

At this point, having done all of this work and now receiving this money we could, if we liked, just buy a nice house and we could have a year off work and take it easy. We could have, but now we had a purpose in life. We knew that if we were to take it easy we wouldn't fulfil our financial dreams or work together, so the thought of getting a job never crossed our minds; not for a second.

I was born to be self-sufficient; if only I'd known that when I left school. I got a job because everybody else did; people are conditioned not to do what they like, but to do what others in their community expect of them.

### *"I think in the 1950s the system educated me and boys like me to be gun fodder for future wars"*

It's a good job that there haven't been any world wars, as maybe I would have served my educational purpose. If I had known at the age of 15 that I was going to be self-employed by the time I was 24, maybe I wouldn't have wasted my time listening to negative verbal garbage from some of the people whom I worked with over the years. Obviously they were the majority, but the minority were great people I learned from; they also protected me in lots of ways. I worked for three years with a man called Arnold Makey, and I would like to thank him for being there for me and protecting me when I started a new job. I worked with him when I was a vulnerable 18-year-old, the youngest of sixty men who thought kids should not be working with them. I know he watched out for me. After leaving this job I was too busy to keep in touch, but I never forgot his kindness, which I have tried to emulate by protecting other people, as he protected me.

# I Didn't Know What I Didn't Know

Life would be boring if you knew everything. Obviously, self-employment came along at the right time; by then I had learned enough to survive, and get as far away as possible from negative people; reprogramming myself became an all-consuming project for me.

SIDETRACKED

I feel for people who have the knowledge to be self-employed and, I must emphasize, want to be, but they won't put it into practice because of their fear of dropping their standard that they have built, plus knowing that they will have to get off their backsides to do something. They very often ask me for my opinion of what they should do, then they say things like, "But..." There is always a **but** and, when I hear that, I think, "Here we go with the never-ending list of excuses." "I have only got 15 years left to get my pension" or "I'm not risking my savings or my house." They say, "I would if I had the money like you." They normally have access to the money but will not use it.

They don't realise they are so experienced and intelligent that they wouldn't fail but, if they did, they have the ability to go back and work for someone else. I would imagine that they could go back in a much better position because, after being self-employed, their perspective will have changed with the knowledge of how one has to work at a business for it to survive.

# Schools Should Teach Survival Classes

I think everybody should have a go at looking after themselves, just so they understand how their bosses think and feel about business. It probably should be compulsory every ten years or so, like conscription should be, in my opinion, even if it's for three months. I am sure that our economy and morale would benefit from this type of education, whatever age you are.

Schools should have real courses on survival; I don't mean jungle survival, I mean in everyday life, like the consequences of getting into debt. I talk a lot about borrowing, but not to buy clothes, cars or holidays; that's bad debt. I'm talking about investment debt used to speculate to accumulate. I have advised many people to invest in a dishwasher, because I can see that they can make more money working on their business rather than washing dishes by hand, so it's not all about the big stuff; it starts with the small stuff.

Now, of course, I was into this situation of being my own boss, being young with a daring attitude, having plenty of energy that meant I could work every waking hour. Also, by then I was totally immersed in business, mentally in that zone, so it never crossed my mind to give it up for an easier life. I say "easier" but I don't mean that, because ducking and dodging anything to do with writing was sheer hell for me.

So, at that time, I would never have been able to climb any company ladder, and why would I want to, having this opportunity to create a business? I just loved every minute of creating our own destiny, not knowing what's going to happen in the next minute, let alone the next month or year. I knew deep down in my heart I could never work for anyone else, because I still thought I was too dumb; besides, what would Marilyn do, try to get a job around the school run for the next twenty years? Besides, we just loved every moment working together, so going back for us wasn't an option. That was a very significant tipping point for us, as from that point there was no return - we had burned our bridges completely.

Back to the sale of the house; at that time Peterborough was expanding fast and the Development Corporation was just building its first satellite township for the overspill from London. People were being paid to move out of London to Peterborough; we found a really nice, new, semi-detached house, which was on a communal heating system. This heating system was just absolute heaven compared to all the other cold houses that we had lived in; this house cost £5,950.

We could have bought this house for cash, still having some money to spare for holidays and the like, but we were in no frame of mind to sit back and relax. We now had a taste for adventure; the freedom of self-employment had got to us. We knew that if we gave up now, our goal of being financially independent would never be achieved, and we could now see that doing what we were interested in was also making us a living. So, at this point, we could have taken it easy or, with a great deal of effort we could push boundaries. Now to us, this was exciting; we soon forgot about all of the hard work and suffering when we started to achieve our ambitions in life, the first of which was working together.

## The Fleas Finally Jumped Out Of the Jar

Looking back to that point in our lives in 1976, I now can't imagine how we had the strength to get through; maybe our backs were against the wall and, with nowhere else to go, you just do it. I remember that, at the time, we could not believe it had happened - the fleas had finally jumped out of the jar and could jump whenever and wherever, and as high as they liked.

## Money Is a Product, Not a Goal for Us

It can be very hard for most people to go and risk all of their money. I suppose we had never had any real money in our hands; it was always tied up in assets, and living in the 10ft caravan was a standard; it did not matter. Money was now a product for us, to be used in the business, not a goal. Obviously, the more you have the more you can do. It was then that we started to use the leveraging of our assets as a means of expansion; it wasn't because we had to do it, like we did before, it was because we wanted to just for fun. Some people have hobbies and interests; business became ours, and the only difference was we were getting paid for this hobby.

Mentally, this liberated us to push our business forward without constantly worrying about debt all of the time; although we were getting into more debt than we ever had before, it was a debt that we thought we could manage and repay quite easily because we were starting to buy more property assets. We were borrowing money to make money; we could see the property market that we were in at the time was on an upward trend, so we went with it.

### *"Money Wasted Is Just That, Money Wasted"*
Neville Wright

SIDETRACKED

There are people who say to me that they wish they had got the money to start a business or money for investments that they are interested in. If I know them, I say to them, "You've got a house that is paid for, or nearly paid for; that will give you plenty of collateral so you could leverage this asset so you really have got the money available to you." Unfortunately, they say, "I'm not going to do that. I am not risking my house." I say, "Of course not; stay away from making money, keep on making excuses for not putting your money where your mouth is; just keep wishing someone else will do it for you."

There are people I speak to who have made the decision to be independent and look after themselves. They are like sponges; they soak up all of the information they can, then they look for ways that the information can be used in their business and lives, always looking at everything as positive. Then there is another type of person who thinks that the business that they are working in is totally dependent on them; they are always thinking that they should be self-employed and have the money that their employers are getting.

Some of them ask for advice, and then contradict what I have said, and always give excuses why they won't do it. They are in limbo land because they won't invest the money needed for this, or even the time needed, or take the responsibility that goes with self-employment. They are the people that are always saying, "We should have," or "could have" and today, there goes another missed opportunity.

BACK

I have found that, when people wish, most don't wish with conviction. I have found that, if you do wish with conviction, you will get what you want and, if it means leveraging your house, you will do it. A house is only an asset; whatever you have in life you are the custodian of that thing, whether it's a house, vintage car, land or money; you are never going to keep it.

I say whatever you have, please look after it and leave it for the next person in better condition than you found it. That goes for money as well, especially money; it should be looked after with pride, not buried deep in the ground, or a bank; money cultivated grows, and makes more money. Using money to make money, I use money three times at the same time.

# We Had No Fear of Failure

If we had failed we would just have started again. We discussed the risks of losing the money that we had worked so hard together for, and we were 100% together on this, believing that, if we ever failed in any business venture and lost our house, we could always go back to living in a caravan, and starting again. Now we didn't want to do that, but we knew we could if we had to so, therefore, having that as a benchmark, a standard, everything above a 10ft caravan was a bonus and, in our minds, everything we wanted to do became doable and achievable.

We put £2,000 deposit on the house in Langley, Bretton, and had a £4,000 mortgage; we still had about £8,000 left in cash. We started to buy cheap houses between £1,250 and £2,250 and then renovated them. As soon as the estate agent said "yes" we had agreed a price with the vendor, we got the keys from the estate agent to draw plans and calculate what we needed for the renovation, and got permission to put materials into the houses ready to start work.

## Do I Want a Wife, Or a Happy Wife?

Enthusiasm and ignorance of the procedures took hold, and invariably we started renovating the houses so they were ready to sell the minute we had completed the purchases. The reason we could do this with most of them was that the people who owned the houses usually lived a long way from Peterborough and the chances of them finding out were pretty minimal, so we kind of knew the risk. We did not think we were doing anything wrong, as the vendor would be the winner if we did not complete the purchase. If they had found out, they could have withdrawn their house from the market, if they had not already signed the contract. They could have then sold it at a substantial profit and we would have been left up the creek without a paddle.

That was the chance we took, oblivious to the consequences. This is what happens in life, you take a chance. We always said we wouldn't do anything if it were immoral or illegal but this, in our eyes, wasn't immoral because we would renovate somebody's house, which was usually derelict, and they could have made a lot of money through our ignorance.

It was only after a solicitor told us that we had to sign first and then get permission, that we realised the problem; we did it that way after that. We didn't think it was illegal as, at the time, we had the money to pay for the houses; so, without knowledge you do these things in life until you get a clearer understanding of the implications.

We came pretty near to that situation on one of the houses and, after that, we made sure we had exchanged contracts and we always got permission from the vendor to start work between exchange and completion. You learn as you go along, sometimes by the skin of your teeth and, as for me not carrying on as I had been doing, it was because Marilyn said so; she interpreted things in a different way from me and inevitably that's the way we went, as I didn't want just a wife, I wanted a happy wife. To get one was easy, I just had to do things in our business the right way.

We then moved into our new house; it didn't take long as we hadn't got much furniture - the kitchen table and four chairs we bought from the Freemans catalogue two years before we got married, our bed, Elaine's bed and a couple of wardrobes which we bought from what I think was the first Indian-owned shop in Peterborough, called *Wahiwala*. I believe they are still there in Gladstone Street, and we splashed out and got a brand-new three-piece suite. It was a lot better than a previous one that Marilyn had bought from the saleroom when I was at work one day; she had paid £15 for it, which seemed a lot of money for a second-hand three-piece suite at the time. I borrowed my father's trailer and went to pick it up; it was enormous, and so heavy. Marilyn had looked at it in the saleroom in the day, but she hadn't considered the size and she couldn't sit on it because it was on some high racking; it took two trips with Dad's trailer.

We eventually got it all in the house. I remember we struggled so much to try and get it through the doors, and then we sat on it; it stunk of dog pee. Marilyn cried, and I felt like crying for her as she had tried her best; clearly somebody in the saleroom had spotted a naïve person and drove the price up. We tried to clean it, but we couldn't, so I took it back to the salerooms the next week; two trips again but, unfortunately, people were a bit wiser than we were, and it never sold, not that week, the next week or the week after that, so we abandoned it to the auctioneers. We felt sick with the pain of losing that money; it still brings tears to my eyes now, thinking of how Marilyn must have felt spending what little money we had on what she thought would be a lovely three-piece suite in our front room that she could be proud of. With hindsight, it was a good lesson learned; as my father-in-law would say, "Open your eyes."

## Learn the Art of Being Deaf Sometimes

BACK

Sometimes it's good to be deaf. When we moved this time, people that we knew couldn't believe we had gone down-market in their eyes, moving from a four-bedroom detached bungalow in what was a very nice area, to a three-bedroom semi-detached estate house, which was half the price.

***"Sometimes you have to go backwards to succeed."***

Neville Wright

This is where business people and non-business people's thoughts differ; we saw an opportunity to leverage assets, being our four-bedroom home, with the downside of not having enough money to heat the large place, and being far too big for us at that time, too. When the time was right, and only if we wanted to, we could then get a much bigger and better house than before, going to a lovely warm, smaller house that gave us, at the time, the money we needed to invest so we would eventually make more money in our quest to be financially independent. It was the right decision.

The person who is not in business thinks, "I am not giving up what I've got." All they can see is the status of big house versus a small one, and location, excellent or just good. Remembering that, only a few months before, we lived in a 10ft caravan, this move was excellent for our financial situation, and also our living requirements and, ever since then, we have had a saying:

### *"We take our luck as it comes, and we fit ourselves to it."*

That's exactly what we were doing; the luck was that we could sell our house at a profit, and fitting ourselves to it was buying the much smaller house with smaller overheads, a comfortable environment to live in, a brilliant and cheap heating system, and a lot less garden to look after, so saving time and money. Plus, we released money that was tied up, allowing us to progress further.

To us a house was a house; it served a purpose. Another example is if you had a Rolls-Royce that did ten miles to the gallon and you traded it in for a Mini that did 60 miles to the gallon, you would have money to spare for other things; but whether it's a Mini or a Rolls-Royce, it will still get you from A to B.

### *"Don't get stuck in your mind, like the flea in the jar."*

Neville Wright

It is inevitable that you will have to go backwards, so the sooner the better. Get used to it then, when the shit hits the fan in life, as it does at times, you can take things in your stride.

We treated life as though it was just an enormous theme park packed with games that you have to play to get you through life, whether you like it or not. When you enter the park at birth you get dealt a hand of your life cards which are completely random. It's up to you to swap those cards while playing the games in the order that has been chosen for you, but you will have to play them all, including the house of horrors; if not, you will not get to your desired destination.

## Creative Thinking Time

I have always had a tendency to carry on until I am exhausted so, over the years, I have literally not woken up some mornings, Marilyn going to work leaving me asleep. This used to occur about every two months; I would arrive in the office around 2pm, refreshed and raring to go with lots of new ideas.

This episode got known to the girls as CTT, my creative thinking time as, when I was drifting in and out of sleep, too exhausted to wake up, I would be thinking of new ventures and why we were doing other things in the business, how we were doing them, and whether there was an easier, quicker, or cheaper way through the process.

Without question, I came up with solutions to the problems, sometimes straightaway; other times the question would be put into my mind and forgotten about, then, out of the blue, the answer would come. But without being so exhausted, I would have never have had the patience to waste on creative thinking time.

## Create a Service

We needed to create a service that was different to what other people were doing in our chosen market at any time which, I must say, seemed to alter every day; there were hundreds of window cleaners about, but not any I came across that would clean their customers' gutters out.

In 1979, Margaret Thatcher became prime minister of the UK. I remember her saying that she was used to doing her decorating herself and anyone can do it. This made me angry but, after thinking about this, I knew that she was right - literally anyone could do what I was doing; probably not so well, but they could do it. Decorating, for me in the long run, was not going to give us abundance in life and everything that we would like.

So, at that time, the one thing that the normal householders shied away from was papering their ceilings, as it can be difficult and frustrating. The other thing, up to that point in time, was that ceiling paper was heavy and full of raised patterns, and which was easily destroyed by the untrained decorator resulting in stress, frustration and near-divorce.

There was a new paper that had a flat back which had wood chippings embedded into it, so it was impossible to mess the job up. I could charge double the amount per roll used, as opposed to papering the walls, yet it was still half the price of what a normal decorator would charge for the normal, old-type of paper. Everyone was happy; in fact, most people who were going to do the rest of the decorating themselves ended up giving me the whole job once I had done their ceiling.

## Keep Moving

Keep looking for ideas. You don't have to look far - as I was papering the ceilings I kept looking at the cheap plastic curtain-tracks that most people had. One day I had to take a curtain pelmet down to paper the ceiling, and found that it consisted of just 4 components that were so easy to copy. Wow! I was now in the pelmet manufacturing business, and I could do this in the evenings. Once the products were shown, the customer wanted them, even though they had never thought of them. Think of a product or service you would like, transfer that feeling and you have made the sale.

# Leveraging

*"Two fleas; one said, 'should we walk, or take a dog?' The other said, 'We'll use a dog - it would take a lifetime to get up that mountain."*

Leveraging the money we had left over from the sale of Alexandra Road, we bought number 220 Belsize Avenue; a 3-bedroom terraced house, for £1,250, and number 62 St Martin's Street for £2,250; this was 5 houses away from where we first started; it was un-modernised.

In those days, 1974 to 1976, you could buy a terraced house in Peterborough for between £1,000 and £2,500. There were literally dozens of these properties about; a lot of them had sitting tenants who had been in those premises since the 2$^{nd}$ World War, 1939 to 1945. A typical situation in the 60s and 70s was that a lot of private-tenanted properties were for sale because the amount of rent the landlords were getting had been fixed since the last World War.

The return on the value of the properties was basically 0%, so we started to buy these properties up as we could see a window of opportunity. Most of the tenants had been in the houses since the War. They didn't want to have their houses modernised while they were living there, but that was the only way that the rents could be put up to a sensible level by law.

## Solicitors

From 1968 to 1976 we had been with our solicitor, Eric Smeeton, of Buckle and Co. We had bought six houses; five of these houses were our homes, one was an investment. We now found ourselves buying another four houses all at the same time; these were going to be investments. Mr Smeeton asked what we were doing buying all of these houses; I said that we were going to make a business out of buying, renovating and selling property.

He told us in no uncertain terms that we were stupid. I am sure that he was trying to protect us from what he knew had been, in the past, a very difficult business strategy. He had clients in this type of business who were a lot older, and had much more experience than us. He said that if they could not make a living out of property, what made us think we could? I did not realise at the time that he was trying to help us. I understand now; what I should have said to him was, **"Thank you; I understand what you are saying but I believe we can make this work."**

I didn't. Taking his comments personally, I took all of the deeds he had of ours from him and went across the road to another solicitor, whom I didn't know. I was still hot-headed then, just like I was in the dole office that fateful day, but there obviously was an instinct in me that was pushing me in the right direction.

## From the Frying Pan into the Fire

I could have been jumping from the frying pan into the fire but, as luck would have it, I went into the safe hands of Derek Walker of Greenwoods who fortunately was on our wavelength; we stayed with him until he retired some 20 years later. Initially, when I spoke to Derek on the phone, I thought he was very abrupt; I thought, "I don't like you."

When I went into his office he was completing a deal with two others on the phones, one on each ear; his office was piled up with paperwork, and the atmosphere felt like something out of the movies. I had nothing but praise for him after that. He cut out the crap - although he did sound abrupt, he was efficient.

## He was another mentor without knowing it.

To be fair to Mr Smeeton, he made me think, and if we weren't to go down the same road as his other clients I had to think outside of the box. Also, Mr Smeeton was looking back, but things were changing and we were at the start of it, looking forward.

### "Always be on the lookout for the next opportunity in your field."

I found out that the local Council had good, vacant Council-houses with bathrooms and central heating, something that most of the old private housing didn't have. If the tenants applied for a Council house they would not only get to live in a much better house, they would also get help from us with moving expenses for new carpets and curtains and things like that, which lots of them decided to do. Everyone loved it - the tenant ended up with a really nice comfortable home; it was a win-win situation.
In turn, this enabled the house to be modernised and sold on, sometimes doubling the value of the property. This went on for a

few years, turning the houses round very quickly and, if the tenants didn't want to move, it was no problem. We would just think of it as an investment and, in time, we sold them on to other investors, normally at a profit but not all of them; some we lost money on, but that's something you have to expect in business - "you win some and you lose some!"

Unlike most builders we never lost any time through bad weather or any other hold-ups, as we used to be working on several of our own properties as well as customers' projects. We would always have more work than we could cope with; something had to give at some point, though, and we were constantly juggling with the type of work we were doing, putting the customers' work first and our own work as a backup if there was not enough of customers' work to do.

That was easier said than done, as we had our cash flow to think about, too; also, our original clients came first as, without them giving us work from the start, we wouldn't have had the business, so we felt that we had an obligation to do their work, even though we could have been making more money elsewhere.

From 1975, Marilyn was working with me during the day on the building sites, and then doing hairdressing in the evenings, taking phone calls, selling grass -that's grass for people's gardens (turf). Not only that, she was doing the bookwork for Wrightway Decorating. I was working as many hours as I could in the day then, in the evenings, I would go out giving estimates to prospective customers. I also would work for a company called Buy and Sell Direct. I was erecting "For Sale" boards on people's houses and persuading other people to sell their houses through this company.

## Change Was About To Take Place

I worked for them for three months and, unfortunately, they disappeared. You know what I'm going to say; I didn't get paid, not a penny for the whole three months. The first two months, we had to prove ourselves, and for the next month we just got fobbed off with excuses. It was pretty much the same with Marilyn, selling the turf for six months; she didn't get paid either; the cheques bounced (**suckers**). Another lesson learned - to do our own thing.

## Our First Office for Marville Properties

In the autumn of 1976 Marilyn said to me, "Look, I love working with you, but I just don't like the remarks that we get from some people when they see a girl working in their house or in their

---

garden, and the same happens with some agents on building sites; so I don't want to do this anymore. I think we should work on our own properties and not for other people; in that way we don't have to answer to anyone else." There was no motivation to get more money, it was just to be in control; that made us happy in what we did and that has been the same for 40 years. Money and wealth have been by-products but, at the same time, we didn't want to restrict the amount that we could earn. Every business has to make a profit, so why not make it a large one?

Marilyn said that she wanted to concentrate on the office work, get the bookwork done in the daytime and have the evenings free. I thought that was a good idea; I could understand everything she said, and we hadn't got paid for most of the work we had done in the evenings anyway. The winter was upon us again and it was really horrible for her working outside, we were getting a lot better-paying jobs, so Marilyn could stop working in customers' houses.

To be honest, she didn't find that working in the winter was a problem, or doing the work; she liked working with me. It was the remarks that we got, such as, "I see you have brought your wife with you; does she help?" I would say, "Sod off," under my breath. It was ridiculous - she could decorate better than me and, at that time, I thought I could do with the evenings at home too.

We knew Marilyn was before her time in that job. Most successful business people are before their time; timing is crucial - if you get that right, then a lot of good things follow. The more quickly we could get away from doing other people's work, the better for us, as there was a limit that we could charge, and we realised by then that, ultimately, we should be getting income while we were sleeping - you couldn't do that whilst having an odd-job maintenance business in the long run. This became another step towards financial freedom. Each small step seemed insignificant to us, until we stopped and looked where we were, and realised how far we had travelled.

If we could only do our own work for ourselves, there would be no limit to what we could earn. We found a terraced house in an area called The Triangle, New England in Peterborough. The houses in that road were gradually being converted into shops or offices. It was great; it had everything we needed, including an entrance into the back garden, as we now needed a place to store building materials.

It cost £3,600 and belonged to Spires's bakery, which is four doors away; I made a deal to buy the property. I was getting planning permission for the conversion of it into an office, at the same time as the solicitors were going through the sale process. Mrs Spires was getting very agitated with me because I was making excuses about signing as, unbeknown to Mrs Spires, I was getting planning permission and, if we didn't get it, the house would be of no use to us; in the meantime, houses had started to rise in value.

Mrs Spires eventually gave me an ultimatum - sign for it or forget it. By the skin of our teeth, planning permission came through the next day and we signed. This was to be the office for the maintenance business as not only did Marilyn want to stop working on the building sites, we also felt it was inappropriate and not conducive to meet people from the Council and other building companies in our house; well, our office, as it was at that time, was in our box room-cum-bedroom, not really appropriate standing for meetings on our upstairs landing looking at samples of decorating materials.

## Marilyn Had Another Great Idea

Before we had moved into the new office, Marilyn had the idea of utilising her time by turning part of the house into a shop as well as an office because, she said, it would only take her two or three hours a day to do the bookwork for the maintenance business, and we could use this excess space for something. So we came up with the idea of a shop to sell second-hand baby nursery items, because we thought that would be quite easy. We had bought second-hand products from jumble sales for our baby, Elaine; at the time, we couldn't afford new. We thought that we could have a shop for second-hand nursery items which would be cheap to start and easy to run. Well, cheap to start was spot on; easy to run was an entirely different matter.

Before we ever went into business we discussed hundreds of business ideas, so having had Elaine and buying some second-hand baby stuff were good enough reasons for us to choose nursery equipment, and it was also a bit more manly than just baby clothes if I ever had to work in there. So who would have thought it, us wanting an office and then getting a shop as a bonus? Now that's a goal within a goal, leveraging not only the premises but the labour as well; we now had two businesses, with the overheads of one.

# Liz and Alan

SIDETRACKED

I had dreamed of owning a shop even before I knew Liz and Alan, who owned a fruit-and-veg shop along Millfield. We knew them because Liz had a daughter who went to Auntie Pearl's with Elaine. Seeing them work together was an inspiration to us; it seemed great that customers came to them instead of us going to the customers.

At the age of thirteen, I wrote an essay on what I wanted to do when leaving school. I said I wanted to work in a pet shop, and I went on to describe in detail what I would do from the minute I arrived to the time I was leaving. I don't know whether the teacher could decipher it but I didn't care; I knew that I wanted a shop, but that thought over the years had all but disappeared into oblivion.

*From left: Helen, Liz's daughter, Alan and Liz, my dad standing, and Joy and John Watkins. John owned the best furniture shop in Peterborough - Watkins and Stafford's.*

# Why a Baby Shop?

BACK

Throughout the years every day has been different for us, and that's what we expect. However, when we opened a shop, friends asked why a baby shop, when Marilyn was a qualified hairdresser; why not have a hairdressing business? Well, as we wanted to be working together I thought that, with my big hands, I couldn't, and also didn't want to do that.

The other thing that was obvious was an estate agency business to run alongside the maintenance business, but I just could not do it. As a dyslexic, there was no chance of working in an office at that time, or going to people's houses filling in agency agreement forms; I had got away with it for the three months when working for Buy and Sell Direct by saying I had forgotten my glasses, and would the customer fill in the form for me? I didn't want to keep doing that.

Around that time my mate Pete, the posh estate agent, and his secretary wanted me to go into business with them. Pete would see the customers, the girl would be in the office, and I would be in charge of maintenance and refurbishments. But I said no, I did not want to do it. However, the truth was I really did; I just could not tell them that I could not read or spell, but I knew that I could do the job standing on my head.

Once again I had run away from something I had wanted because I thought that I was dumb, not knowing that I was dyslexic and that there was nothing to be ashamed of. Whatever you wanted to name it in those days, people weren't educated like they are today. If you were dumb at something, you were dumb and, if you got found out, there was nothing for people to have any empathy about, so you were still just dumb.

I think the great thing about not being as good as others at something, whether it's sports or business, or whatever, you just have to focus on the things that you can do and, in doing so, find yourself; then practise getting better at whatever you put your mind to. So I not only put my mind to what I could do, but also what I couldn't; then I was driven, but you just don't stop at "normal" - you exceed your own expectations and everybody's around you.

# Life Is a Journey and a Series of Ifs

Life is a series of ifs; if I was good at spelling I would have stayed in one of the jobs that I had, probably forever. If the government had given me enough money I would have stayed on the dole. If we could have sold our house before going self-employed, I would have had the fear of losing the money, maybe, and then I would not have had the courage to go into business.

None of these things happened, so I had started the business with 37p, not having the slightest clue of where life would take us. We had not realised that living in that caravan was the best thing that could have happened to us, as it had given us a standard that we could cope with so, above that we were happy, enabling us to burn our bridges over the years, very often risking everything and saying that if this all goes wrong we can go back to living in a caravan. This nearly came true many times over in the first few years, so not getting complacent was never far from our thoughts.

By the beginning of 1977 we were good at buying property. We thought that we knew where we were going, but never imagined how far we could go, and still don't know 40 years later, and where we will end up before we pop our clogs. Property was now in our blood, in our minds and in our hearts; there was no going back. We realised that, at that time, success to us was working together, and the way to keep it on that track was to help as many people as possible get what they wanted, and for them to pay us for what we did at the same time. We also realised that the more we thought about what people wanted, the more we did, and the more exciting it got, and the more we attracted money; this is where we excelled once we started the shop.

# A Builder Buying Second-Hand Prams!!

We were not only working for clients, we worked on our own properties, and were now creating the shop as well. I had now become involved in buying second-hand prams in the evenings. We would look at the local paper adverts then go to the house and buy them. What a contrast, but it was so exciting. Maybe at this point I will make a list of our hobbies; that's easy, there were only three: work, work and, oh yes, work, but every minute was so exciting.

# Life's Mysterious Path

## "Everything is for a reason"

When we were getting the shop ready we had Mum and Dad staying with us for six weeks, because their home had been flooded, so we had that to contend with too. There is always a good side to everything because, when we were out buying prams in our mini-van, Mum and Dad looked after Elaine, leveraging everyone's time. Mum would be in the house with Elaine, and Dad would be in the garage cleaning the prams, getting them ready to sell once we had opened the shop. I can't get my head around why there are so many one-parent families, when it is so great surrounded by family that can not only look after each other, but leverage their time and skills too.

## Marilyn Said, "Neville, You're a Pig"

SIDETRACKED

We were converting the house into an office, and now a shop as well. I was supposed to put the shop window in the next day. I got home at just after midnight, nothing unusual for me. I was starving, so Marilyn made me beans on toast; it all went in seconds.

The next morning Marilyn was up sorting Elaine out for school. She brought me a cup of tea and said, "Wake up." I said, "I am awake and I really feel ill; my stomach hurts." She said, "You are a pig, coming home late, scoffing all that food and then going to bed straight away; what do you expect?"

I asked her to ring the doctor, which she did, and then left to take Elaine to school and then go elsewhere. When she got home at 11 am, her father was there to tell her that I had been taken into hospital with appendicitis. I had my operation that night and discharged myself the next day to get back to work, which was stupid. That said, Marilyn never called me a pig again and always took notice if I ever said that I was ill. I confess I have milked this ever since.

## "If You Really Do Want A Forest You Have To Plant Seeds, Every Day. Yes, Every Day, Forever.."

Neville Wright

A seed was planted that day, when Marilyn decided to open that little shop, that would just grow and grow although, at the time, we never knew just how much effort, care, and love we would have to put into looking after that business. We didn't know at that time what rewards that little shop would give us back in our lives, in the way of lifelong friendships, and an incredible standard of living. The best thing of all that little shop gave us was our two daughters for longer than we could have ever expected in our lives, not only giving us the pleasure of just seeing them every day for thirty years, but for me to work with them was a dream that came true, and was more than anything I could have wished for, to see them flourish and grow into the wonderful adults that they both are today.

## Before We Started This New Business

We needed stock, and finding where to get it from was difficult, not like now, with the Google search. We looked in shops at the sort of goods we wanted to sell and took the address off the products, then wrote to the manufacturers. The very first supplier was called Harrington's Baby Goods; they manufactured nappies, babies and children's clothes, etc., which they sold into high-class stores. the rep made an appointment to see Marilyn before we opened; his name was Mike Turner, and he came to our house as the shop was not ready.

When I got home that night, Marilyn couldn't wait to tell me about this man, literally before I had got my boots off in the doorway. All I wanted was my dinner, but that had gone by the wayside. Full of excitement, she had other things to do that evening; she was like an excited kid, with Mike said this, and Mike said that. They had obviously got on very well; she had taken his advice with the ordering and he had given her some of his samples that he had finished with, which meant a great deal to her.

I was worried because he hadn't seen the new shop and, once he had, that it wouldn't be up to Harrington's normal standard, so I was doubtful that Harrington's would supply us. But I did know, even though I had never met him, that he was a genuine guy who would help us all he could, because Marilyn is the best judge of people that I know. I could tell by her excitement the help he had given while she was doing her first order. He was all right, which subsequently proved right, as he and his wife Ann became life-long friends.

Like so many suppliers over the years, we did millions of pounds worth of business with him. He used to supply many high-class department stores, like Harrods, so he was used to dealing with top people. Over the years, we went out with each other, holidaying and, after a few scotches, he would let his persona down and would say:

"Neville, you two are totally different from any of the customers that I've got, and you are the only ones that I would ever go on holiday with." He was so funny and so nice, but, sadly, he died on a golf course doing what he loved, but far too soon; he is in our thoughts always.

*From the left: me, Fiona, Mike, Ann and Colin.*

I wrote a poem when Mike died, but I was too self-conscious to read it out at his funeral, another reason later on in life why I wanted to fight my fears, and to do public speaking, secretly in memory of our dear friend.

To Mike,
Mike, why did you have to go away when we had one more game to play?

Everyone has a handicap in golf; we both knew that I was yours.

However, you still laughed when adding up the scores, but sadly we can't do that anymore.

Tonight, as all nights, I will raise a glass to you, my very dear friend, and I hope to meet up with you when it comes my turn for the end.

Neville

Mike helped us in that business so much, over the years when we needed it most. Each year we would buy thousands of his clothing samples that were normally too expensive for us to stock, for a fraction of the price, which helped us enormously. He could have sold them to anyone, and at a much higher price, but he didn't, he chose us. We were so grateful to him and the many others who helped us on our way in that wonderful business.

# Life Is Not Predictable

Without some snide remarks from people about Marilyn working in the building business, Marilyn would never have thought of an office. Without the office there would never have been an opportunity at that time for a shop. One thing leads to another; it just does, life is not predictable; that's probably the only predictable thing that you can say about life.

I've said before in this book that everybody with whom we are connected in our businesses plays a good part when it comes to big decisions in our lives, even if, at the time, it appears not to be the case. Over the years we have listened to thousands of people, their wants, needs, hopes and dreams; we have taken praise and abuse literally in the same minute. People have told us what to do and others what not to do; we thank every one of them for making our decisions in life a lot easier.

The shop opened on 6th April 1977, two and a half years after we had first become self-employed. To us, this business was just another extension of our business and, when we were doing adverts for either business, or there was a newspaper article, people would ask when the business started and we would say 1974 because, at the time, we didn't consider that we really had got two separate businesses, although the date got ingrained into the history of the shop. In the first few years, all of the combined income went into just one bank account, as everything we did was as just self-employed; in fact, the first limited company was set up in 2011 after we had sold the last nursery shop. Everybody has assumed that Kiddicare was a limited company, but it wasn't.

# Why the First Baby Discount Shop?

The day before we opened our first customer walked in, as we had left the door unlocked. We said that we were not open until tomorrow, but they said that they were on their way to the maternity ward and wanted to take a present, so we let them in. We had no money in the till, the total was £2.30, and they gave us £3. With us not having change, I gave a pound back, and they were so happy that we decided that's how we would like all of our customers to be.

I have just found this story on us in our scrapbook; it was from the local evening papers that ran an article on Marilyn when we were going to open the shop. This was probably the first time we used a story to advertise our business at no cost to us, which became a normal situation.

## RAINBOW SHOP

The days of carrying bricks and setting cement are over for Marilyn Wright. She is now to take up what many may consider to be a more ladylike pastime, pushing prams and helping mothers.

For Mrs Wright and her husband Neville have been trying for some time to set up a store in Peterborough specialising in prams and hardware. She has been renovating the shop 1229 Bourges Boulevard, Peterborough. Mr Wright is a builder by trade and will continue to run Wrightway Decorating at 31 Langley, Bretton while his wife runs the shop.

After opening the shop, Marilyn managed it by herself and I carried on working in the maintenance business. I found myself being drawn to the shop; or was I just missing Marilyn? I would go into the shop when I was around that area; I wanted to help serve the customers, but I was always in my dirty overalls going from one job to another so I couldn't, except for a Saturday, which I loved. The atmosphere and the delight on people's faces were great, especially when a grandma and granddad-to-be bought their daughter a pram. It was a happy time, yet an exhausting end to the week, or so we thought; this was just the start of us leveraging time.

Not long after we had opened the shop we got a call from the pushchair company, Maclaren, to say the rep would call on Monday. Marilyn was busy so I saw him, as we wanted to open an account with them and, besides, I was capable of buying a pushchair. I met Bill Vasper, the distributor for Maclaren, in our shop. Bill showed me the pushchair and said, "We have four colours, and you have to take two of each." They were £8 each; when I saw Marilyn later that day and told her I had spent £64 plus VAT on eight pushchairs, she thought that I was crazy and saying that we would never sell that many. I said we would sell them in a week. Well, she was right; I think it took us two or three months to sell them.

After that we went through a learning curve on buying that lasted thirty years. We found that the moment we thought we had it all sorted, mistakes would happen as we had to order sometimes up to six months ahead so, by the time we got the stock, things in the market had changed; then we had to figure out how to sell the stuff.

I made some monumental 'cock ups' over the years, which I will tell you about later but, although these things happened, I always seemed to turn the problem around to our advantage. That's part of the fun of being responsible for a business, there is no running or hiding when things go wrong. Others can do that, but not the owners; they have to stand up and be counted. We had no choice other than to get out of these situations by thinking outside of the box and then just doing it.

*Our first shop: 1229 Bourges Boulevard,*

*This business nearly came to an end before we had started it. As Marilyn opened the door, smoke poured out. Stock had been piled up on top of the cooker; she had put the oven on and by mistake turned a ring on as well, and the stock smouldered all night. As the stock was so densely packed together, there was no air to make it burn.*

Marilyn had found security in that little shop; she was in control of her life. I could see that deep down she was happy at last; I believe she had got something to build on, and the dark days of being at home alone with no money and nothing to do were in the distant past, gone forever. I could see that she was driven by the deep desire to succeed; she became so incredibly motivated to become financially secure that it burned deep into her soul, never stopping to rest. She would be continually on the go, working, and thinking of how to improve everything for the customers in the shop, at the same time making improvements in the property business too.

It was lovely to watch this girl who looked after our family and, at the same time, was totally immersed in her own business. Time was of no consequence to her - she would be up half the night stencilling signs for the next day, as we had no computer or printer then. Her shop was all-consuming in her life. It never ceased to amaze me, the transformation from a very quiet, unassuming, shy girl into a businesswoman who, at the same time, never lost her integrity, or kindness and commitment to Elaine and myself. Little did she know what devastating news was to come, after a year of devotion and hard work in the business; it would alter her world forever.

## There Is No Security

Marilyn had been searching for security and had found it in her shop but, of course, there is no security in life; just look at history - over time the displacement of millions of people fleeing for their lives, the Jews in 1914, and again in 1939, the Ugandans in 1972, and now the Syrians in 2014, which will only get worse. There is only one thing in common with all of these people, apart from being persecuted, and that is opportunity; they have found themselves in a situation that they don't want to be in, so they are all looking for an opportunity to be free, safe and secure.

Our lives are like a grain of sand that can be washed away in an instant, and not being in control of your life makes it worse. I think that, at that time, Marilyn had found something that she could control and, by then, she was the happiest I had ever seen her, except for the day two weeks after she had opened the shop. It was about to burn down. The small kitchen at the back of the shop was piled high with stock; we had bought a second-hand cooker on which the knobs all looked the same. Luckily, the stock was packed so densely it hadn't ignited, but did fill the shop with smoke. **"Scary"**

# Which Direction?

## *"Never be afraid to change direction"*

It's hard to describe our feelings in those days of the 1970s. Every day of our life was exciting, because we didn't know what it would bring; at the same time, we were concerned about having enough money to live on. We didn't need much, as nothing was wasted but, in our minds, we needed to be secure as we had seen our parents eking out their money every week and just accepting that was that, and there was nothing that they could do about it, however long and hard they worked.

Of course we wanted money, but not for the love of money. It was for a purpose, which was to create a life that we could work together because separately we were weak, but together we would be strong enough to look after ourselves. And the only way to get from where we were to where we wanted to be was to put every penny back into the business, whether it was for more tools for building, or more stock for the shop. We knew that, one day, there would be a tipping-point where we would have an abundance of money.

I worked on the building business in the daytime and, when I say daytime, I mean my ladders would be up against a window and I would be painting that window as dawn broke. I have scared more than one unsuspecting person when they have opened the bedroom curtains to see me staring at them with a paintbrush in my hand.

In the evenings, when I was working for people in their house, I would just carry on working until midnight. I remember one customer coming into the room that I was working in at 11pm, in their dressing-gown.

## You Will Never Work In My House Again

He said, "Neville, when are you going home?" I said, "I finish at midnight." He said to me, "Neville, I will never have you do any work in my house again." With this, my heart sank; I had worked so hard. I thought that to lose a customer was dreadful - what would Marilyn say? Then with a smile he said, "Well, not while I am here; you can have the keys to the house and I will ring you when I go on holiday." Which he did, and as many others did as well, I was very proud of that trust the customers had in me.

# Decisions That Have To Be Made

Then the day came. A life-changing decision had to be made on where the businesses were going; we were basically working every hour that we could and we were absolutely shattered, so we decided to have a holiday of sorts, and went to Great Yarmouth and hired a caravan for two days. Why? Because we still could not justify a hotel, as they were not only too expensive in our minds, but probably more to the point is that I didn't want to humiliate myself by not being able to fill in the register in the reception of a hotel; and besides, what's a boy that couldn't read or write doing in a hotel? I thought that he did not deserve to be there.

SIDETRACKED

It was cold and horrible; the caravan hadn't been cleaned properly, it was full of sand and, after cleaning the van we sat there in the cold talking for the whole two days. The conversation was about whether we should keep on doing other people's work, in which case we would have to expand if we wanted to carry on, and start taking on civil contracts like roads and what I would call proper building work - houses, factories, etc., which we really didn't know anything about. This could well be a real possibility, as we always seemed to get over things.

Or should we concentrate on our own abilities, buying and selling, renovating, and expand that side of the business? We were only going to get busier doing our own work, so we had to take that into consideration as well. It was probably the hardest decision that we have ever made in that business. The problem was that, if we only concentrated on our own work, we wouldn't be doing any of the normal work for all of the customers who had helped us establish the business; plus the cash flow would stop, as the shop was still being subsidised. Marilyn was not taking any money out, just buying more stock.

The decision had to be made, and we decided it was too risky to go down the route of expanding the business working as subcontractors, doing work that we did not know anything about.
We thought it would be an easier and more profitable option to be in control of everything we did. If you are buying and selling houses, you always have some value at the end of the day but, to be a subcontractor, you could end up with nothing because of the chain you are in.

# Just Work for Me

BACK

I had the job of telling the customers we wouldn't be doing any more work for them, and returning their keys back to them as, in a lot of cases, we did the work when they were away from the house.

I think the hardest part was when people said to me, "Can you just do my work, Neville?" Which of course I couldn't; I still feel bad about that today, because those people were so nice and helped us when we needed it most.

I knew that if I was to succeed in this business I would need to go into a house with six people and renovate it as quickly as possible, without having the thoughts of going away to put a latch on somebody's gate or mending a fence. It was too costly in time for me to be away from the others, as I knew every job that needed doing, and I micro-managed the job so we didn't lose any time. I had to concentrate and focus in one direction.

That is what we did; we concentrated on just doing our own work, and the business then flourished. I could have sent someone to do the jobs but, as I would always be responsible for overseeing them, and Marilyn would have to do the invoicing, it still would be too time-consuming and costly.

To make the cash flow work, we needed to renovate and sell more houses more quickly; then, once we got that right in our first business, we concentrated on the second business, creating multiple streams of income all from that first business. All of this just came naturally to us; by working on building another different type of business that could utilise the same infrastructure as the first, we halved our overheads and doubled our profits.

Over the years, we invested profits into passive income so we could make money while we were sleeping, something that I don't need much of as the time is 3.13am on 17th July 2014, which is a normal day for me; I try to go to bed before 4 am - if I don't, the birds keep me awake with their singing.

# Two Businesses That Are Worlds Apart

## "*Sometimes you go with both ideas because your gut says so*"

We still had the shop after one year; this surprised not only my father-in-law but me as well, knowing my track record.

Marilyn had worked in the shop for around fifty hours a week, and I worked with her on a Saturday; we both loved every minute of being together, creating a business that wasn't dependent on the weather and we would go home clean instead of being covered in brick dust.

Marilyn hadn't had any time to do the bookwork for the maintenance business as planned, because the shop was too busy. In the evenings, along with her doing hairdressing and the bookwork for Wrightway Decorating, she now had the added burden of doing the accounts for Rainbow Warehouse; this was a lot more than we had ever expected. We had stopped selling the second-hand goods after about three months, and went on to selling just new products; this increased the workload for Marilyn. Also, at the same time, the property business was growing to the point of me not knowing which way to turn.

The shop was taking up all of Marilyn's time and, on a Sunday we would be going to the East End of London to the importers, because by then we were selling not only baby clothes but children's clothes too, up to 12 years old. We would also make trips to Leicester every week, buying stock for the shop from a place called Shenu Fashions. The father, four boys and the rest of the family had fled from Uganda with nothing; they had to leave a big cycle-shop and all of their possessions there. They settled in Leicester and, over the years, created through hard work a massive business selling children's clothes; and now, in 2014, the next generation has nursery shops as well.

## Our Toy-Buyer, Age Six

On a Wednesday evening we would go to the local cash-and-carry to buy toys and things for the shop, and food for ourselves. Children were not allowed in the cash-and-carry because of the forklift trucks that were racing about. We asked if Elaine could go in because we did not want to leave her outside. We knew one of the managers, and he said we could take Elaine in because she was choosing the toys for the shop; she was only six and already acted like a grown-up anyway. She was the only child that I ever saw in there, and we must have gone in there for twenty years.

This became our night out, as they had a subsidised café, so the goal for us was to find goods for the shop that had been reduced down in price, and down again as, once we had saved enough to pay for a meal just on that second reduction, we had achieved our goal. We wanted to go out like everyone else, and this was one way we could do it. I remember sometimes Elaine would sit in the café for an hour waiting for us, because it had taken longer than usual to find the goods that saved the money we needed in order to have achieved our goal.

# There Are Only 1,440 Minutes in the Day

We thought that we had been busy before but, to be quite honest, we didn't know what busy was. The shop was shut on a Monday. Marilyn would go into Peterborough town centre in the morning and would search all of the baby departments in the shops, looking for clothes that were just being reduced. We used to get some really nice, expensive stuff for a fraction of the normal price in the sales, and the quality was better than what we could get in the East End of London, where lots of importers were. She would go to Mothercare, C&A, Littlewoods and the Co-op, which were the best ones; she then took the clothes home, cut out the labels, and then put them in our shop.

We would conveniently just have a Mothercare catalogue on the counter so, if people said, "These look like Mothercare," we would look in the book and say, "Yes, they do, but these haven't got a label in." They would see the price in the book, and ours would be 20% lower as we had probably got 70% off when we bought them. There's a saying that the early bird catches the worm; well, she had to be that bird.

Then, on the Monday afternoon, we would be off to Leicester after we picked Elaine up from school; that was the only time we would be ready and waiting at the school gates for her. We found a place that manufactured nappy-liners; we would buy the seconds that the machine had cut wrongly, then my mum would count them into bundles of 100 and put them in an elastic band while watching the telly. At the same time, Dad would be rolling up dusters, tea-towels and dish-cloths into threes, as we had bought them in bulk.

# Rocking-Horse Poo

Thursday, 7<sup>th</sup> October 1976 was an unlucky day for some, as interest rates went up to 15%. There was a really nice housing estate close to where we lived; the houses were too expensive for us but we did admire them. A four-bedroom detached house with two garages on a large plot was about £18,000.

By the weekend after that interest rate rise, a total of 34 people had pulled out of buying houses being built by this particular builder and, by the 12<sup>th</sup> the builder had no choice but to reduce the prices. We jumped in quickly and, on the Wednesday, we reserved a fantastic plot for £14,000. We never gave a thought to how much the mortgage would be; all we thought about was the price of £14,000; it was a bargain. The only problem was that we would need a mortgage; at that time in Peterborough, to get a mortgage was virtually impossible; you would stand a better chance of getting poo out of a rocking-horse than getting money out of a building society.

## Things Happen When You Least Expect Them

Earlier that year, my father had taken early retirement. He had received a £15,000 redundancy payment and, after a few weeks, he gave Carol, Terry and me £1,000 each, just as all of this turmoil with the building societies was going on. The building society where we had already got a mortgage refused to give us a new one, as they weren't giving any out at that time. I asked our accountant, Paul Temple, if he knew how we could get a mortgage. He said that the Halifax were probably the only people to see, so he gave me the name of the manager and said he would speak to him on our behalf; so we went to see him.

He was expecting us, as Paul had phoned him. I had the £1,000 in cash from my dad in my pocket. I told him that I wanted a £7,500 mortgage on an £18,000 new house. he said to me, "Because you are not an existing customer, we will need a substantial deposit sitting in the account; you can't put it in and take it out the next day; do you understand?" I said, "Yes; how much would you like?" He said £1000. I took the money out of my back pocket and acted as though this was just loose change to me. I counted it out and said, "Is that enough, or do you want some more?"

That tactic was a bit risky, because I hadn't got any more, but I wanted to make him think that I had plenty of money. Luckily, he said, "No, that's fine; £1,000 will do." One thing I have found over the years with banks is that if you have got money they will lend you more, but if you haven't got any, or you haven't got any track record of borrowing and paying it back, then you haven't got a chance. **(A chicken-and-egg situation)**

SIDETRACKED

So my advice to anyone, even if you don't want any money at the moment, is to still get a mortgage or a re-mortgage, an overdraft, or some kind of loan; it doesn't matter how small. Then you pay it off, and then you do the same again, and again and again, gradually increasing the amounts, because one day, when you want a large amount of money, you will have gained a track record. If you don't do this, you won't get it. I am talking about proper banks, not payday loans or anything like that. 7% over base is the maximum you should pay, but 4% would be better; I aim for 2%.

BACK

The house we had bought a year before for £5,950, we managed to sell for £9,500. We were still around £2,000 short, so we took out a general overdraft on the business from Barclays, and we used this on the house too. We moved in February 1977, and didn't take the £1,000 out the next day; it was three months before we used the money again!

# We Bought a Caravan for Holidays

By May 1977 we withdrew the £1,000 out of the Halifax Building Society and went to Hunstanton, our local seaside, to buy a caravan so we could get away for breaks from Saturday night to Sunday. Another goal achieved; we had used the money twice - once to get the mortgage, and once to get the caravan.

Now if we had done it the other way, we would not have got the house. It's called juggling money - putting it in something that will go up in value first, then reaping the benefit second.

That Sunday we went to buy a caravan and, once we had bought it, we went for a walk along the promenade. There was a shop that sold buckets and spades, toys and gifts - Johnson's Gift Shops.

We looked around and found some skipping-ropes, which we thought we could sell in our shop, so I asked a boy standing outside next to a till if I bought twelve skipping-ropes, could I have them cheaper as we had a shop? His name was Jim, and he said, "We have a warehouse where we sell to other shops; I will take you there." That day was the start of a friendship that still lasts today.

The warehouse was as large as six garages, at the back of another gift shop that he and his wife Linda lived above, in a flat owned by his father. We could not believe our luck; we filled the car with all sorts of seaside stuff - buckets and spades, blow-up footballs, and things like snow storms. We ended up selling thousands of these things over the years. Today, in 2014, Jim is still in Hunstanton; he now owns his own accountancy business, James Johnson & Co, which has hundreds of clients, and his daughter Emma works in the business with him; his brother now owns Johnson's Gift Shops.

## Another Goal to the List

We now had a new goal to add to our list. Every week that we went to the caravan, we would fill the car with toys to sell the next week. I will give you an idea of how tired I was in those days; we would leave the shop in Peterborough on a Saturday night at about 6.30pm. Hunstanton was 47 miles. Sometimes I had to stop for a rest half way because I was so tired; I would be falling asleep at the wheel. Now, nearly 38 years later, I could jump into my camping car after a day's work and drive seven hours to Scotland overnight without thinking about it. When we eventually got to Hunstanton we had fish and chips; then we would take Elaine to the caravan site club, where she could play with other kids, and Marilyn could relax and enjoy dancing. The next day we would do the accounts, then go and buy toys from Jim and, if we got time, we would take Elaine on the beach or go swimming.

*Marilyn outside the van on Manor Park in Hunstanton. If only we had got this four years earlier, but we would have never got it into the back garden; if we had, we would never have moved into that cold house, and we might still be there.*

## *Holiday with Jim and Linda in Kos in the 1990s*

My friend Jim, who started out as a jockey, is a prime example of someone who has an inner desire combined with a dream of achieving for himself under very difficult circumstances. He has succeeded by going out of his comfort zone midway through his life to learn a new business skill, accountancy, then taken that skill and made a living, not only for himself but his family, helping hundreds of self-employed people running small businesses.

## *2014. Outside Jim's dad's shop, where we met in 1977*

The caravan came in handy as, when Jim was clearing old stock, I would buy as much as we could afford, take home what we could, and store the rest in the van until every space was filled. This was the start of getting multiple streams of income from each business. We started to work with people to get a win-win outcome, and we were learning to use money twice, and started to understand not to waste any of our time. By having a mini-holiday, doing the bookwork and buying stock, combining these things gave us a better life and a chance to get what we wanted out of it.

## Leverage Everything You Can

The caravan doubled up as a warehouse and then an office at weekends, as well as for holidays. We didn't waste time as we bought toys from Jim, avoiding a costly separate journey, and we used our travelling time to listen to motivational tapes once we could get them in the 80s.

## Mark Homer

We have leveraged in thousands of ways. Another person who is a friend of ours is Mark Homer, who owns Progressive Properties with Rob Moore. Mark is incredible; he can go around the world literally for free; now that's leveraging! He has written a book entitled

## *Low Cost High Life*

Mark says there are two types of people: dreamers who just dream, and the dreamers who turn their dreams into reality, working because they want to, turning problems into opportunities, and helping others.

## Rob Moore

Another friend, Rob Moore, has written many books about how people can get out of everyday poverty and into a prosperous life, investing in property in some interesting ways.

## Multiple Streams of Property Income

Rob opens your eyes to the multitude of property income.

# What Went Wrong?

## *"Some things are sent to test your strength"*

We met our accountant to assess the shop's first year of trading. Marilyn was so excited after all the hard work and emotion that she had put into starting the business; she couldn't wait to hear the news. We had talked about having a short holiday as a well-earned reward; after all, Marilyn and I had not taken a penny out of that business in that year, we had been accumulating the money in the business, and now it was time to celebrate.

The devastating news came from our accountant's mouth when the trading figures were put in front of us. He said that we had made nothing, (silence); all we had was £1,500 of extra stock.

We couldn't believe it, what had happened? We had been busy fools, racing about all over the place buying stock and letting the excitement cloud reality. When we analysed the results, we found that it had cost more to go to London each week than the profit we made on the goods that we had bought. We weren't buying enough to cover the costs, but we couldn't buy any more because we hadn't got enough customers in that week to buy the products - a Catch 22 situation.

What a shock! We were lost in our minds, not knowing what to do. We had failed through lack of knowledge of basic business sense; although we had applied the same principles of time and motion as used on our maintenance business, we had overlooked the major point of calculating the profit margins that we needed to make. In our other business, we calculated how long a job would take, then added 50% for unforeseen things; then we multiplied that by an hourly rate, and added the cost of the materials and other overheads - easy. In the shop, we hadn't taken into consideration, when calculating margins, the cost of our time and the shop overheads - simple.

## Decision Made, Move on Quickly

So, feeling low, we decided that we had had enough of retailing as it was too restrictive for us; we needed instant rewards in our life, so shop-keeping wasn't for us. We would sell the shop and concentrate on the property maintenance side of the business. It wasn't until we were going to sell that first shop that I realised what real passion for business was all about.

We put the freehold and the business up for sale for £10,000 with an estate agent called Langford Smith who, incidentally, came into my office last week. He is still working as a surveyor and is well into his 80s. He sold businesses as well as houses. He found the buyer for our shop, a teacher who had come from Uganda along with thousands of other people who had got thrown out of the country in the early 1970s by the dictator Idi Amin.

## Carl Davies Changed Our lives

SIDETRACKED

It was Friday lunchtime and there was a representative in our shop from a company called Tri-ang Pedigree, which sold prams and toys. His name was Carl Davies; he was a very fat man who spoke articulately and loudly - you certainly listened when he spoke. We were sitting in the back of the shop having fish and chips; we always did this when Carl came round and I happened to be about. He used to sell us prams that had been on show in the Boots stores around the country, and I used to try and sell him stuff from our shop which would be suitable for his market stall that he used to run on a Saturday in Ramsey, Cambridgeshire. Somehow he always got the best deal, leaving me feeling deflated when he left; I would think, "However did I let that happen?" **Stupid**

It was a stroke of luck that Carl was there that particular day. Halfway through our fish and chips I said to him, "Well Carl, this is the last time we will see you, because we have sold the shop; we are going to the solicitors at 2 o'clock to sign the paperwork." Carl was an enormous man - he must have been 30 stone. He instantly stopped eating. He looked at me with his mouth open and stared for a few seconds, then said, "Why are you selling?"

I said, "We haven't made any money in a year; all I've done is put a bit more stock on to the shelves and it's just taking up too much valuable time. I think that the shop is in the wrong position." I added, "There's not enough passing trade." With that, he put his fish and chips down, got up and grabbed me by my collar, pulling me out of the shop. I felt like I was being shaken like a rag doll. He turned me round, looked up the street and then turned me back around and looked down the street, with my toes hardly touching the ground. He said, "This is one of the main roads coming in and out of Peterborough. Nobody knows you are here because it's just like all the other shops, offices, and houses down this road. You need to make it stand out from the others."

There was a long row of terraced houses, all with flat fronts. None of them stood out from each other; the houses, shops and offices were just mixed in together, and it was virtually impossible to see our shop. He said, "If you were to hang products outside and put prams on the pavement, then people would notice you."

## My Passion for Business Was Ignited

Carl said, "I've seen Marilyn and you work so hard over the last year, and I can see you are just about to establish this business. You can't throw that away; you need to continue. I can see this becoming a great business." In those few minutes of him shaking me about like a rag doll, and him being so excited and passionate about our business (he was literally spitting out fish and chips as he talked with excitement and passion), my mind was changed. *(**Just like that**)*

I wondered how somebody could be so passionate about something that wasn't even theirs; he was talking about our business. He wasn't thinking of himself; he could see that we were making a huge mistake, and that convinced me not sell.

BACK

It was on that day that my passion for business was really ignited inside of me. I walked back into the shop and said to Marilyn, "We're not selling the business." She asked why, so I told her everything that Carl had said. She said OK, that was fine with her, even though she had done so much work for nothing in the past year. The one thing that I believe made our business successful was that, although we needed to make money, it wasn't the driving force.

The truth is that we just wanted to be together, all of the time, every minute of every day. Marilyn proved it that day, by saying OK after spending a year of her life doing more than you could ever imagine for nothing. To turn around to me and say OK when I said we were keeping the shop, and there was no guarantee that we would do any better tomorrow than we had done yesterday - this is the lovely nature of the girl that I married.

**Marilyn's birth sign is Taurus (the Bull) and, if she had not wanted in her heart to do this, she would have told me in no uncertain terms.**

She later said that she never wanted to sell the shop, as she loved every aspect of creating and the running of the business. However, she also knew we could not carry on without making any money; we just needed someone to tell us where they thought we were going wrong.

## We Turned Unsuccessful Into Successful

Within 10 minutes of Carl speaking to me, I went across the road to the DIY shop and bought a lot of brass hooks; I screwed them into the shop window-frame and hung toys on them - dolls' prams, scooters, bikes. I put prams on the pavement so that people passing by would be attracted by the sight. It was the kick up the arse that I needed. I had made a decision in my head that the business would be successful, and now I had to prove that it was right. Could you imagine how I would feel if this were to fail? What would the conversation be with Marilyn, who trusted and believed in me?

## The First Conflict of Many

With everything in life there are two sides; one side was us just trying to make a business succeed, and on the other side there was the Council trying to keep the pavements clear - so it wasn't long before we were in conflict with the local Council. I have to say, it was the first conflict of a few over the years. Their argument was that we couldn't leave prams on display on the pavement. My argument was that customers could leave their prams outside the shop all-day and there was no objection, so what was the difference? *(stupid people)*

SIDETRACKED

I believe that decision-makers in councils and government should have experience in running their own business before they can ever make decisions on business people's lives and livelihoods - rant over. Now today, shopkeepers in that area put the stuff all over the pavement and nothing is said. I wonder why? Well, Peterborough has changed; there are 100 nationalities now, and the Council probably can't speak the languages but, in the 70s, they definitely could speak mine. Now you would think you were in India; oh yes, and Poland too.

Although I have made my business over the last forty years in Peterborough, I have very little good to say about the local Council up until now, because, over the years as a business person who has employed thousands of people, mostly from Peterborough, I have continually struggled and fought with the Council to build our business. Every step of the way, I have had to overcome red tape, bureaucracy and jobsworths from the planning department, the rates department, and the environment, all of them seemingly not wanting to work to make Peterborough a better place for business.

They seem to delight in making life unbearable for the normal, small local businessperson, even to the point of knowing common sense will prevail but still delighting in delaying the inevitable outcome, destroying businesses, families and lives in the process, all in the name of bureaucracy and prolonging a job for themselves. Maybe if we were called McDonald's, or Costa Coffee, it would have been different.

BACK

Some years later, I was listening to Zig Ziglar's motivational tapes, where he told a story about a businessperson who had invented a fizzy drink that tasted really nice, so he marketed it and it didn't sell. The name of the fizzy drink was 5 up. Anyway, he gave up. Then another person came along with the same recipe and went to work on the marketing; again, it too failed. He had called it 6 up.

Then, Zig says, you know the rest of the story - 7-Up; it went on to be one of the best selling drinks ever. If only the other two people knew how close they were to success; that was the same with us - we did not realise just how far we had come in that short time in establishing the business. Obviously, the man who was going to buy our shop wasn't very pleased - I had to take his verbal abuse over the phone for what seemed like 30 minutes, but that was a small price to pay for, once again, burning our bridges.

We built and sold four baby nursery businesses over the next 34 years, eventually selling the last one and getting £70 million cash for our Kiddicare retail nursery business on 14th Feb 2011.

The difference was that the others were sold not only to make money, but for different reasons; they enabled the growth of the business. The last sale meant that the family business as we knew it, that Marilyn had created, had gone forever, for money we didn't need or want but, having said that, since that day we have made excellent use of it, growing new business.

It's incredible to think that we did this while building a business that encompassed property investment, construction of commercial, industrial and residential, including buying, selling, renting, and flipping all manner of properties at the same time. I really don't think anybody connected to us knew what we were doing and, if they did, certainly didn't know how we did it; this is just one of the reasons why I've written this book.

I wanted to show our grandchildren and future generations what kind of person Marilyn was. She worked tirelessly for the business she had created, and she also encouraged Elaine and Joanne to do what they wanted, and it was nice to see that they wanted to work with her, as I also did.

## Good Fortune Just By Chance

Well, there is something more incredible; without Carl Davis coming to the shop that day, there would never have been a Kiddicare, as we were about to go in a completely different direction but, whichever direction we had gone in I am sure the girls would have worked with us, as it doesn't matter what you do in life.

After Carl's talk with me, I put my thinking-cap on every day, and we pushed the baby business forward; but we didn't have enough money for stock if we wanted to make the business profitable so, in order to grow both businesses, we decided in the autumn of 1978 to go back to Langford Smith. We asked him to sell our commercial premises and to find us some other premises to rent that would be suitable for a shop and an office for the maintenance business. He obviously was curious and asked why we wanted to do this.

We told Langford that we needed to get the money out that we had put into buying the premises; we could use it to buy more stock for the shop and more houses to work on. We hadn't got enough variety of stock for the customers and, in order to achieve more sales, we felt we had to sell the premises that had tied up our cash. We could then rent because, at the time, all of our money was tied up in the property; we knew we could earn more by renting premises and releasing the capital to invest in the business.

He advised us to stay where we were because we had established our business in that position, and it would be difficult to find suitable premises for both businesses as we were using the back garden as a builder's yard. He said that we could have something called a sale and leaseback. For this arrangement, he would find an investor to buy our premises, which would enable us to stay there and finance more stock; we would, in return, pay rent on what was originally our own premises. We had never heard of this before, but it was certainly the best thing we could have done. Once again, we were leveraging our assets. We sold that asset, the office-cum-shop, for £8,000, we put £5,000 into more stock and we had £3,000 left over to buy more property.

We leveraged that £3,000 with a £1,500 overdraft; this hadn't been considered when we were doing this deal, so it enabled both businesses to grow quicker. I remember the day we got the £8,000 we could not quite grasp that anyone would do this, he gave us £8,000 and we gave him back £20 for the weeks rent. The £5,000 worth of stock we bought made £5,000 in a year and the rent was only £1,040. With the other £3,000 we had left from the sale we got an overdraft, making £4,500 to buy more property. We bought and sold an extra six houses a year and made £1,000 profit on each.

I started to juggle my time between the two businesses, which was hard, as we then began to advertise in the local paper and then word spread that we had branded stuff at knock-down prices; customers started to flock in. I put the Maclaren pushchair that we couldn't sell for £12.99 to £9.99; we were making £1 on each, which wasn't enough, but it would work if we sold a rain cover to go with it. Nobody knew the price of a rain cover; they only knew the real price of the pushchair. We could sell the rain cover at normal prices so, together, the profit was sufficient for the time spent with the customer, but we soon realised we had to become sales people in order to achieve our aim.

We became Bill Vasper's biggest customer, selling hundreds a month. Then, in time, it went to thousands and then hundreds of thousands of Maclaren products over the years, and the rain-cover manufacturer couldn't believe how many we sold, even in the summertime. Well, we did have a special on them.

Within a year, business was booming. We had a bus stop outside our shop; that was great because cars were not allowed to park there, so we unloaded our lorries in the bus stop. We would try to time it so we missed the buses that were every half hour. I just wish I had a picture - the bus stop would have 100 boxes in it. By that time we had some staff - our sister-in-law and Ray, our next-door neighbour, and a girl that had just left school. We would all be franticly running about trying to find places to put the stock; this in turn would attract people passing by in their cars, and they would stop to see what we were selling.

By now the nappy-liners that Mum used to count into 100s were selling like crazy and we were having them produced for us, as we had a big wholesaler buying them from us 50,000 packs at a time. Timing was crucial; we would arrange a time for them to pick up from the front of the shop, and then arrange for the manufacturers to drop them off 1 hour beforehand, praying that it wouldn't rain, because there was nowhere inside for them. We were making the same money on this one deal as we were in a week in the shop. Unfortunately, one day it all went wrong; the delivery was late and the collection was early; the collection driver saw where they had come from and, from that day, the wholesaler went direct.

To be quite honest, I reprimanded myself for that, but such is life, and by then we had outgrown Marilyn's little shop. We were running around like headless chickens; it was like a comedy. The shop would be so full of people, no one could move. By then, we had rented a house on Lincoln Road, Millfield, to store stock and we had a van to ferry stock in between, but we really needed to move now.

## A Dangerous Situation

My father and I had taken down the internal walls and repositioned the staircase, so now there was one room on each floor instead of two. Remembering that this building had been built over 100 years ago, for a family, we had weakened the structure. Now we were bringing in customers, lots and lots; they just kept coming until we couldn't move, people having to wait on the pavement for people to come out before they could get in.

One day, when the shop was full, I was literally stuck on the domestic stairs that we had put in, not thinking that there would be any more than two people using them at one time. There was a line of people going up and one coming down, two people on each tread. I thought the stairs were going to collapse; I could also see that the ceiling was bowing and the fluorescent light-tubes were bending to the point that they would pop out of their sockets. This was scary, to say the least; I was sweating with fear, and I was glad when that day was over. I knew then we had to move, and move fast.

# Business Changes Every Day

## *"We all change every day; that's life"*

So, by 1978, four years after we had started the window-cleaning business and three years after Wrightway Decorating, we were just finishing off the last of the customers' work that we had promised we would do. We had progressed in that short time to working only on our own properties; the name Wrightway Decorating and Property Maintenance wasn't conducive to what we were now doing.

## Marville Properties Was Our New Name

If we were going to concentrate on buying and selling houses, and by now we were thinking about building a large portfolio to include commercial premises as well, we needed to review the name. The local estate agents probably would not have taken us seriously with the existing name, so it had to be changed to reflect what we were doing. The business has always been a 50-50 partnership so, on 27th September 1979 our names, Marilyn and Neville, became Marville, and we just added Properties on the end, with the tagline of residential and commercial investments.

We had traded properties from 1975, buying and selling one or two properties at a time. Now we could step up and buy more. We used to go into estate agents and ask what they had for £1,500 or less; they would go to their filing cabinets and have a rummage around, and probably bring out about six or eight properties, all under the £1,500. We knew virtually all of the properties that they would show us.

We knew all the streets in Peterborough, because we would never go to the same place twice without going on a different route, looking out for sale boards. I would make ridiculous offers on all eight properties, even though I'd never seen inside them. I would offer the price of a virtual rebuild, so I used to think that any condition above that was a bonus. The agents would say, "If you were fortunate enough to get all of these, would you be able to buy them?"

Do you think I was going to say no? Of course not! I used to say, "Yes", of course, thinking there was no way that all of these people would accept my offer. However, just in case they did, I was confident enough that I would find the money from somewhere. The chances were quite slim that I would get any at the prices we had offered but, if we were lucky enough, then we would probably end up with one, and one a month was good.

## I Want It

There was one estate agent who, as soon as he thought we were really keen on a property, would slide his hand along the counter that he stood at. Every time he did this, a phone on the desk at the back of him would buzz, and the person who was sitting there would pick the phone up and say that Mr so-and-so was on the line wanting to buy, and he would say the address of the property that we were talking about.

The agent would say, "Tell him that the house is probably sold." Then he would say to us, "You don't want to miss this one, do you?" Incredibly, we bought a couple of times before we realised what was going on - that's the power of 'if someone else wants it, then I want it.' These were great days, when we were learning to be in total control of our life, and new experiences and decisions were being made every day.

## Buy three Houses, and Get One Free

Buy three houses; get one free. If we bought a house for £1,500, we would spend £1,000 on renovating it, then sell it for £3,000-£3,500, making at least 30% profit on our initial investment. So, for every three houses we bought we got one free, literally. If we could renovate them in between signing the contract and completing, before we had actually bought them, we could do a lot more - one a week, instead of one a month.

We were limited only by the amount of work that we could do with our enthusiastic crew of part-timers; plus, we had subcontractors to do the electrical work, plumbing and new roofs, if needed. We did the rest ourselves to keep the cost down, which brought the profit up, so we could expand.

The number-one goal of establishing financial freedom as quickly as possible had its ups and downs, as we tried to hold on to as much property as possible and receive an income from it. By holding on to it, cash flow was affected and, consequently, properties had to be sold. It seemed hopeless to us, but an outsider would have seen it differently; they would have seen the substantial number of properties we had at any one time.

The business was growing, but we just hadn't got to the tipping-point of keeping investments; we even had properties that could produce 20% income but, of course, this would have meant keeping them for five years to get our money back, which we couldn't do. Sometimes you have to give up what's good in the short term to get what's great in the future.

By now we were buying small commercial properties and renting them out, mostly to new businesses like Indian and Chinese restaurants. Then many just disappeared overnight without paying the rent, although this was minimal and there was always someone that would take their place.

## 1979 - We Needed To Expand the Shop

By the end of 1979 we were desperate to move, so off we went to look for a much bigger shop. No sooner had we started to look than we found one in a place called Orton Centre, a new satellite town on the edge of town. There were about thirty small shops, one supermarket, one big DIY store, a school and about 3,000 new houses. This new store was five times bigger than the one we already had, so we signed up for a 25-year lease. We then put Rainbow up for sale again, this time just the business, as a going concern, together with the lease, which had 18 years left to run, for £10,000.

One year previously the freehold and the business was that amount; the business had gone up because of its takings, and the profit had improved because we had invested more money, thought and energy into it, plus we were getting more experienced.

We had two offers straight away for the asking price, so we sold it to a couple who had a taxi company and who needed to move as they were trading from home - I thought they would have a better chance of running two businesses from there, as opposed to one.

We had spent £5,000 on buying and converting the shop; four years later we sold the freehold and business for £18,000. When we sold it, we told the people before they bought the shop that we were staying in the business of selling nursery goods, and also where we were going. We also said that we would supply them with stock until they got their accounts opened up.

By 1980 we had the new shop; it was five times bigger than the old one and it was ready to open the doors the day after we sold our first shop, Rainbow Warehouse. All we had to do now was hand the keys over to the new owners; I was worried about the new owners, as I had tried to get them into the shop for training.

I said that we would give them a month's training to learn just how we had run the shop, but they said that they would be all right. Again, I asked them to come in a week beforehand just to go through things and so that we could introduce them to our suppliers, but nothing came of it. I really could not understand them.

### *You can sell a business, and include all of the training that's needed for the business to be a success, but you cannot make people do it.*

We wanted to do things properly. We had told them that we were staying in the same business, as in those days people could have a shop a few miles away and not be in competition with each other, unlike today with the Internet. Marilyn had made them a folder that had all of the information inside regarding what each of the suppliers sold and the terms of business, our discounts and so on.

We left extra free stock for them to compensate for any losses that they might have; we also told them that, if any customer was to bring stuff back, they should just exchange it and we would pay them for it. Also, we agreed to supply them with stock at 5% over our cost until they got their accounts opened, as we had informed all of the suppliers of the situation, so we felt we had done all that we possibly could do.

It was a Monday; the shop was closed on a Monday. Marilyn went through the operating of the till with the lady and I went through the stock. All fine, then a customer walked through the door - we hadn't locked it. They asked for a baby-walker. The new lady owner just looked at us; we showed her where it was and helped her with the till. The next customer came in and the next; by now the shop was filling up.

I didn't know what to do, as she had refused the training offered and we had now got to go to Leicester. We were late, so we asked, "Will you be all right?" She said she would, so off we went. That's when I realised that we had sold the full package but they hadn't taken us up on it. "You don't know what you don't know," and I certainly didn't know why.

I could not have put everything together and done any of this without Marilyn; she was brilliant. It certainly brought it home to me by then that we were a team, and that the way forward in anything we did was to combine our abilities, making things possible together where it would be impossible on our own in the long run. At this point, we decided that the two businesses would be run completely by both of us, with my ability to think outside the box and making instant decisions, and Marilyn's strength to keep the businesses grounded and to tie up all the loose ends.

## A New Shop! With New Opportunities

The new shop opened on the Tuesday, not to the sound of bands playing, but to the sound of compressors and diggers that were outside our doors. The builders hadn't finished the Shopping Centre so, consequently, only the bravest of people found us for the first couple of weeks and, in that time, there were some raised voices from me to the Council about the situation.

Luckily, we hadn't hired any extra full-time staff at that point, just some part-time staff in the shop so the day we moved in we wondered what the hell we had let ourselves in for. We were the only shop that had opened up, and to get to our shop people had to walk over planks of wood through a building site, as there were no paths. I went crazy at the landlord, the local Council, and got the pavement sorted out - but where were the people?

The few people who were around did not want to spend the amount of money on baby dresses and clothes that we were used to in our first little shop. We served people in that old shop personally, presenting each baby dress or romper from out of a glass counter. When you are giving personal service, by doing it that way and engaging with the customer, there is a rapport. We regularly sold four £12 baby dresses to one person in 1979; however, in 1980, in a self-service environment, people ignored the higher-priced garment and went for £2.99 ones instead. That was a steep learning curve that season, as we lost a lot of money after buying for the whole season; in fact, five times more, because we had five times the space. We soon discovered it doesn't work that way.

## Rainbow to Kiddicare

We couldn't call the new business Rainbow Warehouse, as we had sold the name, so we had to think of another and, as we had always admired Mothercare because we thought it was the best baby nursery shop in the country and, 40 years later, we still do, we called the new shop Kiddicare. We aspired to be like them and any other businesses that we thought were the best in what they did.

None of these businesses can be beaten, so we never tried to, although most people thought we did. We tried not to be in direct competition but, with so few brands in the market, it was a job not to, so we tried to sell the same things but in a different way.

## Prams for Elephants

Just as we had settled into the new shop, Peterborough got itself a new shopping centre in the town which included a John Lewis store with a brilliant baby department. Now they were competition for us, their spies would come into our small shop every week to check on our prices, which made me mad, so I would confront the person and say, "I will show you round and then, when you go out, I will reduce everything that you have on your list." They would stand in front of me and deny that they worked for John Lewis; how stupid could they be, the same people sneaking around every week with their note-pads.?

Some years later I did ask a spy from another shop if her daughter was an elephant, and she gave me a funny look. I said, "You have been telling me every week for four years that your daughter is pregnant and you are just getting prices of all the equipment for her so, as we don't sell equipment for elephants, you are banned from my shop."

## Nursery Imports Were Just Starting

We found ourselves on the radar of all the big nursery suppliers, as the shop was now in a shopping centre. Baby equipment sales were rocketing, and imports were just starting to come into the country; these were more stylish and cheaper than the home-manufactured prams and pushchairs.

Although they were cheaper and more stylish, we soon found they came with a hefty, unforeseen cost. By now, Maclaren pushchairs were selling at £18.99, so we bought 100 Cindico imported pushchairs to sell at £12.99; they flew out of the door - fantastic. What we did not realise was that they would soon all be flying back; the wheels were falling off and, because we sold them so quickly, we had ordered another 100. These new ones were already modified, so Cindico clearly knew about the problem.

So we exchanged the 100, all within three weeks; now, by that time, we had ordered another 100. The second lot was now coming back with another component broken. I decided enough was enough, so I bought 100 Maclarens ready to exchange so, as customers were coming through the doors with the faulty, cheap ones, we would get a Maclaren and give it to them saying, "I'm sorry you have had a problem; this one is much dearer, but you can have this for the inconvenience  caused." It defused an argument and the customer became an advert which promoted us, instead of just a customer.

If customers had a problem, we sorted it without any fuss so, instead of telling other people what rubbish products we had, they recommended us for great customer service - a bad situation turned into great advertising. As the time went on over the next year, we became established and, once again, the shop started to boom. Customers were coming from as far as London, because their family had moved to a new township in Peterborough as overspill from London.

Most people wanted products instantly, with the exception of prams, so it was no good selling something and then ordering it; we needed stock as a back-up and the only way to do that was to re-invest the profits, and get a bigger overdraft. Everything comes with a price, because the more stock we got the better reputation we had as, at that time, most nursery shops only stocked samples and took orders for when the baby arrived.

## Lay-A-Way - What's That All About?

We tried this thing called "lay-a-way" because the customers and the reps all said we should as the customers wanted their prams storing until the baby had arrived; we had got up to £10,000 worth of prams put away, with £500 deposit on the whole lot.

These prams were taking up too much room in the back of the shop, so I took them all home and put them in our garages. No sooner had I had done that than a lady came into the shop with a friend and asked me to show her friend the pram. With that, I had to go home and get it. She then came in the next week and did the same with another friend. Another lady put a £200 pram away for six months with a £10 deposit, and then said that she needed her £10 as someone had given her a pram. The pram I had put away six months ago was now an old colour that was going out of fashion; I had to sell it for £99, which was a lot lower than cost.

## Everyone Said We Wouldn't Survive

That was it; our days of lay-a-way were over. People in the trade said that we would never survive without doing this and we would go bust, so I put my thinking-cap on once again. To overcome this, which apparently was an age-old problem that nursery shops had, I delved into the reason and discovered it was an old wives' tale of being bad luck to have the pram at home before baby was born.

Prior to us entering the trade, manufacturers would make a pram and deliver it to the shop built-up ready to use; then the customer would fetch it when the baby was born. Customers went to a local shop that was in walking distance so, if they took the pram early and didn't need it, they would be stuck with it, as it would have been wheeled out of the shop - in other words, it was used.

When we came into the trade, everybody had just started to put the prams into cardboard boxes in two parts, as the chassis were made differently from how they used to be, so now they could get more on the van. To sort out this issue and to get the customers to take their prams before the baby was due, we just gave them a written guarantee that was from the date of when the baby was due to be born, and we suggested they stored it at their mum's house if they were superstitious. That solved the problem - we not only survived, we were now starting to prosper.

Rapidly, the shop filled up with stock; then our house became full of stock, and we had three garages full. We were desperate for more space, but this is a normal process that a small business goes through, and I never thought twice about filling our house up with stock, because it was free space.

We developed an "anything is possible" mind-set, and still have it today. Since we had started the businesses it had been hectic, with no time to spare; working 7 days a week, we were running on adrenaline, literally always running everywhere. We were also buying and selling commercial property, as well as residential.

SIDETRACKED

As we needed more stock, we would buy bigger and bigger quantities to enable us to get the price down; but, in doing so, we found we never had enough money to be able to pay the bills, as we never sold the larger amount quickly enough. The inevitable happened - we ran out of money, and now we had bills that we couldn't pay.

I was putting money in the bank, which was three doors away from the shop, up to four times a day. One day, the lady at the counter said to me, "Why do you deposit the money so many times a day?"

I said, "Each time we make cheques out to suppliers, we put the money in the bank so you have it, and we don't go overdrawn."

She said, "Mr Wright, we only cash up once a day, at 5pm, so you don't have to do that." There we were, four years after starting the business, and we didn't know this; and we thought we knew everything.

## Cyril Shorts Was More Than a Rep

Cyril Shorts was a rep for a company called Baby Relax, which imported and manufactured nursery equipment. Cyril used to call on us every month. He came in as usual and, as we were talking, he always asked how things were going. I remember that I had said that we were having cash-flow problems, not thinking anything of it.

I have always been open with people and, who knows, sometimes other people have solutions to problems, although I wasn't thinking of that at the time. He must have asked how much we were short of because, two days later, a building society cheque for £7,500 came in the post, with a note saying, "Keep it as long as you want, with no interest." I was so grateful to Cyril for doing that; in fact, what happened was reverse psychology.

Once more a kick up the arse to get my act and responsibilities in gear; I paid the money back in 30 days, and I paid £300 interest, equivalent to 50% p a, which he didn't want. I did this because if I had paid nothing it would have taught me nothing. I can tell you, it was the most valuable and best mentoring I have ever had. It taught me to be responsible for my actions. The trouble is I was going down a road with my eyes closed and, as my father-in-law says, "Open your eyes." Also, I had forgotten about the game of chess - what will happen if I do this or that?

## An Education from a Great University

BACK

We started to learn a lot about business. It was fantastic, although some days we didn't know whether we were coming or going. We did not have to go to university to learn business economics and any other things that university business studies entail; they all came to us in the form of a verbal slap in the face every day from customers if we didn't come up to their expectations - just like Mrs Corton did when she wasn't happy with me in those early days.

We learned from the university of hard knocks, whether it was employing people with their own specific wants, needs and dreams, or basic business needs like keeping the accounts in order every day. I also wanted to know everything about our suppliers' business, to give me more ideas for ours.

## Thieves, Conmen and Chancers

The majority of our customers, I would say 99%, were lovely people who were a delight to serve. The minority of 1% taught us how to run a profitable business; these were the thieves, conmen and chancers. Without these people we would not have had to stretch our minds to solve the problems that they were creating for the business and, in doing so, taught us to close the loopholes and steer the business in the direction that cut these people out as much as we could, knowing that this is a moving target and would be a full-time job for someone in the future. This turned out to be right, when a guy called Barry Herbert came to work with us some years later.

I was back playing chess in my mind. The thieves made a move; now, what do I do to stop that happening again? If I do that, what will they do? We only wanted to run a baby shop because Marilyn had some spare time and we had the space; now I was an unpaid detective, so I had better put the knowledge into use in the overall plan of the business.

The business plan was sketchy at that time, as it changed in minutes to suit us on that day; having said that, we were getting very consistent as we now had responsibilities - the staff and overheads that you have with a 25-year lease. I liked it, but the freedom that I had whilst working in the property business had gone. I sometimes felt like I was the flea back in the jar hitting my head on the lid every bloody minute, all 1,440 of them in the day, but it was just another learning curve that goes around.

We still had our financial goal as our number one priority. I would be thinking about that every day; I don't know whether it was because I was scared of failing and ending up back on the dole, or the thought by now of wanting to be a millionaire. I have tried to analyse this. I know it definitely wasn't for the love of money, because I never hoarded any; as soon as we got any it went into stock, more staff and property, plus by now nice cars, mainly as a reward for the hard work that we just couldn't get out of even if we wanted to.

There was a never-ending feeling of burning our bridges to get to the next goal; that usually involved helping other people, whether it was in investing thousands in a new brand of prams that people were asking for, or building houses or shops to give people accommodation and us an income.

## We celebrated our first year as Kiddicare by rewarding ourselves with one of our goals, a new Mercedes Benz car.

At the time, a new Mercedes car was really out of the question, and I had told my brother Terry, who was a car salesman before starting his cycle shop, that I was saving up for the car. He said that by the time I had saved that money, with inflation at 16% it would keep pushing the price up and I would never get it. I should get HP, because it would be cheaper than inflation and I could have one now instead of waiting. How brilliant - we got our goal that paid for itself.

Our thoughts were always that if it all went wrong we could go back to living in a caravan and, as long as we were together, it didn't matter. Then we realised that we actually had all the freedom in the world, because we were doing what we wanted to do; it was an unbelievable feeling because, personally, we hadn't got anything, so we wouldn't miss it if we lost the business.

*Advertising Kiddicare in Orton Centre Peterborough*

## The Rep Who Only Got One Order

One day when Marilyn was out, a rep walked in selling baby shoes and, instead of saying, "Come back when Marilyn is in," I bought 12 of each shoe, or so I thought, in each colour. No problem until they came in; I had ordered 12 of each in 20 styles in 6 colours, 1440 x £2. I still feel ill now, thinking about it, so you can imagine how I felt then. I thought that everyone was like Cyril; he used to tell me if I was buying too much stock. He would say, You can always buy some more, but you won't be pleased if I come round in a month and you still have the stock left from this order."

Well that rep was both silly and greedy when he knew I was not a shoe-buyer yet still sold far more to me than we needed just to get more money in the short term. We never gave him a second chance, even when we became the biggest independent in the UK and could have easily sold many more than that initial order. Greed had shot him in the foot, and that day taught us a lesson that stuck with us from then onwards; we only did business with people and companies that we liked.

In 1980 the first Peterborough local radio station was launched, Hereward Radio 225; the rep came in selling air-time, which I thought was great. They were selling one-minute ads, which were the normal time. I asked if they could do thirty-second ads and they said yes, so I had a small campaign. Then I decided on a twenty-second ad, which they said wouldn't work. I created a rhyme and the studio did a voice-over that sounded like a child's - it was a great success.

## *"Mummy had a baby, a tiny little thing; we took it down to Kiddicare and bought it everything"*

*Sale time*

I did what was the first ever ten-second ad at that time, and I kept asking for a bigger discount, so they sold me all of the spots that they could not sell to anyone else every 24 hours. Other retailers didn't want ads in the middle of the night, but our customers were up feeding and changing their babies, and the teenagers who would soon be our next customers were also awake. I got these ads for £2 each. We got 100s a month, which was great until the station got busy, when the prices went through the roof. It was good while it lasted, and got us established for next to nothing.

***Cyril Shorts showing us some of the new Baby Relax products on show at the Harrogate Pram fair 1983.***

Cyril became a friend, mentor and adviser and a second father figure to me. Over his long career he and Letty, his wife, ran numerous businesses selling everything from birdseed to car batteries, running a restaurant to renting out baby-weighing scales. He also loved to gamble; we can remember many happy nights with them both at the Sportsman Club in London, near to where Cyril lived on Tottenham Court Road.

# Look After the Pennies

## *"And look after the pounds as well"*

For years I have asked people to answer a question in 5 seconds:

Which one would **you** pick?

1 million pounds cash right now, or

1 penny today, and doubled every day for 31 days?

Just so you understand, without any doubt; on the first day I would give you 1 penny, the next day 2, the next 4, the next 8, and so on. On the eleventh day it would have accumulated to £10.24.

Which would you take?

Answer now - 1 million or 1 penny?

When it comes to money, lots of people like to keep it, hoard it away for a rainy day, or just because they feel safe seeing their savings in a bank ready for them to live on when they don't have a job or don't want to work.

Now think about this: if, after working and saving for thirty years, you find out a thief has been stealing a bit of your savings every week you would be very angry, so why are you not angry about inflation doing the same thing every week? Inflation is just robbing you so that your money deflates, leaving you unable to buy what you could have just a year ago. So I say that your money is being stolen. Most people don't see it like that and, if they do, they don't understand just what it's doing to their savings and the diminishing returns they can get on their money.

Another question for you, in 5 seconds please.

Who is the winner when it comes to money?

The person who saves their money in a bank?
The bank which lends that money to a customer?
The person who is the borrower of that money?

The answer, in the vast number of cases, is the person who borrows. You see, different times call for different strategies, but the person who puts their money into the bank, usually to protect it, loses out to inflation in two ways: £100k today in the bank, with inflation, say, at 10% next year, is worth £90k which, in 5 years' time, will be worth under £62k.

Meanwhile, the person who borrowed their money has an investment worth just over £161k, which they can leverage against, say at 90%; that's an extra £54k of investment that they can buy and reinvest, making a £215k investment that can buy passive income for them.

At the present time, the net passive income would be £12,500, plus the appreciating asset would keep up with inflation, whereas the money in the bank would have an income of £500 and would be eroded by inflation.

## *So speculate to accumulate*

"Money makes money, but only if it is invested with caution." "The rich get richer and the poor become poorer." But there is no need for that.

Most people don't give this a thought; the richer you are the more you can do for other people. Don't be ashamed about accumulating money; besides, money is the direct result of helping people and the by-product of this helping is money. If you don't believe me, ask any business person in the world.

## Things That Must Be Avoided

There are two situations to avoid. Firstly, buying anything that is at the top of the market and, of course you need to know your market, or get good advice from someone that does. In 2006 we sold some of our properties at the peak of the market and used the money for another business for five years, then picked up similar properties in 2011 for half the price. This rarely happens, but be ready when it does, because it will.

The second thing is lending to people who say they will pay it back when the bank is willing to replace the debt or when the business makes money. Naturally, having the debt should put their back against the wall and, in so doing, put every spare penny back to the loan - that should be the first thing they do to prove they are worth the next and bigger loan. But some pee every spare penny up the wall and then go bust; that's my prediction on one business that I know of today, 4th June 2014.

Now, if you have some money or are planning to accumulate a large amount in the future, and when I say the future, I mean the next 40 years, believe me it's not long and you will need a lot of money for two reasons: one, to live in comfort and two, to have something to do with your brain, looking after and growing it.

Once we were making enough to live on, we then started expanding. I will give an example of what we have done since 1974. We invested in equipment so that we could take on bigger and more profitable jobs. Then, over the years we continually invested all of our money into stock for the shop, enabling us to sell more, as in retail, if you have stock, people will buy, but if you have to order anything the sales go down dramatically, as people look for immediate gratification. If we had enough stock for the shop we would go on to buying property and, if we needed money fast to obtain a bargain, we would borrow from the bank with the assets as collateral.

## Just One Small Step at a Time

Over the years, we found the money we needed to live on as a percentage of the profits came down dramatically, from 95% when we started to 5% a couple of years later, because we were still living at the same standard as when we started. This gave us a tremendous amount to invest. We knew that, if we could just hold out living a very sparse lifestyle, at some point there would be an abundance of money.

As time went on it became harder to cope with having so much money tied up in the business whilst we were living on virtually nothing, but that all changed in 1982. That was the tipping point, which took 8 years to achieve; I would say it was the hardest time we had encountered in our lives but, as Marilyn says, the pain is soon forgotten once the baby is born, and our baby business by this time was fast growing up.

There are thousands of things people can do to start earning money today, in 2014. People are moaning about zero-hours contracts when, in fact, it can give them more freedom to explore other avenues of money-making opportunities, because if they had a full-time job there would be no time to look for new ways to make a living. So, in fact, today's labour force is actually better off than the workers of 40 years ago, but most cannot see it.

We now don't put any more money into the bank than we have to. We borrow money if we can, and put it into assets that generate an income. Leveraging assets is good at the right time; why buy one house when you have the ability to buy two, three or even four? The same goes for buying stock.

We worked and invested the money over and over again, until we had enough money to support our needs out of the income without touching the capital. We looked after our pennies first, and then looked after our pounds; then we only threw away the ones that we didn't want to work for us. I am joking, but I am surprised at the number of people who do throw away money, even though they say they haven't enough of it.

Back to the first question; why take a lump sum of a million when, if you had just had the patience to wait a few more days, you would have had 10,736,418,24 that's 10 million, 736 thousand 418 pounds and 24 pennies.

| | | | | | |
|---|---|---|---|---|---|
| 1) | 0.01 | 12) | 20.48 | 23) | 41,943.04 |
| 2) | 0.02 | 13) | 40.96 | 24) | 83,886.08 |
| 3) | 0.04 | 14) | 81.92 | 25) | 167,772.16 |
| 4) | 0.08 | 15) | 163.84 | 26) | 335,544.32 |
| 5) | 0.16 | 16) | 327.68 | 27) | 671,088.64 |
| 6) | 0.32 | 17) | 655.36 | 28) | 1,342,177.28 |
| 7) | 0.64 | 18) | 1,310.72 | 29) | 2,684,354.56 |
| 8) | 1.28 | 19) | 2,621.44 | 30) | 5,368,709.12 |
| 9) | 2.56 | 20) | 5,242.88 | 31) | 10,736,418.24 |
| 10) | 5.12 | 21) | 10,485.76 | | |
| 11) | 10.24 | 22) | 20,971.52 | | |

You and I both know that we are not going to get that return, but it's a good lesson, a principle that can have a great impact by looking after the pennies. Remember, we had 37 of them and we invested them in that piece of scrim; it all started from there.

This next picture is a typical example of what we were investing in during the 1980s. We built a hairdressing salon that opened on 1st March 1989; it cost £26,000. The land was free, as it was a back garden on a corner plot. We let it for an average of £7,000 a year; 25years x £7,000 = £175,000 in rent, and the value of the building today is 100k (not bad). We started with small projects like this one.

**"I could have had that." "No you couldn't."**

The salon was built on the back garden of a house that we had bought. In the 1980s, we would buy houses on corner plots then divide the garden and build, so basically getting a free plot of land. This one we saw in the Friday paper at 6am; we had looked at it by 8am; then we were waiting for the estate agents to open at 9am and subsequently bought it.

A few days later, we were talking to some people who lived not too far from the property, who said that they could have bought it. So I asked why they didn't buy it. They said because by the time they went into the agents at 10am it was already sold. They couldn't believe that it was already sold. I said, "Well, in that case, you couldn't have bought it," but they still insisted that they could.

## Doing Nothing, Sleeping, Eating, and TV

It is one thing having the money to buy anything but, like in our case over the years, whether it was houses or prams, you still have to be first. So many times we have succeeded just because the other people that wanted the same things were sleeping. This is where enthusiasm comes in; we didn't have to be brainy for this basic stuff, we just needed to get up and be first - simple.

We started early and finished late, if we wanted to succeed with the money that we had. The person who says, "It's all right for you," uses too many of the 1,440 minutes a day in bed, too many watching TV, too many eating, and too many doing nothing; then they wonder why others have more than they do.

The next picture is of a building we bought in 1986, as a going concern, for £19,000, complete with fittings; we then found a tenant and sold the fittings for £1,500, making the purchase £17,500. We then let the building for £5,000 a year for four years, and then sold it to the tenant for £32,000.

This deal gave us a return of 85% from our money in four years but, better still, we got another 28% a year rent. We did this time and time again, buying shops and restaurants, thinking we were getting nowhere when actually we were - we just could not see this at the time. We always wanted to do bigger deals, as we were totally driven, not by the money, but by the exhilarating feeling that it gave.

We started to grow the business, buying not only houses, but also now small commercial buildings. This phase went from 1974 to 1984, and then we gradually stepped up the size of properties. By this time we had completely stopped doing any building work for other people.

By then we had got enough of our own work, and the shop too, that was a full-time job on its own. I used to think that we should be in the circus on one of those one-wheel bikes, wobbling about trying to keep from falling off and, at the same time, juggling those big things like a pin, as in 10-pin bowling. I think they call them clubs.

## Windows of Opportunity

Whatever industry you are in, there will be some businesses doing well and some going bust. On the face of it, they are all doing the same thing, but it usually comes down to changing your business every day, even if it's just a tiny bit because, if your business is not changing, someone else is, and that's one of your competitors.

## 75% Profit in One Month

We bought a shop for £12,000 on the first day that it went on the market; it seemed, as far as the agent was concerned, the going price that the area had been in the past. It was very rare that any shops came up for sale in that area, and this is one thing he had not taken into consideration. I immediately put it back on the market and sold it for £21,000. We knew what every property was worth in Peterborough; some people have a hobby, but this hobby of ours was one that we got paid for if we acted on the information that we gathered daily.

## Me, Lost For Words!

Hundreds of words just vanished from my vocabulary in minutes, this happening in 1981. Elaine was out with me one day; I was buying a new van, and then we were going on to Langford Smith Estate Agents to get some keys for three houses we had just bought. But when I was half way through buying the van, I found that I could not speak; one minute he was writing an order, the next I just walked away.

I couldn't get any words out at all. I went on to get the keys for the properties, but first I had to take Elaine to the properties to show her the addresses so she could go into Langford's office for the keys, as I wouldn't be able to talk. We went home, and then Elaine rang the shop to tell Marilyn that I had a problem and, within 10 minutes, Marilyn and an ambulance were there. The medics thought that I had got malaria, but it wasn't.

We would be in a restaurant when I would say to the waiters, "Could I have...," then I would be stuck. People around the table who knew me would start saying things like red sauce, pepper, oil; then, once they got it, I would say yes. I just could not find the word, so I would say "yellow stuff," meaning mustard; it became a vicious circle.

# Heartbreaking Days

## *"Things came to try us"*

It was now October 1981. Marilyn was pregnant at the time; we were so excited - we had been longing for another baby. We were also looking for a new house, something that would match our income and lifestyle, when I discovered a 47-room mansion in an isolated village. The price was around £240,000, the equivalent house today is £2.5 million; to put that into perspective, we were buying brand-new four-bedroom detached houses in Peterborough for £25,000. This was ten times that price; we had come from a 10ft caravan that we classed as our standard of living, at our lowest point in life in 1973, to this, in eight years.

## You Have Only One Life

SIDETRACKED

What's The Worst Thing That Can Happen? Here I just want to say how we dared to do the things we did by taking what most people would call massive risks, literally risking everything. Maybe I have said this before, but I will say it again.

Although we had lived and survived in that little caravan with a three-year-old, in the snow and the freezing cold, it had done us no harm. It had taught us to realise that possessions were far less important to us as a family; we were the only things that mattered. If we lost everything but still had each other, then that's all we would need. Of course, having lots of money at the same time is better, because it gives you the freedom of choice.

## If You Have Made the Effort Once

So when some people ask for my advice on how to make more money, and I tell them, some say to me, "It's all right for you, with all that money. I have just my house, and I am not risking that." I say, "That's fine. When you die, your dream of having wealth has gone with you, but you have lost your house anyway, so don't get hung up on possessions. Your God gave them to you as a reward for your effort, so why have you stopped making an effort? The loss is obviously greater than the reward that you are seeking; maybe you need to relook at what you want because, when the reward becomes bigger than the potential loss, the effort will be made."

The house was very spooky, and too far away, but that's how crazy our minds were at the time, well mine was, anyway. The thing was, it was like a mausoleum - too big, too dark and too isolated for Marilyn. She soon put me right about living there, so we just kept looking, as we needed a home with privacy, security and on its own.

Unfortunately, Marilyn lost that baby a few days later. Our lives were so hectic, with not a minute to think, and she was back at work the day after discharging herself from hospital. In fact she had to, because we had to go to London for two days to the Nursery Fair. It was at the Russell Hotel, Russell Square, where all of the new products for the nursery industry were shown for the year and, if you didn't put your orders in for the next six months, you wouldn't get any stock.

Marilyn was the only one who could do it, as we didn't have any staff with buying capabilities at the time. How she got through those two days I will never know; buying prams is a very girly thing, you have to be in the mind-set of an expectant mother with an understanding of the emotions, needs, and wants. Marilyn was in that mind-set the day before we went to the show. I can't imagine what it was like for her; I tried not to look at her, but every time I caught a glimpse of her face her eyes were filled with tears. She just kept her head down and did the ordering non-stop from 9am to 7pm, constantly looking at and buying the new products.

## The Highlight of Our Year

Those two days back then, once a year, were the highlight of our year in the nursery business. In the 1970s and 1980s there were more than 2,000 independent shops selling baby products in the UK; now, in 2014, there are around 200 left.

Everybody seemed to be so happy enjoying themselves; the hustle and bustle of trying to get appointments with manufacturers, seeing and talking to other shopkeepers who we had met at other trade shows, and staying in a hotel in London, even though it was just for one night. This trip was like a luxury holiday to us; we used to get the bedroom just above the entrance, because it had a little sitting area next to the bedroom where they would put a bed for Elaine.

**The Russell Hotel, Russell Square, London**

SIDETRACKED

We went past there the other day on our way to a meeting at one of our new businesses in London. We looked up, and the memories came flooding back and, for a few minutes, we were transported back 33 years to those two days in 1981; then, with tears in our eyes, we quickly went to our meeting in our meaningless new world.

BACK

Normally on the way to the London show, we would be chattering to each other non-stop about what we hoped to see and who would be there. We would discuss over and over again the amount of money we had to spend which, of course, never worked out, as we always spent much more than anticipated, and then struggled for the next six months to pay. On the way back we just wouldn't stop talking; we were so excited about the things we'd seen and what we had bought and how we were going to sell the products, but that year was different. There was silence there and back; we were just heartbroken. We couldn't look at each other without Marilyn crying.

# Business Carries On, No Matter What

When you are in business, things don't stop for sentiment; there are always fires to fight and projects to complete. There was no time for fuss, but I remember the next day, when we walked into the shop, Marilyn saw the pram that she was having for the baby. It was a gorgeous cream and brown corduroy pram with windows in the sides of the hood so you could see the baby; a very special pram. She burst into tears then went straight into the office. It didn't cross my mind to phone the shop while we were away, to tell the staff to put it out of the way so she did not see it. What a plonker!

No sooner had we got back to Peterborough than our heads were in the paper as normal, looking for property and, within days, we had found another house close to the new shop in a village called Alwalton, next to the A1. I think we paid about £70,000 for it.

### *The house we never moved into; we didn't like it anyway.*

The thing was the neighbours were really horrible because we wanted to double the size of the house, put an indoor swimming-pool in and have six garages. The neighbours said it would make their houses look inferior, so they objected to our plans. I said to them that it would actually put value on their houses, but they were having none of it; it was a very close-knit community and, when you're living in a place like that, you want people to talk to you in the local pub and I could see none of that happening.

At the same time, the shop was so busy that we needed to hold more stock and, as the shop was full, I had the bright idea of using the empty house and garages because our house was full of stock. Anyway, our neighbours were used to seeing me loading and unloading my van but, because we weren't living in the new house our new neighbours complained to the Council, so again we were fighting bureaucracy and had to get all of the stock out of the house.

When you are in business you are constantly bombarded with red tape. It's a wonder anybody bothers to build a business, but then again, it's probably easier than ducking and diving working for someone else when you want to be in control. You see, if I were in control, I could employ others to do the things that I couldn't do and, as long as those people were happy doing that, everyone was a winner. So now we had two houses; one we lived in along with the shop stock, and the new, empty one that we had planned on rebuilding, that also had stock in, but the local objections got so unbearable that I really did not want Marilyn and Elaine in that environment - but what could we do?

## A Great Year for the Shop

In May of 1981 we were the first shop in the country to start selling Mamas and Papas prams and, at the same time, we got the agency to sell Silver Cross prams too. Up to then we had written to Silver Cross every year after each Nursery Fair for five years, asking them if we could sell their products; always we got the same reply, "We have three accounts in Peterborough and that's enough."

That year one of their accounts, Fairways department store, closed down, followed by Alexandra Thompson department store which, I believe, was due to the opening of John Lewis that came to Peterborough in 1980. But with these gone, it opened up new opportunities for us.

## Wow, Expecting Again

By June of 1982 Marilyn was 4 months pregnant again when we saw an advert in the *Sunday Times*, a house for sale in Stamford, Lincolnshire, with an indoor swimming-pool. It was £225,000, so off we went to look at the swimming pool, so we could get some ideas of how to build ours in our newly-purchased house, which we hadn't moved into as Marilyn did not want to move house until the work was completed and the baby was born.

We learned to move fast on things; we would make some mistakes, but the successes always outdid any of our failures and besides, we got so much experience from all of the mistakes that we did make.

We did not have to know everything about the nursery trade; there were more than 2000 competitors who could teach us, and we assumed they were all making a living. It amazes me that, with all the experience out there, we the newcomers become the most successful - why?

That's an easy one to answer - just carry on when other people stop. Obstacles are just something that gives you time to think, and being responsible is a learned thing; once we were over 24 and looking after ourselves with our brains that had matured, we became completely responsible for ourselves. Then, we naturally grew into becoming responsible for others around us; once we learned and accepted this, it was a great feeling.

I can't believe now, looking back, that I was, at the age of 30, looking at a 47-roomed mansion that had not been touched for a hundred years. I wouldn't do that now but, if Marilyn had said yes, I would have found a way to have bought it; what was in my mind?

Marilyn always put her business before herself and carried on regardless, knowing that one day she would be secure; I suppose that's why she went along with my mad, scary, crazy, nutcase but sometimes-brilliant ideas.

## *"You only have to be right 51% of the time to be a success in business."*    Neville Wright

## Money Just Kept Rolling In

The money just rolled in so, financially, we were much better off now, because the income was very consistent from the shop as well as the property side, which had been erratic, but good. The average wage in 1982 was £7,500 pa and, by then, we were making £60,000. Having said that, our personal drawings were a fraction of what we were earning; the surplus stayed in the business. This actually got a hold of me; I tried to live on next to nothing while at the same time re-investing as much as possible into the business.

I still had this dreadful fear of failing, and that dole queue was never far from my mind. I have just spoken to a person today, who told me that he bought all of their nursery equipment from us in the 80s. He said, "We had a choice of where to buy and the reason we chose you was because there was just something about you two - the way you cared about the customers and the passion you had for the products that we didn't get in other shops."

# 1982. A New Life

## *"Running at 100 miles an hour"*

10th November 1982 outside our house number 70 Hyholmes, Bretton, Peterborough. Marilyn going to the maternity unit, having booked in to have Joanne on that day so as to be back working in the shop by Saturday 13th, as that was the shop's busiest day of the week and no one was allowed to have a Saturday off. Well, Marilyn made the rules!

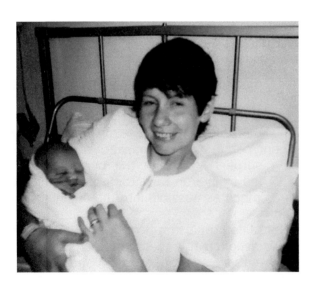

11th Nov. I took Marilyn a bowl of Angel Delight as she had asked for some food and, at that time, that's the only thing I could cook. Marilyn looked at it and said, "I asked for food."

Of course, I took a briefcase with 30 invoices in it, too; they needed to be paid, and all by cheque in those days. I licked the stamps for her, and the bowl.

Marilyn was back at work on the Saturday. The next week, one of our suppliers, Gordon Brooks, came in; the first thing he asked was, "Are you a new dad yet?" I said, "Yes, the baby is in the office with Marilyn." When we went through to the storeroom he looked in the office and said to Marilyn, "Where's the baby?" Marilyn was on the phone, so pointed under the desk.

Baby Joanne was in a carrycot under the desk and our dog, Prince, was sleeping at the side of the cot; there was nowhere else for her.

At that time we started to meet lots of people in our industry, many becoming life-long friends, like Gordon and Pat Brooks, who always had time and advice for us even though our business in those early days was very small compared to their other customers.

*13/11/15. Out for lunch; at the age of 88, Gordon has the same sense of humour as he had in 1976. In the 90s we went on holiday with Gordon and Pat to our home in Tenerife. One day, we took a wrong turning and got robbed by four men; scary, but we can laugh about it now. Gordon sadly passed away on 29/1/16.*

## Is It a Toilet? No, it's an Office!!

Marilyn spent most of her time in the office, looking after the bookwork for both of the businesses. We had leased two units in the Orton shopping centre and knocked them into one; each had two toilets so, in one of the units, we took the toilets out and took the doors off, making one into a kitchen and, in the other, we took the door and fixed it to the wall, which made a desk-top for Marilyn.

At times three people worked in this tiny space that we called the office, standing in a row to cash up and so on. Our dog would be on the floor under the desk all day; we were only reminded it was there when someone would put the one and only stool on its tail, when an almighty yelp would scare the life out of our unsuspecting reps who were there to take orders.

## Walk a Mile in the Customer's Shoes

SIDETRACKED

A few days before Marilyn was due, I went to maybe Peterborough's best camera shop and asked for a video camera. The guy asked a few questions; I told him that my wife was having a baby in a couple of days and that's why I wanted it. The best camera came out, a monster of a thing with a lead attached to a heavy video recorder that you put over your shoulder.

He took me to the till to pay, and I asked if there was anything else that I needed. "Yes," he replied, "a tripod." I asked what else might I need, and he said a microphone. I asked, "Will it pick up sound six feet away?" "No." "What then?" "Oh yes;" and this went on and on. Well, I came out with £2,400 of equipment.

Obviously he didn't know what he was selling. The halogen light that I bought burned the housing and blinded people in a second, but the biggest problem was that he didn't sell me a spare battery.

I wanted to capture the moment when mother and baby bonded for the first time but, as I went to film them, the battery went dead.

When I went back to buy one the next day, he said that most people didn't buy them because they were too expensive.

We taught our staff at Kiddicare the value of our products, not the price, something that other shops competing with us did not seem to understand, together with the in-depth sales approach we had with the customer. Competitors thought it was purely on price; nobody understood the philosophy that was behind everything we did; why would they? People want things that they generally think are too expensive.

# Objections

It was our job to show them how to justify why they should have them; it was easy to break the price down into how much the extra amount of money would be to have exactly what they wanted, as opposed to what they thought they should spend, so anything they objected to on price would be broken down into the amount of days the product would be used.

So, if a pram was £100 more than they wanted to pay, we would sell them on 14p a day extra over 2 years, and then say to the couple, as we would always stand next to the woman but looking at the man, "14 **pence a day** to get what you want." Sometimes the man would say that a hundred pounds extra was too much. I would often answer that by saying, **"Do you want just a wife, or would you prefer a happy wife? It's only 14p."** As long as you had been with that customer for a while and had got to know them, and also got the voice inflection right, there was no objection and the sale was made.

## Some Things You Just Have Got To Have

BACK

Well, guess what? When we looked at the house with the indoor swimming-pool in the *Sunday Times*, as soon as I went through the big electric gates and down the drive I fell in love with it. We looked at each other and said, "This is nice," but inside of me I was saying, "YES; this is the house we have been looking for;" but I had no right thinking that way.

**Park House in Stamford, Lincolnshire**

Although this house was £225,000, it was only first fixed; it needed another £100,000 spending on it. It was equivalent to nine brand-new, 4-bedroomed houses in 1982 (today around £3.3 million) and besides, we had just bought another house for £70,000 and had not sold our own - where would we get the money from? We walked to the door and as soon as we went into the house I recognised it; I had seen the plans on a wall in a builder's office a couple of years back. I had gone into the office when I was just passing, to ask if they had any plots of land that they could build a house for us on.

I was dressed in my overalls covered in plaster; the lady in the office immediately made up her mind that I could not afford to be in there. "We have nothing that would suit you." I took no notice and persisted; I said, pointing to a plan on the wall, "That's the kind of house that I want." She said, "That's **not** a house, that is **just** an extension for a swimming pool, and that is costing £80,000." I thought, "Sod you, you bitch," or something like that.

*The indoor Italian marble pool area*

The reason that the house had not sold was that it was too expensive for the people who had looked at it, and it only had first fix in it so it needed finishing off, bathrooms, kitchens, etc. Another £100,000 needed spending on it but, when I saw the house, I thought, "I'm having this one, just because of that woman's shit attitude towards me." It was an instant fulfilment of a goal within a goal, and besides, I loved it. Paying for it, however, was going to take some doing.

## We Offered What We Could Afford

It was like going back to 1968, when we bought our first house in St Martin's Street, Peterborough for £650, not because we thought that was what it was worth, but it was what we had at the time of the offer, and the same principle applied here. By coincidence, it was in an area in Stamford called St Martin's Without.

Once more we had gone into a recession in 1982, but the good news is we bought the house, which was advertised at £225,000, for £143,000 from a bank that had repossessed it. The crazy thing was I had spoken to the owner about a week earlier, in August, and he said he would take £180,000; I was ringing the agent to say we would have it, when he said the house now belonged to the bank and they were dealing with it. I then offered the bank £130,000 in cash, which they rejected, but said they would come down to £180,000; after this, we haggled.

I haggled down and they haggled up until I had got to £140,000. They totally rejected this and re-advertised in the national paper. Luckily for us it was October, and the housing market had virtually come to a halt. Finally, they said they would take £145,000. I knew the house was easily worth £180,000 but I was a sod in those days, I had to squeeze the last drop, and I didn't want to jump at their figure, so I offered them £143,000 and they took it. Unbelievably, the timing was right - for a while I did think we were going to lose it.

The fear of loss is a terrible thing when you're negotiating, so my thoughts are that if you have never had it, you won't miss it, but I wanted this; it was probably the best and the most expensive house in the region for sale at that time. Oh yes, Marilyn was crazy about it as well. I think now that I was quite foolish to risk that deal for £2,000, something I haven't done since.

## We Sold Five Houses to Buy One

In 1981 we had bought three brand-new houses outright, as the businesses were starting to generate lots of income. So, for a very short time, we had three tenants living in brand-new houses that were better than the one we were living in ourselves and, to top that they weren't paying their rents, which made me think I might be doing something a bit wrong here. So we sold them, as we thought that we might as well get the benefit if we weren't getting the rent, and we sold our other two houses, making a £21,000 loss on the one that we had never moved into.

# Was I Dreaming, Or Was This Real?

The 27 years that we lived in this wonderful house were amazing, and gave us everything that we wanted from a house that matched our income; it was just an unbelievable place. Every day, when I drew up at the electric gates, I had the feeling that it shouldn't be mine; I felt like I should be working there, not be the owner of it. It took me about two years to get over that feeling.

The decision to buy this property was made easy for us. Firstly, the woman, who really had nothing to do with the house apart from being involved with the builder who built it for the client, looked down her nose and disrespected me, so my buying it was a tick in a mental box. Secondly, we had to sell five properties to buy Park House, but it didn't matter because we sold the three where the sodding tenants were not paying their rent - a win-lose situation for them, but only in the short run.

Why should we have the money sitting in these properties that were better than we were living in ourselves, and yet not receive any rent? Why not have the investment in our own home and enjoy it? The third reason was that the house suited us down to the ground. Also, it was a brilliant investment that shot up in value, making it very easy to borrow against when we needed money at the drop of a hat - certainly a goal within a goal. And as for the one that we never lived in, the £21,000 loss was a small price to pay to have kept away from such negative people as lived in that village.

# I Was Educating Elaine

SIDETRACKED

Back to 1981-1984; as the years went by we gradually stopped doing the house renovations ourselves - time wouldn't allow us to - and we concentrated on buying the properties and running the businesses. Every day, I was supposed to take Elaine to school.

We always travelled a different way each day, looking for property that was for sale or, if I had seen something in the paper, or an estate agent, I would want to have a look, which didn't seem to bother Elaine, as attending school wasn't on her priority list. I can't think where she got that from!

Of course, Elaine never got to school when she should have, as I would get too engrossed in seeing agents and solicitors. Making deals was an everyday event so, when she was 11 to 13 years old, I would tell Elaine what to look for when buying property. It got so that I would ask her to make decisions on which property to buy, and on what basis she had come to that decision. By then it sometimes would be too late to take her to school, so I would drop her off at one of the shops.

***Elaine with Joanne, Saturday 12th March 1983***

BACK

We had got ourselves two natural-born sales people. Some days I would go into the shop where there would be a crowd of people gathered intently looking and listening to Elaine, this little 11-year-old girl who had a high-pitched voice, telling the customers all about a pram or pushchair and showing them how it all worked. She loved helping out on a Saturday and in the school holidays.

They would ask Elaine questions, and she had all of the answers instantly, as there was nothing that she didn't know about what she was demonstrating. It was a sight to see, an 11-year-old selling to adults on their level. Jo would be there in her pram, and Elaine would say, "This is my baby sister," just the best sales person we had and, whatever pram we put Jo in, that line sold out within days.

Elaine sometimes had been to school in the morning and popped into the shop for her lunch, and when they had got busy she had just stopped to help the staff and serve the customers. I didn't mind, as I knew she was going to work with us when it came time to leave school. I also thought that she was getting a better education with us, but Marilyn and the headmaster thought differently from me. On the days that I actually got her to school on time, I would drop her off at the back of one of our shops that was in the same complex as the school.

It was quicker for her to go through the shop than walk around. Invariably, at some point in the day I would ring that shop and who would answer the phone but Elaine. She would say that they were short of staff so she had stopped in the shop instead of going to school.

## Marilyn Was For Education, and So Was I

Marilyn would say that Elaine needed proper education, and I would say that that was what she was getting. By the age of 13, Elaine would say, "I'm not going to school to be with kids who just mess about; I would rather work." The teachers could see that Elaine was not a truant, because they would see her in the shop working.

The headmaster called me for a meeting, so I took Elaine along to see him. He suggested that I should get Elaine to school or there would be trouble, so I tried, but that lasted only three days before I got side-tracked and she did not get to school that day.

Back I went to see the head again; it was then decided that Elaine would go to school when certain subjects were being taught that would help with her career, which was fine for two weeks. Then came the summer break - she worked every day in the shops for six weeks, loving every minute of it.

Marilyn said a couple of days before the start of the new term that they would go and get some new school clothes. Elaine just refused, and I didn't help matters; she just would not go back to school. The school called me back in and said that they would make me take her to school; I said that they did not do that with travellers so what was the difference? And besides, they could see that she was being looked after; it was not like she was roaming the streets. That was it - she didn't go back, and nothing happened.

From 1983 our lifestyle was changing rapidly, all due to prolonged hard work. It was incredible what it could achieve; it just drove us on, as the rewards were fantastic. We began to travel the world with our constant companions, our mobile phones; the more we were away, the more we had time to think, constantly giving us new ideas.

Communications technology was on the rise for the ordinary person. I knew that this would be the future, but how to take advantage of it was to prove invaluable. We were now taking advantage of the mobile phone in our business, which was the one thing that would help to drive it forward to get the rewards while being on holiday.

## Learn From the Past

At this time, in 1983, it reminded me of when I talked to Mr Smeeton in the 1970s about investment property; he was still looking back when property was on the turn and we were looking forward. It was the same situation with communication in the 1990s, when people were still stuck in the 1970s, not understanding what was happening with progress.

We have always tried to think what things will be like in five years time, and then preparing and pushing our business to go in the right direction; this has always been a challenge in getting it right.

The house was on the market for £225,000, the dearest house for sale in the area in 1982. We bought it from a bank for £143,000, a 36% discount; about normal if you are prepared to look around.

The indoor swimming-pool cost £80,000 in 1979. We went to look at the indoor pool only because we were going to build one in our recently-purchased house, and fell in love with the house immediately, and I have already said there was another incentive for me. I understand that builder went bust; I wonder why?! That's what you call karma; treat everyone with respect as you are going up the ladder, as life has a tendency to repay you for what you have done, good or bad.

From the moment we got the house, Mum and Dad came and stayed with us and, as the years went on, they spent more time there, entertaining their hundreds of friends from all over the world who were associated with the many cycling clubs Dad was involved in. In 1982 Dad helped me complete the building work; then, in 1995, we decided to convert the massive loft space, and Dad helped me again.

After Mum died, Dad would spend a lot more time with us. Then, after he stopped driving, we used to pick him up on a Friday evening after work and then drop him off at his home on Monday morning. I wanted him to live with us, but he said he wouldn't leave the memory of Mum after living in their home for nearly 50 years together.

**Arthur Clarence David Wright, my dad, with Armani and Paco Rabanne.**

*My lovely mum, Winifred Mary, our Great Dane, Rex and Prince. Every weekend they had free they would spend from a Friday evening to Monday with us.*

## Rex Was a Big Man Who Had a Big Bark

Our Great Dane was a stray that we named after Rex, the Maclaren sales director in the mid 80s. He was a big man with a huge chest. He had been a cross-Channel swimmer. He had a loud voice with an overpowering character to go with it; he visited our shop one day, and I said, "I am glad you have come; your sales rep and company are not crediting this faulty pushchair which we have exchanged for a customer, so please can you take it back and credit it for us?"

He point-blank refused to take it, saying that he hadn't room in his car and that it would not be credited. In those days I was used to dealing with conflict with a pickaxe handle so, when he refused to take it, I called Ray to get a hacksaw; then I told him to cut the pushchair up into small pieces and then I would put Rex and the pushchair into the car. I didn't have to cut it up, as he found room; he took the pushchair and left a credit note.

I suppose I've always been an odd-job man, and the 80s brought debt-collecting along as a new business. But collecting money needed total focus and determination. This was never going to be my daytime job. Then inevitably, by 1992 Marilyn insisted I leave that type of business to other people, as the retail business was more conducive to family life; so I dropped that, knowing there would always be work for me if I ever needed to start another business.

A few months later, at the Earls Court pram show, we were invited out for dinner as Maclaren's guests. Well, the Maclaren team all got pissed out of their brains; on arriving back in the hotel they all went swiftly into the bar, where the owners of Maclaren were. Rex went up to a very nice gentleman and slapped him on the back and said, "How are you, you old poofter," in his normal loud voice. The next morning, when I saw him going into the show, I shook his hand and said, "It's been nice to know you; good luck with things today." He was dismissed shortly after 9am that day.

# Security

SIDETRACKED

After we had bought Park House, local people whom we met told us that there had been problems with the people who owned the place. One of them was kidnapped and held for a ransom, and there were rumours of gun-smuggling going on. Who knows? But in the first few months we did have some rather dodgy characters visiting the house wanting money, and who made Marilyn very uncomfortable.

We decided to get an Alsatian as a deterrent was needed, so I went to the local dog pound; a win-win as normal - I would get a free dog, the dog would get a wonderful life, and Marilyn would feel safe.

I explained what I was looking for to the lady who ran the pound. She said that they didn't have any Alsatians, and then I heard a dog start barking very loudly. I said, "That sounds like what I want." The lady insisted that the dog was wild and vicious, but I insisted that I see it; then, seeing the dog in the cage, I immediately called it Rex.

I said, "This dog is not vicious, it is starved." The poor thing couldn't even sit down without being in pain by the look of it, as it was just skin and bones. It was a job to persuade the lady to let me go into the cage, as she was frightened that I would be attacked. I kept calling it Rex; the lady really thought that the dog was mine until I told her the story. I called for a van to pick the dog up, as it was way too big to get into my car. The lady told me that I would never be able to look after the dog and I should bring it back tomorrow. There wasn't a chance in a million that I would ever take it back.

Rex was the most placid dog you could find until a car drove up to the gate, and then all hell would break loose. This dog would stand on its hind legs just like when I first saw him in his cage; this massive dog with a loud bark - it was enough to frighten anyone away, yet with the children he was so calm, he seemed to know what he was there for. We had that beautiful dog for six years, and then nursed him day and night for four weeks before he passed away.

# Expect the Unexpected

## *"There were no plans to expand"*

We had no intention of opening another shop; all we wanted was a building to store stock for the Orton shop, as we were getting very busy. Well, busy is not the word, more like crazy; we could not store enough to satisfy the needs of the customers and, again, we had filled the spare rooms we had in our new house. We saw a building advertised in the paper, saying, "Building for sale with car park in a village near Peterborough, suitable as Garden Centre" at £100,000.

I made an appointment to go and see what I thought would be a farmer's barn in a field, as that's how I read the advert. It was November; there was thick snow on the ground and there were Marilyn, Elaine and two-year-old Joanne. As soon as we drove up to the place I saw Roger Newton outside waiting. It was a 5,000 sq ft Co-op supermarket, which was still trading. There were hundreds of kids coming out of the school across the road. We looked at each other and said, "This is not a warehouse, it's our next store."

We all got out of the car; then Roger said the staff did not know it was for sale, so he had told them that we were doing a survey, which was right to a certain extent, but I wasn't going to leave the others in the car as I wanted their opinion, so it was a little embarrassing. The staff probably wondered what all of these people were doing with me, especially the baby; anyway, I got out of there as quickly as possible and bought it there and then.

In 1984 we opened our third shop, which was over twice as large as the second and ten times bigger than the first one. Now the real juggling started. We thought we had been busy before, but now we had twenty-five staff in that business, besides everything else to contend with; and to think the shop was supposed to stop Marilyn from getting bored in between the office work or slack times.

All this was new to us; we had never had any training in retail or employing lots of staff, stock control, buying, warehousing, retail customers, accounts, mass public health and safety, and on and on it goes. It was all new, day after day, never knowing what was to come next, which was probably a good thing, as we took the unexpected in our stride.

## *We instantly knew this was for us*

That shows how our minds worked; our business changed instantly in just a few seconds without any prior thought whatsoever and, without having any intentions of going in a certain direction, our lives took on a whole new dimension.

# A Major Change

This was probably the most exciting thing that we were embarking on in our Kiddicare lives. It was so fantastic that, in just eight years in that business, we went from a two-up, two-down terraced house, where Marilyn thought she could supplement our income by selling second-hand prams, to the biggest baby supermarket shop in the Peterborough area and, in fact, for miles.

There was only one problem - the money; so we went back, as we seemed to do most weeks, to Brian Ellis, the manager of Barclays, Old Fletton branch to sort it out, which he did, because we were probably the best customers that the branch had.

We deposited all of our takings there from Kiddicare, and all of the money from Marville Properties went in; plus we gave them all of our deeds, whether they needed them or not as collateral. We really burned our bridges by doing that but I thought that, if these people were good enough to have faith in us by lending us some other person's hard-earned money and trusting us to pay it back, then that's what was needed to enhance a good working relationship.

# They Said a Baby Shop Was a Mad Idea

I was getting the shop ready to open, painting under the front canopy, when a local scavenger called Dinesey came along and asked me what **they** were doing with it. I said that **they** were going to have a baby shop here. The next day he came around again, looking at what wasn't bolted down, and told me that the whole village said the people who had bought it were mad and that a baby shop in a village would never work and they would go bust. I said that I would let **them** know! Once again we opened the third shop without any fanfare; we were exhausted, as we had pushed ourselves to the limit again and, as normal, were doing it all on a shoestring.

# Do Business with People, Not Companies

After about 18 months, our insurers insisted we installed more fire extinguishers, so we looked in the Yellow Pages and found a local firm called Newflame. A young lad called Steve Best came in and said that his dad had owned the business for some years and they would look after us. So I let him get on and install what the insurers wanted but, within a couple of weeks, a "fire inspector" came in to check our fire equipment. He immediately condemned them all, saying they did not comply and that the extinguishers were only half full; he said that he would supply new products to the proper regulations, so I agreed, but I said that I would see him the following week.

In the meantime I rang Steve, telling him to take his rubbish out and to give me a refund. He said that there must be a mistake and the so-called "fire inspector" was a fraud. Steve convinced me that I had been conned, so we arranged to meet the next week when the conman would be there. It was 17$^{th}$ December when the man came in for his appointment; I made sure that the offices were very busy, and then I found an office that looked empty. We went in, and Steve was ready and sitting waiting in there, so I said to him, "Can we use this office?" He said, "Yes; you won't disturb me, I am just looking at some accounts."

The man sat down next to Steve and across the desk from me. He got the papers out for me to sign and, as he was doing so, I just casually said that I couldn't believe that I had been sold inferior products by Newflame. He said, "Yes, they are rogues." I said, "Do you know the man who owns Newflame?" He said no, so I said, "Have you ever met the owner of Newflame?" He said, "No, not personally, but I have heard a lot of bad things about them." I said,

"Let me introduce you to Steve Best, the co-owner of Newflame; he is sitting next to you." With that, the conman got up and shook hands with Steve, said, "Merry Christmas," and ran like hell out of the building, never to be seen again. As for Steve, he remains a life-long pal, still doing all of our fire systems - another friend whom I can trust with my life.

*Left, Steve Best, Marilyn, June Best, and me at one of their brilliant Christmas parties, sometime in the 1990s*

## Surplus Stock Became Our Business

Our first encounter with surplus stock was back in Rainbow, about six months after we started, when a rep offered us 500 pairs of ladies' cork-bottom sandals with denim top, which were just going out of fashion. The price was only 25p per pair, and we sold them for 99p. We had found a catalogue with the same shoes in for £9.99, which was great for advertising, and we sold out within a couple of months; we had people coming in a year later asking for them.

As the years went on, the buying got much bigger and there was never enough to satisfy the demand that we had. By now we were taking lots of staff to the nursery shows so they could understand the whole process of the business. This would also bring out the ones who were interested in their job and the ones who wanted to do more interesting things; they would see what was on offer besides just what we bought, and they would give their opinion, which helped expand the offering for the customer.

One year there were seven of us going, and I had a plan. Normally, we would go onto each stand and do the buying; then, if they had any surplus or discontinued old stock, they would tell us, but only if we asked. Sometimes, they would say that they had had some, but had sold it to the other customers who had got there first.

That particular year I planned that, when the doors opened at 9am, we would be first in; we would all split up, with each having their own list of suppliers to see and ask if they had clearance stock.

Each one had a phone, so we could make an instant decision. That was fantastic - we bought all of the surplus and old stock within the first hour of the two-day show. We heard that other retailers were not happy, but it was a window of opportunity and the early bird catches the worm.

I had put the same principles into action in the nursery trade as I had done in the property business years before; from a few second-hand prams to buying literally all of the nursery industry clearance in one go, just eight years into this incredible journey, which I often described as a box-shifting business as, once we had the volume of customers, we could have sold anything to them. Which we did, but we always came back to the core products of the industry.

SIDETRACKED

Then, in 1984, we bought a piece of land for £15,000. It had planning permission for a pub but, at that time, pubs were having a bad time and there were no takers, so we got planning for three shops; we were going to sell the land on to a builder. For about four months the builder messed us about, saying that he needed to get an anchor tenant to make the build viable.

As soon as we discovered he had got permission for six shops and two houses, we gave him a deadline to exchange by midday on the Friday, or we would withdraw. The deadline passed, so we withdrew, and contacted an architect, as we would do the work ourselves. Within one hour the buyer came into our office with the money, but it was too late - I had made my mind up to build them ourselves. Some people are too greedy, wanting everything in place before buying, but not sharing the rewards. Anyway, they got the permission, and that time, it was us who got the rewards.

# Another Unexpected Shop, the Fourth One

A step nearer financial independence was achieved when we built those six shops and found there was no need to sell them; the shops cost a total of £72,000, and now they are worth £450,000, and we have had over £600,000 in rents from that investment. So, just to recap, the investment is worth £450,000 and the income is £39,000 per year; this is from an initial outlay of £72,000. At the same time we did a deal with the contractor for £15,000 for the two building plots, so another win-win situation, as he built the houses at the same time and made that profit for himself.

*Rachel showing off the latest matching trends, and Elaine in the shop doing what she loved best, selling.*

When we built the 6 shops, prospective tenants found out that we owned Kiddicare, as they came for a meeting in our office in the store. They asked us to open one of the shops as a Kiddicare, and we thought why not? Elaine was 13 at the time, and still technically at school; there was a girl called Rachel Barnett, who worked for us as a schoolgirl when she was 14. They took two weeks off school and, between them, fitted the shop out with shelving and all the stock, and then opened it for us. Unfortunately, they were missed at school and had to go back, so we employed two more staff to run that shop.

Once Elaine was back at school, she wasn't happy; she couldn't wait for Saturday to arrive each week so she could be at work selling prams alongside Marilyn and myself, with Joanne running about in the shop with Prince, our dog. Prince used to go for a walk around the shopping centre; sometimes the people who owned the fish-and-chip shop would leave their back gate open and Prince would get into the rubbish bins, and then come back to the shop stinking of fish.

## Swedish prams

One day, shortly after we opened up the new shop, a man walked in who sold Swedish prams; his name was Peter Crane.

*Irene, Peter and Marilyn at one of our many fabulous parties. He has just celebrated his 80th birthday.*

Peter had been in business in Leicester for years selling TVs, toys and prams in his 6 retail shops, and now he was selling the prams wholesale. He said he had them in his van, so we went out to the car park, where there was a caravan full of prams. It appeared that he was going round selling to shops and, at the same time, sleeping in the van. Well, we bought some, which started a relationship that has lasted ever since.

We sold thousands of these prams over the years, and when Peter retired and his son Andy took over, I thought that we would continue to grow the business. Unfortunately, our business went down fast; Peter and I had a common goal which was a win-win for both of us, whereas his son had been a very good tennis player and, unfortunately as I see it, he brought that win-lose trait with him, and it felt like he always had to win in any negotiations that we had.

I do see this in a lot of successful people when they are young. I think that maybe I had the same trait at some time, but we didn't become the top independent retailer without a win-win attitude. I think that I was very lucky because, when I wanted to win at any cost, the older people in the trade, such as Mike Turner, Gordon Brooks and Cyril Shorts, sorted me out; they weren't afraid to tell me where I was going wrong with my attitude. I think that Rodney Cottrell and his wife Christine, who had owned and run some very successful businesses, have always been a team and still are to this day. He has taught me the most about compromise, and give and take, and I would say he taught me the art of winning without the attitude, or being an arsehole, resulting in very long relationships with lots of nice people.

## Our World Had Changed

Until we had the shop I never understood how people could make a living wearing a suit, because I had come from a manual working background, and here I was, wearing a suit and not getting dirty, earning more than I could have ever have imagined. Back in 1966 we thought that if we were to win the Premium Bond jackpot of £25,000 we would be set up for life and here we were, a few years later, earning that in just a few weeks. We had a great lifestyle; however, we never lost sight of the golden goose that the business had become and the lifestyle it was now providing us with.

# This One Made Us Millions

## *Ek Pialla Garam Chaar*

"One cup of hot tea;" my dad told us this when we first started in business. This one sentence, once implemented, has made us millions of pounds. When he was in India the shopkeepers used to invite people into the shops, and then ask if they would like a cup of tea.

He said that the process was very, very simple. The tea was a free gift; the hotter it was, the longer it would take to drink, meaning more time for you to wander around the shop. The more you would see in that business, the longer you were there, and the more the shopkeeper would befriend you; then, everything being equal, if there was something that you wanted, why not buy it from him?

My Dad told us about that on our first day; however, it took something like 5 years for us to implement the strategy, and only when we got our third shop. We put a small reception area in the middle of the Nursery department that doubled up as a tea-and-coffee bar; we then went one step further by adapting this to our business by adding hot chocolate, soup in a cup, orange and biscuits, all free, something for everyone, adults and especially kids.

## The Law of Compensation

The more we gave, the more we received - "speculate to accumulate." Local people who would go for a walk around the village would stop for a free coffee, a win-win situation unbeknown to them. Just by being there they were helping us to sell to new customers coming in for the first time; the thought of a shop in a village, packed with people, it must be good and, of course, every aspect of the business was.

It doesn't always work, though; we met a bus driver when we had a rare holiday in the Isle of Wight, who said he took coach trips to the new shopping centre in Peterborough and he would do detours to our shop if we crossed his palm with silver. Well, the first coach came - 47 people had free drinks and a whole case of biscuits, and then someone asked for a sandwich. Six loaves and a ton of ham later they left, with not a penny in the till; that was the first and last coach that we entertained.

# Juggling Balls and Spinning Plates

## *"My eyes and ears were everywhere"*

If you have ever been to a circus, you will have certainly seen the clowns juggling balls and spinning plates. Both come to mind in the early days, when we started building the business, especially in those first few years. To be quite honest, I probably worried about it, but then, after the excitement set in, it became a normal part of growing a business and I can't say that it ever stops; or rather, we would not want it to stop.

Metaphorically speaking, after smashing so many plates along the way, we did get a bit cynical and, therefore, I ended up using plastic ones; hedging our bets, in other words. I often felt I should be dressed up as a clown to go to work, as my world consisted of juggling balls and, verbally and mentally, spinning plates.

*All of the staff dressed up every Christmas for 3 days; it was party time, and always a great end to every year through the 80s & 90s.*

# Having Fun and Making Money

What better way is there to make a living, than doing something that you love to do with the people you love to be with?

*Elaine, Marilyn, me & JoJo.*

## Every Job Was Another Plate

If you have seen a clown, they get one plate spinning, that's fantastic; then they get another one spinning; no problem to get the third one spinning, they cope with it, then the fourth, then they have to start going back to the first, second, third and then the fourth. They then get ambitious and they do a fifth, and back they go to number one, all over again.

No time to rest, no time for holidays. No time for long lunches. This was us; after a while, we were there spinning eight or nine plates. It got easy, we got used to it; it's so easy thinking we were invincible, piling on ten, eleven, twelve, thirteen, fourteen but realistically, in business, to get up to this number quickly you would have to involve the bank.

We were leveraging our assets with the bank and had no problem giving them all of our assets, including our house; we also extended our credit that we had with our suppliers, many times. If our suppliers wanted to sell us their surplus stock, we would want to pay for it once we had sold it. This amounted to leveraging our souls, which I became uncomfortable with as I liked to pay for goods when we received them, as the other way round is risky business, to say the least.

## Rob Peter to Pay Paul; Then What?

Every growing business goes through this at some stage. If you know that you will sell more stock, say in January, you have to buy it in December; the supplier wants to let you have it in October and says pay him at the end of January. Of course there are many scenarios and two are, firstly, that you sell the goods by December but take your credit time.

Then, secondly, you find you have used the money on other stock when it comes time to pay. In the event of you not achieving the anticipated sales, panic sets in, and you sell the stock at a loss to make way for new stock that you think will sell; this is then leaving you short of money. Unfortunately, we were no different and, at times, just constantly juggling. Because our business was constantly growing, this was what we had to do; eventually, however, this situation turns.

Having reps that knew our business, and who knew us personally as friends, they could fight our corner with their company so as to provide us with more stock to trade out of the situation. It really would have been hard for us to expand at times, without the faith that everybody had put in us. Many suppliers would give us ten times our insurance limit because of our payment track record in the past; most also knew as well that we had property that we were not afraid to sell if it came to the crunch. Our suppliers also knew that we had a team around us that understood the business in terms of what the business needed to achieve and why, which was found to be invaluable.

## Well Done Everybody; Now Let's Get On

After getting through some of these very difficult situations, there was a time then for reflection; you may call it a debriefing, scrutinising everything we had done to get there, understanding how and why we did it, and then enjoying the rewards before a new challenge would appear the next day.

This can only be done if members of staff have a complete understanding of your goals to make it become a success; without excellent people on your side there would be no business. We were blessed then, and are blessed now, to have people with understanding of what the businesses are all about.

There are two unfortunate things about this process: one is that some people haven't got the stamina to keep going, and the other is that some want the money before they have earned it. They may well have worked hard and been paid for their work, but the golden goose has to be fed, which takes a lot of the profit and, when some people see the profit, they want it for themselves, starving the golden goose.

# A Time for Rewards

At this time I needed more material things to keep me motivated. We were buying two new Mercedes cars each year; I wanted staff to share in the success of the business, so we used to lend the cars to our staff to go on holidays, and also paid for the holiday for their families, and extended families too. Like all good things, however, a few people got complacent and took the perks for granted and ended up disrespecting our hard-earned possessions and our hospitality, so that, unfortunately, had to end.

SIDETRACKED

From the mid-80s things started to change rapidly. We started to keep more investments and we went on to holding on to our own houses, commercial units, small shops, offices, restaurants and warehouses. We rented them out to tenants and rapidly expanded the business but, when bad times hit us, we remembered where we had come from, and we were not afraid to act immediately; we would sell anything that we could lay our hands on to keep the business going.

One day in 1985 we needed money quickly, so we went to the local Ford garage in Stamford, sold the Mercedes cars for £19,000 cash, and came away with two Ford cars on HP. That's just how we were at that time - looking after the business first.

I say "were"; we are still like that today - we know what feeds us, so we look after the business and feed the golden goose as a priority before we feed ourselves, knowing the golden goose will look after us forever; but if you starve it, it will destroy you, guaranteed.

# At Last, Millionaires

### *"Well on paper anyway, but that's a start"*

In 1986 another step towards our goal of being financially independent came along; after twelve years of building the businesses we found that we had achieved one of our greatest financial goals of all time - becoming millionaires. But of course, this was only on paper, taking everything into consideration, everything that we owned, including the diesel in the truck and the loose change in our pockets.

We really mentally needed this goal to be achieved as a milestone after thousands of tiny goals along the way; these tiny goals were essential to keep us going but sometimes we wondered whether it was all worth it. As in all businesses, we had been robbed by either unscrupulous clients or contractors, and very rarely staff; but it did happen, although it was more likely to be the everyday opportunist thieves.

Unfortunately, this can be a daily occurrence in business, and anyone who says they don't get robbed has got their eyes and ears closed, because this has happened to us for the past 40 years.

I do think that, after ten years in business, you either go blind to this or become sceptical of everything if you're not careful.

When I was younger I thought of millionaires as having a big pile of cash and never having to work but, of course, that's not the case; our million was all tied up in stock, either in the shop or in property, and our valuation probably would not be the same as a bank's fire-sale price but, as we weren't selling, it was my valuation that counted. It made us feel good and spurred us on.

## Celebrate Achievements

We felt that we couldn't tell anyone about our wonderful achievement because it would have been seen as showing off; that is, apart from Alan Bird, the European representative who sold Silver Cross prams. He had become a friend of ours, and stayed at our house each month when calling on us for his company.

We were attending the annual Nursery Fair in Harrogate when Alan said to us, "I want you two to be the first to know that I have just taken over a company that supplies Silver Cross with accessories and, to celebrate, I want to take you two out for dinner to share this with the only people that I know will be delighted for me." We said, "Alan, we also have something to tell you, so it will be a double celebration tonight."

## I Wanted To Become the Best

I started to put notices up in the office to motivate myself. Over the years I would put them everywhere, but not so the public could see. I would put them on the office walls, in warehouses, in the staff kitchens, all over, as I thought they would motivate the staff but, most of all, I wanted to motivate me, because I was the one who people expected to have the drive and the answers to every question. The motivation had to come from somewhere, and constantly; these were not your normal reminder lists, they went something like these:

***"I must do the most productive thing possible at every given moment"***

Tom Hopkins

***"Don't count the days, make the days count"***
Muhammad Ali

***"If I were a garbage collector I would shift more bins than any other person alive, and I would do it before they got out of bed"***

Muhammad Ali

***"Focus on your goals, do not deviate, don't get side-tracked, work, work, work but remember if you only 'work' you will do it for evermore, and in the process will end up poor"***
Neville Wright

***"Sometimes you have to go backwards to succeed"***
Neville Wright

***"I can work 12 hours a day with enthusiasm that would bore me to tears if I thought that I would have to keep it up for a lifetime"***

Neville Wright

***"I am better today than I was yesterday, but tomorrow I will be better than I have been today"***

Neville Wright

I put this one up in the shop, but it wasn't very popular with some of the customers. Maybe it was a bit too close to the truth for some of them. There is normally a knee-jerk reaction to this one, but a little more time should be taken to think about it:

***"There are no naughty children in this world, only naughty parents"***

Neville Wright

I made hundreds of signs, all aimed at me, to keep me calm. Staff thought that I was doing it to motivate them, but it was me who needed the signs as, every time I fought another fire, which seemed to be several times a day, I was mentally exhausted, very often wanting to give it all up and just go and get that pig farm and look after ourselves in our own little world. That wasn't going to happen, as I needed people around me; those negative thoughts only lasted the same time as it's just taken to read this bit - that's how quick my mind was.

This was the path that we were on; I was the one who chose to employ others, so I was responsible for my actions. Having a business meant that we were in control of our lives but, to have the life we wanted and achieve the goals that we had set for ourselves, it would be impossible to do it on our own; so I needed to know more about everything in business, but I hadn't got the time or money to do it all at once. I decided that the number one priority for the business was to help customers make a buying decision, and that decision was to buy from us. My thoughts were that if we sold more the business would grow, we would be able to invest in people who could do all the other things that I hadn't got time to learn and do myself; all I needed was the vision for the future, of where we wanted to take the business. **(Simple)**

# My Car Became a Classroom for Me

My thirst for knowledge took a hold of me. If I was going to do something, I wanted to be the best that I could be. I wasn't competing against anyone, only myself; what was the point of doing anything without pride? After all, that's what my dad had taught me.

So, from the first moment that Cyril Shorts lent me his motivational tapes, I have listened to them for thousands of hours more, ever since that day, every day. In fact I didn't use the radio in any of my cars for the next thirty years. Every single motivational tape recording that I listened to inspired me to put the ideas into practice; they paid for themselves literally overnight, as is the case with the books that I have read as well.

There is a vast amount of knowledge out there for everyone to tap into if they want; a lot of it is free, and the stuff that you pay for is normally a fraction of what it is really worth.

# We Had Lost Our Way

After 5 years of becoming millionaires we had hit a low point in our lives. I suppose we thought it would have been easy after achieving our goal of a million, but it got harder; we had three shops, I was trying to put a management structure in place as I was racing around training, and trying to put out fires every day. This got ridiculous as, every time I thought that I had one shop sorted, I would go to another only to be called back to deal with a problem, leaving the other shops in chaos.

One day I said to Marilyn that I had had enough and, for sanity's sake, we should go back to having just one super shop where we could have a controllable system overseen by us at all times, and where I would not waste my time travelling around getting nowhere. Two shops were put up for sale as going concerns, Orton shop and the small one that Elaine and Rachel had opened two years before. That one sold within a couple of weeks for £10,000 plus some stock; the person who bought it didn't want the name, which I thought was strange, but they had their own name as they sold children's wear on a party-plan basis and wanted to expand with a shop. But party-plan and shops are two entirely different things; with party-plan you have a lot of freedom but, with a shop, you are committed every day; so that didn't last long.

The other shop at Orton Centre was up for sale as a going concern too; we rented it from the local Council. We were asking only £100,000, which was equivalent to two years' profits and really cheap, but it did not sell, so we reduced the price to £10,000 and still had no takers. After 3 years I had no option but to keep it. We refurbished it, putting in new flooring, taking off the light diffusers, which brightened up the shop, and decorating, all for a cost of £1,000, as we had about ten years left on the lease. No sooner had we done that than agent Jones rang me and said, "Will you sell, and how much, as I have got someone looking for a business in Peterborough?" I said £100,000; they walked in and bought it within ten minutes.

## Love What You Do While You're Doing It

I realised that lots of people had looked at it before without buying because it looked worn out and uncared for; they couldn't see beyond the holes in the carpets. I never let that happen again. Arthur Dye had told me when I was 13 years old, some 32 years earlier, "Speculate to accumulate," which I normally did, but not that time. Bill had told me years before, "When selling, present your property as a picture, and the garden as the frame."

All basic stuff that I ignored when wanting to sell that shop; I think that I was lazy or too busy, no matter what I learned and, once again, if I were to succeed I could not become complacent. I had to tell myself to love what I was doing while I was doing it, just like the man in the Co-op bakery told me when I was 17 years old, all those years ago; then just get on with it, and just do it.

I really did not want to sell the Orton shop once we had refurbished it, but Marilyn said that we wanted a nice life where we didn't have to work every hour, and she didn't want the staff to do it either, as they were running between the shops. She thought it would be better to have all of the staff under one roof, where we could all work as a team, all focused, going in one direction.

By now we had got a new Mercedes again, plus a £72,000 Porsche 911 Turbo, and I was looking to get my first Bentley too. So our philosophy of not being afraid of going backwards to go forward paid off many times; but a funny thing always happened each time when we went backwards, we found in doing so we always went forward with far more speed than we had in the first place.

We would be constantly paying off debt, thus giving our banks confidence in us, knowing we had a mindset to pay what we owed and more, enabling us to then get a bigger overdraft or mortgage when buying another property, if we wanted it.

## Why Buy One, When You Can Buy Five?

Crazy days. I remember in 1987 we went back to Hunstanton to buy another caravan for weekends; as usual, it didn't stop at a caravan, and we came home with a three-bedroom caravan and four flats that were up for sale on the seafront.

*In this picture I was on the balcony painting; Ray is on the left down below. Marilyn took the photo; that's her Mercedes.*

The builders' van was round the back; we stayed in the caravan while we painted the flats. That week we all lived on fish and chips, and some fantastic meat pies that a lady had made and sold from her house opposite the campsite. In those days it was heaven to get fed like that, as cooking was not one of Marilyn's priorities in life, and I could not do it; as far as food was concerned I never even thought of cooking. I would never have ever thought in a million years that, in two years' time, I would be cooking all of the meals for the next twenty-eight years, and loving every minute of it.

## Our Word Is Our Bond

Our word was our bond. This was put to the test in the crash of 1989, when we were buying properties which we knew were suddenly overpriced; we went through with the purchases because we didn't want to let the estate agents down, or our own reputation either. In doing this we lost a lot of money and those estate agents ceased trading, a lesson learned for us in the future.

We found that there is a balance to achieve in life, and keeping that balance is the difficult thing when every day changes. I found at this time that other people we were involved with wanted to be partners in the property business, doing joint ventures together, which I agreed to; but, when things got tough they would lose their commitment, and then they would want out, and we would be left holding the baby, with all of the responsibilities that goes with it. Inevitably we would pay them off, and struggle on by ourselves.

I do think ambition and responsibility go hand in hand - "If you want to drive the car, you have to pay the insurance" - but a lot of people whom we came across and whom we helped did not understand the commitment needed to run a long-lasting business. Just look at the way some CEOs, who are looking for big pay packets, can change companies, then end up leaving them in chaos and, incredibly, getting millions of pounds in compensation for being a failure.

## Keep On Juggling

It's basic: invent your everlasting gobstopper, and then work like crazy; invest the extra income, probably with some leverage, until you are receiving passive income. Then you have a choice as to whether you want to work ever again, live off the passive income, or invent another everlasting gobstopper for today's market.

All the income you will need will come along as a by-product of what you are doing, but only if you do it better than anyone else in your field. So, if you do it well, you will have an abundance of money, if that's what you really want.

## Our One and Only Shop

Around 1987 we built a 2,000 sq ft extension costing £21,000 onto our shop in Werrington Village; then, in 1988, we bought an orchard that backed on to the car park from a neighbour for £15,000. This was to make a larger car park. Then, in 1989, we bought the back garden land on the opposite side of the car park for £25,000 and built four houses.

## Think With the End in Mind

In 1989 we also applied to rebuild the shop to make it bigger, as we were so busy. The plans got refused, and that's when the fun started as the Council said that a new shop, although a traditional building, would be out of character in a conservation area. I could not understand their logic; the building that we occupied was a

1960, flat-roofed retail store, more like a cheap industrial unit, and it was in the middle of a conservation village.

## *"So I painted the old building to show them what 'out of character' was"*

## Sorry!!!

We went back to planning, with no luck again, so I got the first five of twenty TV aerials and put them on the roof. Then I put flags on them. I then got into trouble with the locals - unknowingly, I had put the Union Jack upside down. They said that I did it on purpose and I was being disrespectful, but I didn't know there was a right and wrong way - the lines all looked the same to me, flapping about in the wind; another 15 to go, some with skull and crossbones, etc.

I had an artist, Bob Pickersgill, a customer of ours paint the building with a Noah's Ark and animals down the side, and the front with a cottage and a big rainbow. No one could miss it when they came down the road, which led to increased business for us. The Council were not pleased, but there was nothing they could do.

*"We loved that shop and everything about it"*

## Golly, Bob, What Have You Done?

Then someone spotted that Bob had painted a golly in one of the cottage windows, so we had a nasty, threatening letter from a customer who was offended; he came into the shop and repeatedly asked a member of the staff what the picture on the wall was, trying to put words into her mouth. He was told by one of the part-time schoolgirls that it was a golly... it was a traditional toy, and we had the knitted dolls on sale. In those days the general culture was changing, and words and names that people had grown up with, and with no understanding of what other people thought about them, were gradually ending.

These dolls were everywhere, and you could also collect stickers from the Robinsons jam–jars. Well, I got Bob back and asked him to change it, but he insisted it should stay as he could not understand the problem, so I paid him to change it. He was back in the office within ten minutes - he had changed it into a monkey and everybody was happy, except Bob the artist.

Bob, the artist from Liverpool, caused a stir in the village, but it was the Council that prompted us to do it because we wanted to demolish the old Co-op flat-roofed building, which was out of character, and replace it with a traditional-looking building that blended in with the street scene.

My thoughts were that, if they didn't like the new one, they certainly wouldn't like the painted one. I was right, they hated it, but there was nothing that they could do about it. In the meantime our customers loved it and we attracted even more, making the reason to rebuild more compelling.

# What Is Normal?

## *"Whatever it is, keep away from it, don't let it get you"*

By the 1990s we had now learned and gained the ability to be flexible, with the attitude of "The answer is 'yes', now what's the question?" That meant that when customers said, "Can you...?" we would say yes before they had finished asking the question. We still worked hard, only now we were getting incredible rewards for it, so we started to have the things that came with surplus money - worldwide holidays, good cars, my first Bentley.

SIDETRACKED

Marilyn did not like the Bentley, but my mum and dad loved it, which meant so much to me. When I say Marilyn didn't like it, it was because one day when out in the Bentley, we drew up to the traffic lights on the bridge in Stamford where we lived; some builders in a van in front of us opened the back doors of the van then dropped their pants in front of us. I just laughed, but Marilyn was embarrassed and refused to go in the car again, so I put it in the garage and just forgot about it.

We could now afford nice food, in nice restaurants, although that didn't mean that we were extravagant. We only ever lived on 10% of what we made, the rest going back into the businesses, as their growth needed more and more money to feed them.

BACK

Eating out every night became a normal necessity of working life, because the more money we earned the more responsibility we had, and the harder we worked, the less time we had at home; everything that needed doing at home, like cleaning, gardening, and the help in looking after Jo, was done by two lovely people, Sandra and Clive Kent. They looked after us so we could work extra hours at the drop of a hat, which happened most days.

We were getting so busy that it was not possible to see all of the reps during the day; we would see some of them in the evenings, and some would stay at our house instead of a hotel. We could get the buying done without the disturbances that inevitably would happen in the shop during the daytime. There would also be more time to chat and find out what was going on in the trade.

We were very careful not to compromise any of the reps when asking questions; it was very important to us, as we didn't want to be just another retailer, we wanted to be the best. We would ask, "What's your best sellers?" then, "Where are we in your list of customers?" without naming them, which we wouldn't have expected them to do anyway; and, if we weren't their top customer, I would say, "How many do we have to sell to be at the top of your list?"

We had to know what to do to be top of their list; this was crucial to me. Usually, if Mothercare or Tesco or someone like that were in front, I wouldn't mind, as we could not, and had no desire to, compete with them on location but, if any other retailers were selling more, we compared what they were doing differently from us.

It was usually something simple that we could put right immediately and then become number one for that rep. I seemed to be more concerned that the rep came top in his company than me being top in the league of independents; it was my secret goal that all of our reps were the number one salespersons in their companies.

SIDETRACKED

Things don't change - we still carry on working now very much as it has been for years and I am writing this book mainly between 10.30pm and 3.30am; it's the only time that I don't get interruptions. One thing that has never bothered us in business is the 24 hours in the day; it's not broken into work, and then other time zones - we have been available in the business 24/7 because we had no choice at the start, and we just naturally carried it on the same as it is today. Once you get the rewards, you realise that the effort that was first forced on to you by necessity is all worthwhile. I suppose at this point, if there is any advice that I could give to my grandchildren, it is:

# *"Don't let the flea trainers get you."*

I saw my father-in-law yesterday (2014) and he asked if we would ever retire, because he couldn't wait to leave his job as, at the time, he was doing twelve-hour shifts, something he hated.

He fought against selling his time, although he needed the money. I do think a lot of unrest was in his mind; he wanted to be in charge of what he did in work, and that's the difference - you have to accept taking orders from one person when employed or, as in our case, having to take orders from thousands of customers each day.

# Nothing Is 'Normal' - Why Should It Be?

BACK

A chap called Richard worked for a commercial agency called Barker Storey Matthews, from whom we have bought and sold properties through from the 1980s. Sometime in the late 1980s, one Friday night, Richard rang me and said he had got a client who wanted a commercial property that we owned; Richard thought that we would be able to do a deal with him.

Richard said that his client would like to rent one of our properties; he wanted to turn it into a tearoom/café, and he wanted to live above it with his family.

I said that was great, although I didn't think he would be able to make a living from it; however, it would be nice if he could do, so I told him that if he wanted to do the paperwork we would go ahead.

Richard replied, "It's a bit more complicated; he needs to sell his house before he can move," and gave me the address of the property.

I said that was fine; we knew the area so we would buy it.

Richard replied again, "There's a slight problem; he is in arrears with his mortgage, and he will be repossessed next week if he doesn't pay £3,000 by next Monday. So could you give him the £3,000 by next week and take it off the price of the house when you buy it?"

I said of course, I could do that.

Once again, Richard responded; "That's great, but there's another problem; he can't legally sell the house for three months. He bought this house cheap as a sitting tenant and, if he sells before June, he has to pay back the discount he got."

I said, "That's fine, we will just do the paperwork with the solicitors and then complete in June." Richard said, "That's not legal, so you would have to take it on trust." I said, "OK, I will see him tomorrow."

Then Richard said, "And there's another problem; he's getting married in a weeks' time. Tomorrow he needs £1,500 to pay the caterers or they won't do the catering at his wedding on Saturday."

I said I would take the £1,500 to him, and then I asked Richard, "Would there be anything else that he has a problem with? Ha-ha-ha."

Richard then said, "Well, actually there is another thing; before he gets married on Saturday, he needs to get divorced first, but his wife will not sign the paperwork unless she has £3,750."

I said, "OK; so, as I see it, I am going to buy a house in three months' time, and I am going to give this man £3,000 for his arrears, £1,500 for his wedding catering and £3,750 for his ex-wife."Richard said, "Yes, that's it."

I said, "That's fine, on one condition. I will also give him a year's lease valued at the £11,000 for the commercial property that he wants, and take it off what he thinks his house is worth."

He wanted £39,000 to get himself out of trouble, but obviously I had to value the house first, and it would have to be a win-win situation for both of us, not just him. We concluded the deal. The following day he wanted £39,000; we agreed £34,250, made up of £16,000 for the house, which was what he paid for it, £11,000 for the year's rent, £3,750 for his wife, £3,000 for his arrears and £1,500 for the caterers. He moved into our premises and we bought his house in the June. I then renovated it for £5,000 and sold it for £47,000.

The funny thing was that, when the tenants came in to the office to sign the paperwork, they found out that we also owned nursery shops and, unbeknown to us at that time, they decided to open a baby shop instead of a café. Within eight weeks the man and lady came in to see us, saying they wanted to leave that day, and would we give them £600 for two months' rent on a house that they had found? So, that afternoon, I met them at the estate agent, W H Brown, and handed the £600 to the agent.

They left that day, knowing that they could have stayed there for another 10 months without paying any more rent, but they did not want to; a win-win for us, because they knew that they could not have a refund as they had taken a year's lease, and they never asked us the question, so we could let it to another person.

We could have refused the £600, but that would have been a win-lose and that wasn't on. That was a normal day's work; we made £17,000 on that deal for an outlay of £30,000 for six months - that's equivalent to 57% profit. I still can't understand why he wanted to move so quickly.

# Mobile Phones Were Essential For Business

We married our business and slept with our phones. By the early 1990s business was in our souls. We lived with our phones - we learnt that it was an easy way to make money. If we went on holiday with anybody in those days, some of them thought that we must have had a problem, and very often got awkward with us for being on our phones, well especially me on my phone, throughout the day, every day.

We always made extra deals and, without fail, we have done deals that paid for the holiday that we would not have got if we had ignored our phones. I remember that each week we spent away in Tenerife, the calls alone would cost at that time around £600; all part of the holiday, as no deals meant no holidays.

By having the mobile phones with us we have made many thousands of pounds, by buying either nursery products or property that we wouldn't have done the deal on if we had thought 9am to 5pm. These same people who had left their phones at home had no problem in asking us if they could borrow ours to make a call home so, for us to be successful we married our businesses, and slept with our phones.

Consequently, when opportunities came along we were the first to hear. So many times, people would ring us with property just going on the market, saying that we were first on the list as we were readily available at any time with the ability to make a decision; plus, we had the money or the facility to get the money, which is every agent's dream - all they had to do was bring the right property to us; well, all properties are right, it's just the price that's not.

## Auctions! You Must Do Your Homework

I remember one day in 1988, when we went to an auction in London and did not get what we wanted. Not wanting to go home empty-handed, we bought a railway station in Norfolk.

On the way home from the auction, we went on a detour to Norfolk to look at it and, as we went over the railway bridge expecting to see this fantastic Victorian railway station that was shown in the brochure, all we could see was this railway line, and a cleared site where once the magnificent railway station stood.

We then looked at the auction brochure. It read "former railway station site" and, with me being dyslexic, I did not read it properly.

I had looked at the picture and, having just a few seconds as the bidding started, I assumed I was bidding for the station shown. As my father-in-law would say, "Open your eyes." As luck would have it, a builder came into the office the next week asking if we had any sites for small industrial units for sale; we sold him the site and made £30,000 on it - in fact, we were doubling our money, not bad in the end.

Another time, a very large property was purchased at auction, only because we had an hour to spare and the auction was only about 10 miles from our office. We had no intention of buying the building but, when the bidding was coming to a close, I recognised one of the bidders as a person that had once said something derogatory about my brother some years before and, for no other reason I outbid him at the auction.

**13 Market Place, Market Deeping, Lincolnshire. "Lucky 13"**

I started bidding against him and then, when he saw me he started to go red, probably because he thought he had got it, or maybe because he knew me, and we were on his territory and now I was making him pay more for it.

I drove up the price, which had now hit the guide price of £80,000; then on it went, up to a whopping £130,000, around 60% more than I thought it was worth, but the feeling was good.

When we walked out, Marilyn said to me as we were walking down the street to our car, "How on earth are we going to pay for it?"

I said, "I don't know," and then we looked at each other and just laughed, knowing that we would find the money from somewhere.

## *"A spare hour, and lucky that man was there"*

By this time we had got to be experts in juggling and finding money just in time, by the skin of our teeth. Then, as luck would have it, when we took possession I realised that there was an overgrown piece of land and another building not described in the sale particulars. We immediately sold the land for a car park to the pub next door for £50,000, and then we let the small building for £3,000 pa. That left the main building costing only £80,000, and which we rented for £15,000 a year. We got £18,000 pa rent from this investment for the next twenty years, and then sold the freehold for £650,000.

## The Next Opportunity

We were always on the lookout for the next thing; once you have found it you have only a limited time to exploit it before everyone is on to it. We went through a time when we bought freehold restaurants where the owners could not make them profitable because of their mortgages. We bought them complete with all of the equipment, and then we would sell the restaurant business and lease the property.

If only the people who sold the freehold had known about sale and leaseback deals, they probably would have never sold. A lot of people in those days did not think of selling their business and, incredibly, even today people don't; that's where we came in, buying the freehold then selling the business, which was worth 25% of what we had paid - in other words, a 25% discount. We did this on all types of businesses by just hitting the right time and thinking outside of the box, seeing opportunities or creating them where none existed.

This was the start of what I would say was a second stage of our life in business; as we weren't scrimping any more, we could now expand the business more quickly and easily. It had always been fun, but this was a more relaxed fun, without the pressure being on us, although once I started on expansion I put pressure on myself naturally.

All this was done from whatever shop we were working in. We would be buying nursery equipment and, at the same time, taking calls about property deals; this has been continuous over the years, every minute of every day, always lots to do and, if there wasn't any work, I would make some. ***"Nothing changes"***

It is now Sunday; no, it's Monday morning, 18th June 2014. I have just travelled from Lincolnshire, where I live, having set off at 11 pm to arrive in Devon at 3.30am, visiting some friends. There are 1440 minutes in my day and I intend to use them all. My thoughts are that this is normal, but I get challenged by people all of the time about this type of behaviour not being normal. Umm! Let me think about that one. Marilyn has told me it's my birthday.

# Embrace Problems

I think that, if anybody wants to be really successful in business, they have to be thinking all the time of how to solve problems.

Start with the ones you have got and expand from there. When you are in business you don't have to look for problems, they will come looking for you, thick and fast. All you have to do is figure it out in a simple but unconventional way, so stop looking at a 9-5 solution and start feeding your mind with these problems; then it will come up with a solution, as your mind works for you 24/7. Don't block it, embrace it.

If you read this book ten times, and look between the lines, I guarantee you that you will become a millionaire if you implement what you have read - all the answers are in here, but some are in disguise.

I must add that you will get what you want only if you desire it enough to make you focus on the subject and without procrastinating. Just get on and do it now, and do it without stopping until you have completed your task.

# A New Shop

## *"This would last us forever"*

Over the next four years our architect did lots of plans and, each time we submitted them, the conservation officer said that he didn't like them. I would say, "What would you like?" He would say, "It's not up to me to tell you, it's up to you to alter the plan." This was getting us nowhere. There was no common sense; we had spent £15,000 on the plans, which was a lot of money in those days, so enough was enough.

By then we had bought a 5,000 sq ft warehouse and we had to ferry the goods backwards and forwards all day long so, in frustration, I rang the planning department and asked if our plans were going to be approved, as they were out of the time limit and should have been decided. The people in the department didn't want to speak to me, so the operator would say that there was no answer. One day I got so fed up that, when the operator hung up, I stayed on the line, as in those days you had to put your phone down before another person could call.

We then called on another phone; the same thing happened, so we didn't put our phone down. We did this seven times, blocking seven lines; each time the operator tried to use the line we would say, "It's us, and we are not going until someone from the planning department speaks to us." It worked, but the person whom I spoke to was very uncommitted, so I asked a very simple question.

# A Red, White and Blue Car Park?

I asked the question, "If I were to spray-paint our car park red, white and blue, would there be any law to stop me doing it?" The person said, "You wouldn't." I said, "I am going to do it today; now, please answer my question - is there a law preventing me painting it?" After going around in circles for ten minutes, the person said, "There is no law, but don't do it, as I will see if we can't look at the plans now."

Planning was granted, with a provision that no murals, flags, or any other painted areas would be allowed without consent, etc., etc. So now we could look forward to 35 weeks of real chaos for the business, for the staff and, most of all, the customers; but surprisingly, everyone was fine and, I think, quite amused at how we were doing it.

## *In 35 Weeks We Sold 1.2 Million Of Stock From A Building Site.*

The car park was in the middle of the village. If I had painted it, there would have been such a lot of publicity from it. News reporting, TV; helicopters would have come with the reporters; the shop would have been put on the map. Sadly it wasn't to be, as we got the planning permission, albeit four years late. I suppose better late than never, but who wants hassle like this? And in that time we could have employed another 40 staff.

We rebuilt the back of the shop whilst working from the front, and then we rebuilt the front whilst working from the back. Goods were stored in the houses that we had built next to the car park and in all that chaos we still did a £1.2 million turnover in 35 weeks. We used two of the houses that we had built next to the shop for storage of stock, and the gardens to sell container-loads of garden furniture every week that summer.

## Take the Money

Saturday was always the busiest day of the week; the rest for us was a bonus in a way, as we were so busy with the rest of the normal business transactions that went on. Sundays were just getting popular, but Marilyn would not open Sundays or Mondays. She wanted the staff to have two days off together and be able to be with their families on one day at the weekend; this gave us a problem competing with shops that were open, but it turned out to be an advantage.

The customers would look at the products and basically make up their minds, but wanted time to think about it. Lots of our customers lived a long way off, so we knew that the husbands only had the weekends free and, if they went away, we knew most of them wouldn't bother to come back; so, after the salesperson had spent maybe an hour with them, just to see them walk away with nothing was both disheartening for them and costly for us, so we came up with a plan that worked.

## Create a Buying Frenzy

I wanted to cause a buying frenzy, and get customers to make up their minds. I thought that this could be done only by a series of things; one was to fill the shop with people, because we all know that if you went into a shop that was out of the way in a village and it was packed with people, there must be something good about it.

## A Playgroup Every Week

*Every week Elaine would organise another playgroup to come in, which primed the selling pump for the buying customers.*

At the time, we gave a lot of toys and equipment to playgroups, so now, instead of just letting them pick these things up at any time, we set 10.00 am each Saturday as the time for a different playgroup to come along each week to be presented with the toys.

Invariably, they would bring along the group with their children; Elaine was put in charge of this task, and she got the local newspaper involved; they would be taking pictures of the staff giving away free stuff and, at the same time, this was giving us some free advertising.

Some customers would just procrastinate when it came to buying, saying they would think about it, or that they would return tomorrow. But we wanted the sale right now and, if they did come in on another day, invariably they would bring a different person in, and then the salesperson would have to start all over again which, in my brain, was a waste of time and money for us. ***"Time and motion"***

There was a lot of excitement going on when customers started to come in around 10.00 am; this kick-started the excitement and put them in a happy buying mood. On the other hand, and especially on a Saturday, we would oversell lots of products because, with ten staff all selling stuff like crazy, we were bound to run out of some products.

## Raving Lunatics

All hell would break loose at the collection door in the warehouse. Customers would be shouting that they had queued along the road in the village before getting into the car park, queued to be served by a member of staff, queued at the till to pay, and then queued at the back door to get their goods, only to be told that we were sold out. Oh, shit! Most retail staff would have hidden away, but not ours!

Good staff is all you want, and we had fantastic staff at the back door where the collection point was; John Thompson, the manager, together with Roger, Dick, David and Stewart, they could all charm the birds out of the trees. A free bottle of bubbly, a promise of extra discount and a fast-track around the store, accompanied by a department manager to decide what their second choice was; they were taken to the front of the queue to pay, before being escorted to the back door to pick up their new goods, once again jumping the queue and getting VIP treatment, turning raving lunatics into raving customers. I will tell you more about this soon.

# Countdown Tickets

The shouting and the screaming just couldn't go on; we had to get our act together, and quickly. We bought a £7,000 duplicating machine on a five-year purchase plan, together with a laminator and guillotine; Scott connected the duplicator to the computers, and off we went.

We made what we called countdown tickets, putting them onto each of the items like the prams, cots, highchairs and so on, so that when the product got down to a stock level of only ten, we would start to mark it off with a dry wipe in front of the customer when they had bought one. Other customers would see this, and would try to get the attention of a salesperson as the more the product quantity was marked down, the more the customers wanted it.

The fear of loss made them make up their minds today, instead of leaving it and risk losing it. This new system stopped the arguments at the back door, well, almost 95% anyway, and I would say in doing this it was a silent salesperson, and what doesn't speak doesn't lie. This seemed daft - we did this to alleviate queues but it increased them, as we sold more.

## If it is Right for the Customer...

If it is right for the customers, then our sales people should not disappoint them. The next thing we had to get over concerned the stubborn ones, who knew what they wanted but wanted to keep their money in their pockets a bit longer, saying, "We will come back tomorrow." We would tell them that we were closed on Sundays and Mondays, so they would say, "I will come back next Saturday." We would say, "That's fine, but you might be disappointed because the chances are that the products will all be sold, and then you will have wasted your time;" which was true. Inevitably, they would buy there and then.

Then we still had the ones that wouldn't buy. Usually they were accompanied by their mothers; the staff were taught to recognise what the problem was so, very subtly, they would put into the conversation that the guarantee did not start until the baby was born and, if they had no use for the product, then we would refund their money. That usually brought out the mother, who would say, "Well, in my day you couldn't do that, so I suppose it's all right," and they could go ahead with their purchase without any worry; then, and only then, they would buy.

# Do Your Job Properly

If it is right for the customer then our sales people should not be letting the customer go home empty-handed; this was our attitude. It may sound pushy but, when you heard a disappointed customer saying, "I should have bought it last week when you had it in stock," you realised you hadn't done your job properly.

The shop got so busy that, when people would ring to see if we stocked certain products, we would tell them to avoid Saturdays if possible, unless they got there at 9 am. Some people would not believe us so, when they got there at 11 am, the car park was full, and, by the way, on a Saturday all of our staff would park in the streets around the village to give customers more parking.

Customers would say to me, "You're busy today." I would look down at the floor and say, "No, we're not busy, I can still see the carpet!" On the busy days you could see only shoes; it was unbelievable and so exciting, it made everybody happy.

When we moved out in 2002 and left the village with a fantastic building that now serves the community as a doctors, opticians, and pharmacy, what could be better?

## It's Not a Baby Shop, It's a Cash Machine

In the 1980s and 1990s we would take the week's takings to the bank on a Saturday evening, and deposit bags of money into the wall safe. This was OK, as Marilyn and I did this after leaving the shop; we would deposit the money and then go on to the local seaside, where we had our caravan, about 50 miles away.

## We Loved Saturday Nights

For insurance reasons, two people were allowed to carry only £10,000 in cash to the bank but, as time went on, these sums got larger, so John would meet us there, then Rosie our secretary, then Shelly, one of our managers. We started to take so much cash to the bank that it got a bit scary, especially in the wintertime, when it was dark.

There would be two of us with pick-axe handles standing on the pavement, while three others were depositing wallets of £5,000 into the wall safe, one at a time, which took around six seconds to do.

We would deposit about ten wallets, and every time we opened the safe drawer there would be a loud bang, then we had to put the wallet in, and then bang again, then we would open and close it again to make sure the wallet had gone through into the safe. If not, the next one would get stuck; that's four loud bangs every time that used to echo down the street, attracting attention.

It looked like there was a bank robbery going on, with all of us around and making so much noise. It got to the point one Saturday when there were eight of us; Marilyn said it was getting too dangerous for the staff to do this. The following Tuesday we got Securicor to collect the money from the shop three times a week. I missed the thrill of the adrenalin rush from not knowing what would happen, and counting the number of bangs that the drawer made each week. It was a goal of mine every week to push for more each day, wanting to hear two more sets of bangs each week, knowing that we had taken another £10,000.

This was one of those times when our overheads were relatively low and our profit margins were high, because of the way we could buy our stock and the way we put our product packages together.

*Marilyn, in her new office that incorporated a kitchen and toilet; I designed this with time and motion in mind.*

# Drugs and Alcohol

## *"I felt I was a burden, but someone must have thought different"*

By 1992, when I was 42, I was constantly in pain; it was excruciating, and went from my back, going down one leg. I had a constant feeling like a red-hot poker going into my foot. When I tried to stand upright, one foot was two inches off the bloody ground. The pain was 24/7 and had reached its tipping point for me.

From 1980, when I was 30, my back was becoming a real problem; inside I was a total wreck, but I managed to hide it from other people. I was pushing myself beyond my body's limits but, with overwhelming desire, need and enthusiasm, and a one-track mind focused on going in one direction, the pain was suppressed by adrenalin; or perhaps it was alcohol.

The doses of painkillers and muscle relaxants steadily increased, until I took anything that was going; but still the pain persisted. It was always in the background, and I just got used to it; therefore, it didn't register so much to me while I was engrossed in work. However, once each task or the day was completed, then, bang, it used to hit me. It was like being stabbed in the back.

In 1993, the rapid progression of the problem over the previous two years had got to me; I just could not see an end to it. I had spent twelve years in pain, four of those in severe pain, and the last two years in excruciating pain. I slept on my own for those two years; Marilyn would put pillows, towels and rolled-up blankets around me so I did not move in the night and, if I did, I would scream out in agony.

I had kept it under control even by using mind-over-matter programmes, just to see if it was mental. By this time, however, an operation was hopefully the only answer, as nothing I did was working.

I had seen nine different types of doctors, and quacks. I let them try anything, but with no success; it took me up to twenty minutes to psych myself up to get into my car, a Porsche 911 Turbo; what a stupid car to have in my condition, as I knew what pain it would cause to get in, and the same to get out of that car but, in that twenty years, I missed hardly a day's work.

It got so that I would lie on the floor of the office when I had meetings, and I stopped going to restaurants because I could not sit down for more than 2-3 minutes at a time; it was so embarrassing.

The last straw came when there were eight of us in a restaurant in Stamford. I was in so much pain that I lay down on the floor while they all had their meal; that was the last time that I went to a restaurant for years.

## Still Expanding, Why?

SIDETRACKED

I can't believe that, when all of this was going on we were still expanding the businesses; it was just in us. Perhaps it eased the pain for me, thinking about other things. At one point I went to a private hospital for a few hours a week; I would lie on the bed and be strapped to it, and then they would pull the bed apart to try to release my trapped nerves - but it didn't work.

To take my mind off the pain I was in as I was being stretched, and to relieve the boredom of being there, I calculated in my mind the worth of everything we had in the world, then I multiplied it by 10%, and then compounded it in my head. Up to the age of 65 we would be worth £12 million if we just carried on working.

Now, I thought, what if we made more effort? So the next week I recalculated while I was lying there. I never had a calculator because I had to lie still so, by the time the session was over, I hadn't finished the sum and, when the nurse came to me and said, "Are you all right?" I said, "No, I could do with a bit longer." She thought I was being funny because of the pain, but I hadn't got any pain to speak of as my mind had been distracted away from it.

That day the pain was distracted until I went to get back in my car, when it remembered what pain was. At that time I had a Bentley and a chauffeur who worked in the house; why didn't I use them instead of driving myself? The next week I finished the calculations off, and the figure was that if I made an extra effort for the next 23 years, and increased the margin from 10 to 20%, we could be worth £115 million by the age of 65. When we look at the results of compound interest it's incredible so, over the years when we have had money, we have put it into things that we thought would increase in value. Of course not all do, as we have had some disasters along the way, but we have always managed to turn them around.

The drugs were taking hold of me. By this time it was commonplace for people to try to help me with my sentences by guessing what I wanted to say. I would start the sentence and get stuck, and then they would come out with what they thought the next word or the last piece of the sentence was, until they got it. This was really bad in the early 80s, but seemed to find a level in the 90s and never went away until we sold Kiddicare in 2011; then, within a matter of days, the problem disappeared,

## Where Was My Mind?

I remember we had lorry-loads of army camp-beds turn up one day that I had bought. I vaguely remember someone in our car park who had bought a sample in; I lay on it in the middle of the car park and bought thousands of them. Apparently, I had rung an army surplus place that advertised them for sale in the *Sunday Times*. I also tried to buy a lorry-load of real frogs from a garden centre, but they didn't deliver them. *I wonder why? Whatever was I on?*

## The Power of the Word "Free"

These beds were made for the Second World War; they had got 1939 stamped on them and the mattresses were made of a thick, green fabric that looked like it was waterproof, and stuffed with something like straw. They were rolled up in layers of brown paper that had tar in between for protection, and were tied with string, which made it impossible to get into a car without unwrapping them and filling the car.

There was no way that we could sell them, as I would be too embarrassed to take people's money, so I had an idea - we advertised them in our January sale: "An adult size bed and mattress worth £50, free when you spend £50 on baby goods."

What else could we do with them but give them away? One crazy mistake turned into a fantastic and cheap advertising stunt that got people coming to the shop in droves. Most of the customers loved it, but some turned their noses up at them, saying, "You can keep that crap," but even those people were happy with what they had bought.

**The van with the roof rack on it, piled high with stock.**

We had a Suzuki mini-van that would hold only 12 beds at a time, and it took a one-hour round trip, eight trips a day. The mattresses would go in the van and the beds would go on the roof rack; if only I had a picture of it, looking like something you would see in India.

The sales went crazy; people were coming from a 100-mile radius. One day a busload of people came from Leicester just to get them. We could only give 96 away each day because when they first arrived we had nowhere to put them, so we had to send the lorries to our house in Stamford. We stored them in our house and garages, and even in the sheds, summerhouse and the greenhouse.

The village came to a standstill. People were waiting for their free beds, as we had run out, and the van was stuck in the traffic, so we walked the customers down the road and unloaded the beds on the pavement. The van turned around and went back for more and the customers had to carry their beds back to the shop. It was utter chaos. We hurriedly loaded the 12 beds in the cars and got them out of the car park to get another 12 in; it was like being in a Carry-On film. Most of the customers loved the carnival atmosphere.

***Roger on the right, and me; he worked in our service department and practised reflexology in his spare time.***

Every member of staff dressed up at Christmas. We had fairground rides, a hot-dog van, and Grandad's free home-made wine and mince pies. Christmas was an exhausting time for us.

We would have two days off and, very often, would spend that time ill in bed with exhaustion. I remember Pete and his wife Harriet calling in one Christmas Day as they were passing; they came in to our bedroom. What a sight we must have looked! We felt dreadful. Ever the optimist, I said, "At least we are ill while the shops are closed." Elaine was looking after Joanne.

## Kiddicare's Gone Crackers

At Christmas 1992 every single member of staff dressed up as usual in children's character dress. It worked; we would take £70,000  a day, equivalent nowadays to £130,000. Not only were we giving the beds away, we also had our first wraparound newspaper advert, that was a cover page, back and front, in all of the papers in the area. Looking like it was the actual front page of the paper the headline said "Kiddicare's gone Crackers."

*1992. Dad was our Father Christmas for years, providing gallons of homemade wine for the customers and staff. I've just realised why we all had such a good time.*

We were running out of baby clothes, so we rang the owner of Shenu Fashions from Leicester, but he was closed for the holidays as nobody did any trade over the New Year. Marilyn and I took the van over to his warehouse after the shop had closed and, by 10 pm, we had the van loaded and were on our way back, getting some fish and chips and eating them on the move; we then spent half the night pricing the stock up ready for the next day.

## I Still Managed To Get Into Trouble

Every year we would go to a company called Jean Sorelle, which had a factory just on the outskirts of Peterborough, as they sold off all their surplus toiletries in December that were used inside gift boxes for Mothercare, Boots and other High Street stores. We could give them away but not sell them, so that year, as usual, we advertised them as a free gift to everyone who came into the store, no purchase necessary. The only problem was that this year we had done a deal to take everything, about 20,000 items in total, which was far too many to give away in the sale.

In February, after the sale, I decided to sell the rest of these products at 20p each. Common sense told us that some of our customers worked at Boots and Mothercare, and we knew John Lewis spies would be in checking our prices. Well, the shit hit the fan only two days later for selling the Jean Sorelle products and we had to stop immediately. We had sold only about £2 worth so, for the next two years, we were giving the bloody stuff away. Local customers would say when they were given this free gift at the till, "I don't want it; you keep giving me this stuff quicker than I can use it."

## Money Go Round

The pictures below show just how the world of money goes round and round. The more that you have, the more you spread the money. At the time, we had a new Bentley; we gave thousands of pounds to charity. One particular night that I remember very well was where guests came to a ball that we were sponsoring, and had a great evening.

At the end of a great night I was standing outside, waiting for Marilyn. Our car was parked there. About twenty people stood waiting for cabs and cars, when a guest standing next to me said, "What 'C' would have one of those?" pointing at my car. My thoughts were that I was giving prosperity to the manufacturer who produced it, to the garage that sold it to me, to Colin from Colebrook's, who maintained it for me, and most people liked to look at it.

I stood there and said nothing, as I wasn't going to get into a fight with a drunk. I was just thinking, "I hate people," but of course I didn't really, apart from that ignorant bastard who was only thinking of himself. I sometimes wonder how much he has given away.

## The Chernobyl Disaster

The Chernobyl Disaster was in 1986, when a nuclear power station blew up, leaking radioactive material. Hundreds of children were affected. One day, someone asked if they could have some prams and cots for the children; they said that they took a lorry over to the Ukraine regularly with supplies and I had no reason to disbelieve them, so I agreed and set about loading up 20 cots and mattresses, 20 prams, all sorts of pushchairs and other equipment, plus toys.

Once the truck was loaded, we gave them tea and biscuits and asked for their card so we could keep in touch with them; they hadn't got one on them, but said that they would send all the information on. We asked for photos so that we could collect money from our customers for the children; we got nothing back from them, so maybe it was "con-obyl".

*The late 80s started a lifestyle that we could never have imagined. Below is what surplus money can be used for; I show this only to inspire the people who want this sort of thing.*

**The new 1989 £72,000 Porsche 911 Turbo I bought, thinking it would motivate me as I was going through a period of coasting, but all it did was make my back worse. The plane belonged to one of our suppliers, Peter Teichman. The lifestyle seemed attractive to us in 1999 but, after flying in small planes, we knew it wasn't for us.**

**Ever since seeing the man in the late 70s sitting in his Rolls-Royce waiting for his wife who was buying our house, I have wanted one. Well, my goal was achieved in 1989 when I bought a bright red £115,000 Bentley. Then, a few years later, in the 1990s, we built a villa in the mountains of Tenerife at the bargain price of £1.4 million.**

**Once Roy and Sue introduced us to motor-homes in 2002, we have travelled around Europe. Boats have always been an**

*attraction, we even have a 180-mooring inland marina in Oundle, Northamptonshire.*

## The Last Straw

By May 1993 the last straw came when I could not get upstairs. I was on my hands and knees, and Marilyn was trying to help me up the stairs; I was screaming with pain, even though I had taken everything going for relief. The next day I was still out washing mud off lorry wheels before they left site, so as not to get mud on the road. At the same time, in my head I was planning my exit from this life because I felt that I just couldn't carry on.

At that time Marilyn was overseeing a huge project of rebuilding what was our main store in Werrington village; the store was being rebuilt in three sections while we were still trading there. This project was taking 35 weeks, plus fit-out, to complete; it was a logistics nightmare for her. On top of that she was organising Elaine's wedding; the reception was to be at home, and we were having a 48ft conservatory built at home with a massive new patio, new walls, new planting - the works. On top of this, she was looking after me.

## It Wasn't Time

I couldn't stand the pain any more, and there was no way out. I was drinking so much alcohol along with the pills to ease the pain - I just felt life would not get any better for me. On the other hand, I felt like Marilyn's life would only get worse looking after me.

I had kept my thoughts from everyone; besides, what could they do about it? The next morning at 11 am, as I was washing the mud off the wheels, my knees and back bent, eyes streaming because of the pain that was getting worse by the minute, Marilyn appeared. She said, "I've rung a surgeon who has a waiting list a year long, but his 1 o'clock appointment has cancelled; if we get there he will see you."

I went with Marilyn to see him in the Peterborough Hospital. Going down the corridor I was literally holding onto the walls and radiators; I wanted to crawl on the floor, but that would have made me look like a twat. Even though I was ready to kill myself, I still had my dignity. He said that we needed to get to the local private hospital, as they had a MRI scanning machine there. Back down the corridor we went; how I managed to get to the end I don't know - the adrenalin had gone completely. I was ready and wanted to die.

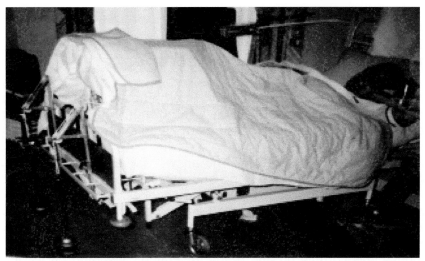

*The operation eased the pain and then it took thirty months to heal completely.*

## Marilyn Grew Two Heads

I went in to get scanned and didn't come out until fifteen days later. When I was in hospital I really can't remember much; they had to knock me out for the scan because I could not keep still then, for the next nine days, they hung counter-weights on my legs to pull my vertebra apart, which pulled my legs three feet off the bed. I don't remember, but I do have the photos.

All I do remember is that the hospital ceilings were multi-coloured, the walls were covered in pictures, and Marilyn had two heads, which scared me if she came too close. Drugs can do some scary things to your brain, as the ceiling was actually white and the room had only one picture on the wall.

Marilyn tried to take me home from hospital but I was having none of it; I was stopping in my room, and there was no way I was even putting one foot outside that door. I was so full of drugs I was just happy to stay in there forever. It's scary to think what can go on.

Anyway, a nurse and Marilyn eventually persuaded me to walk in the corridor, and within an hour I was home. Once home, and with the drugs out of my system, there was no time to lose in getting on with the business. I now had a second chance at life and I was going to make sure I did as much as I could.

# Another Cycle in Life

## *"And back to what was normal for us"*

The shop was now completed, and I felt fine, apart from just a constant niggling pain, but I was back to normal. I had disrespected my body in the past, but now I had been given another chance.

Would I do anything differently? The answer is yes, of course; how many people do something wrong and get a second chance? I just feel so lucky in getting so many second chances in my life. Nobody knew how close (just a few hours) I was to ending my life, and it's all down to Marilyn ringing that surgeon; maybe she knew!

The house was completed and ready for Elaine's wedding on 4th July 1993, only a few days after I came out of hospital, and twenty-three years to the day after Marilyn and I were married.

*Elaine and Scott, 4th July 1993*

It was a great day; the sun was shining, and Marilyn had organised everything perfectly. I took Elaine to the church in the Bentley; well, Colin from Colebrook's, who serviced our Bentleys, drove us there and back home after the wedding, where we held the reception. It was such a fantastic day; we ate outside in a very informal atmosphere.

It was great to meet Scott's dad at last, and his three wives, for the first time. I found that fascinating, but Marilyn told me afterwards that he was only married to one at a time, and obviously the drugs that were given to me in the hospital had affected my brain. The following day we jetted off to have a holiday in Menorca with Jo, Elaine and Scott; some people thought it strange that we went on their honeymoon, but a holiday is a holiday, and besides, they had lived together for years.

We were producing phenomenal profits at that time and I had loads of ideas of how we would spend some of the money and, at the same time, take the business forward. One of our goals was to build a place in the sun, a villa in Spain or somewhere, as we could see that we were going to be able to take more time off. We had got some terrific staff who were in tune with the business and us; it was a great time again when a group of people gelled together, and who worked as one.

## A Natural School Leaving Age Is 13

Elaine was 22 years old; she had now been working full-time in the shop since she was thirteen - yes, thirteen - and, by the time she was sixteen she would be in charge when we were away on holiday. Joanne left school, again at thirteen, just like her sister. She would be educated by us at work; school hadn't suited either of them. I think it was because they were brought up in an adult and business environment, as we never seemed to have time to really get into school things because the business had to take priority, so they both learned a great deal about real life and business.

I think that, when you have a business that your children want to go into, their minds can be distracted from school; they think that it is a waste of time and, of course, very often it is, and there is little you can do to change those thoughts, so we embraced them. Well, I did; Marilyn had a different opinion, but the facts were that Elaine hated school, she was ready to be educated in the real world of business, and Jo was being bullied to an extent where we had a duty of care for her and would have been wrong to have made her stay. Marilyn didn't want to rock the boat with the education authorities but, once the girls were working with us, Marilyn loved every minute of it; she just thought that this way of life was so natural.

There were other times when things came to really try us, like the fighting with the Council over expanding our business. It was like knocking our heads against a brick wall, but it was all worth it in the end. Sometimes one of us would think of selling up, but we always ran the thought of giving up out of our minds within minutes; one of us would pull the other up when one was low, and then we used to laugh and say, "What the hell would happen if we both felt down at the same time?" But we couldn't let that happen as, by then, too many people were relying on us for their livings.

# My Mum Died

SIDETRACKED

Dad had looked after Mum for about 12 years, cooking and doing everything around the house, before she died on 8th December 1993. She had always been what you might call a bit frail. She smoked, like most people of her generation did; after all, the tobacco companies portrayed smoking as a healthy lifestyle.

Dad and Mum belonged to lots of vintage cycling clubs all over the world, and for years they would be somewhere different most weekends, attending rallies. Dad would ride, and Mum would sit around their caravan talking to her friends, until the last few years; then they spent more time with us.

Mum had contracted TB when she was young, rendering one lung with only partial use, which meant she had to be very careful; so, all of her life, she had a reason not to exert herself but, with having three kids to look after, I think that went out of the window. She died, aged eighty, from stomach cancer, after being ill for just a few days. After the funeral I went back to work that afternoon; I worked in the warehouse sorting pallets of stock out. I mentally did not want to accept that she had gone.

I was chastising myself for not making enough money soon enough to give my mum a life with no worries about money. I couldn't give her everything that I thought she wanted; although my mum and dad were relatively poor in terms of money, they always lived a lifestyle within their means. I learned a few days after she had died that it wasn't money she wanted in her life; Dad said that all she wanted was to have her three children get on, and be happy with each other. It still haunts me today to think that I didn't portray that love I had for my brother and sister to her; I thought there were more important things in life than that. What a shit.

*I thought I knew everything when I was young, and Mum knew nothing. Well, turns out the opposite. Mum used to say, "You will miss me when I've gone." Oh boy, was she right.*

BACK

In 1995-6 we had a few relatively small companies make approaches to buy the business. We used to think it was probably the thing to do - sell up and retire - because that's what is expected in this country; and if you didn't, you were odd. We were now 45 years old; even then, after twenty-one years in business, we had in the back of our minds that retiring was the thing to do but, of course, we were becoming odd. Many business people in those days retired in their 40s; I thought what the hell would we do? We had no hobbies and, besides that, what would Elaine and Joanne do?

Elaine had a baby girl, Sophie, born on 26$^{th}$ May 1994; she had worked, just like her mum, right up to having Sophie, then back the next day into work. We had Elaine and Joanne, the next generation; now the start of the third generation was with us, giving Marilyn and I motivation to keep going. We were now very proud grandparents.

Although things were now going great compared to a lot of businesses, our real independence was eroding away. We didn't know it because, in a very short time, we had come from nothing, making decisions that affected just the two of us, to now being responsible for all of these people and their livelihoods. The stress started to affect me, and my calm nature changed to one that I didn't like.

## Adapt to the Circumstances

My thoughts were that if I were going to look after people, providing a job, then they should look after me by committing every waking hour to the business like I was; but of course, that's not the case. I didn't understand; I was on a massive learning curve that lasted for years as the business continually grew ahead of me, yet I was the one who kept on pushing it forward. The more that I did that, the more I expected everyone to do the same; of course Marilyn, Elaine, Joanne and the main staff did.

## Working for an Idiot

I think that I was on a treadmill that I wanted to get off, but I couldn't. On the other hand, Marilyn would say, "Neville, you should calm down or you will have a heart attack; you are expecting too much from people." I know that I lost the plot; for a long time I was a madman working for an idiot, who was me.

Although this was happening, it was just par for the course. We were on a never-ending conveyer belt of continuous learning; at every step of the way there were new obstacles and challenges to overcome. The main thing for me was finding staff that could be on my wavelength; since 1974 and up to 2014, we have been fortunate to have groups of like-minded people who have gelled together as teams within the business, taking instructions and responsibility, and knowing what our aim was for them and for the business.

We have been blessed with many incredible people who took a job with us; then, somewhere along the way, that job turned into something else for them. It really amazed me when I saw people changing their lives in Kiddicare, from just turning up for the job each day, to one day changing into part of the fabric and the heart of the business. Sometimes it took a few months, sometimes a few years but, when it happened, it was amazing to see all of these people taking responsibility for themselves, the company and their actions. Seeing this was the one thing that made running the business all worthwhile. Another thing that happened was that so many people got together and became families, which Marilyn and I thought was absolutely brilliant.

## Strive for Perfection

Every day I would strive for perfection on anything that we all came across, no matter which department it was and, although we were happy with things, we all still looked for continual improvement. To some new people it looked like I was not satisfied with anything; I have been called a slave-driver, but most of the staff understood that, if there were not continual improvement in the business then, at some stage in the future when the going gets tough, the ones who have coasted in business would not survive.

# A Touch of Complacency

## *"Life was just too easy compared to the early days"*

From 1994 to 1997 life was so good, but we were coasting compared to the early days. We were getting more work done with less effort; I suppose it was because we got wise, or maybe just a bit wiser, doing more of what we knew would work. I thought taking it relatively easy was something that we should do, and I suppose it's what our society expects; I even retired to write a novel, as I thought I had a great imagination. Three days later, trying to read what I had written was too much like hard work, so I sneaked back to the shop without anybody noticing that I had ever been away.

## Idle People Attract Trouble

We went on holidays at least six times a year for up to three weeks at a time, keeping in contact every day with some very, very long faxes; but to us this way of life didn't feel right, it really felt like we were wasting the most precious thing that we all have, and that's time.

So an expanding business was always going to win; aiming at a moving target, very often in new territory, was so exciting and rewarding, as idle people inevitably attract trouble into their lives.

## Been There, Done It

When I say a moving target, I mean that we were always experimenting with new lines that were sometimes only just outside of our core business. Failures in these products were thick and fast; just because we were brilliant at selling baby things, it didn't mean that we could sell household products, or even baby products, that were sold in all of the supermarkets. Although we went through thousands of different items, we really managed to sell only nursery products in vast quantities, and vast quantities were all we wanted.

## An Odd Product

It's just come to mind that there was one product that we did sell for some years which had nothing remotely to do with babies; it was garden furniture - tables, chairs, parasols and cushions, all in a variety of sizes and colours. We would store them in the garages and houses that we had built next to the shop; one year they were full of other stock, so we had to store thousands of chairs in the garden at Park House, our home. They were packed in 20s that were shrink-wrapped, so I thought that they would be protected from the elements.

## If the Price is Right

We would always buy when the price was right; well, buying garden furniture in the spring was expensive so I bought it in the autumn, clearing left-over stock at a fraction of the price. We had four 40-foot containers turn up from Italy; the drivers were bewildered because they had arrived at a private house, not a warehouse as normal, and then when they saw where we were storing the product they were more than a little bit amused, to say the least.

We put this mountain of white plastic chairs wrapped in polythene under some trees, as they would be less conspicuous. We had to make pyramid shapes, which wasn't easy with 20 chairs in a long, plastic bag constantly moving about; it was an art on its own to keep them from falling apart, but we soon got the hang of it, with three people carrying each parcel of chairs down our drive.

When Marilyn got home she was not pleased to see what looked like a recycling mountain of rubbish in her wonderful parkland garden. All I could say was that we had got a fantastic deal, but that fell on deaf ears. When it snowed I tried to make light by saying that we were the only people around with our own ski slopes.

Then, when the spring came, the polythene had filled with water and, in a very short time, when the sun came out the algae grew rapidly; stagnant water under polythene - great, I needed something to do on a Sunday evening. I jet-washed those bloody chairs for weeks, cursing my stupidity on every chair I washed; oh yes, plastic chairs don't like to be jet-washed - they turn into aeroplanes and tend to fly away under pressure.

## Expansion Was Out Of the Question

We had no intention of expanding into areas that we didn't know, because at that time expanding meant opening more shops in faraway places that were covered by Mothercare, John Lewis or usually a very good independent, so what was the point? Besides, we were making all the money that we would ever want.

The money was coming in every day. We had only the one shop and it was busy, to say the least. I see from our accounts that in 1992 we bought vehicles for the four managers plus two for ourselves, and then we renewed them in 1995.

Times were good and the entire staff gelled as a team; everybody had a smile on their face - it was a happy time. Our customers would drive to us from up to three hours away because of the free, no-catch petrol offer we had advertised; I don't think there was anyone who went home without a car full of purchases.

# I Expected To Be In Pain For evermore

SIDETRACKED

Two years after my operation we were on holiday in Tenerife. On 12<sup>th</sup> October 1995, this photo was taken about one hour before what I would call a miracle occurred. I had stopped for a rest and I had hold of my back because it was hurting, as usual.

Then, as we were walking on a building site looking at potentially building a property, Marilyn said, "What's the matter, Nev?" I said, "Nothing; why?" She said, "You're walking in front of me." Normally I would be walking twenty paces behind her, and now I was in front without any pain. I just couldn't believe it - the pain had gone.

The next morning, as I woke up expecting to be in pain again, I was delighted but sceptical that it would last. I subsequently was very cautious, not aggravating it for the next 18 months but, gradually, I got back into golf, running and the gym without any trouble at all.

# Now Anything Was Possible

BACK

John Thompson and his team were experts in fitting everything into cars; many times we would take people to the train station, the grandparents loaded up with stuff. They had travelled to us in the car with their children and the car was jam-packed with goods that they had not thought they would buy.

They were left with no space in the car, leaving the grandparents without a seat. It gave us all a real buzz seeing the last one go at 7pm on a Saturday night, on their 3-hour journey back; inevitably, their friends would come well-prepared - another week with vans, trailers, and roof-racks. Can you imagine any other shop staff doing that for customers?

There had got to be a better way to serve more customers, but how was it to be done, and at what cost? I had to explore other ways.

## Stand Back and Think

SIDETRACKED

At one point we owed £1,075,000 to the bank, as we had started to keep most of the properties for passive income. This amounted to a lot of money then, a lot easier to borrow than to pay back when, or if, something happens. The tipping point came when a friend died at the age of 39, leaving his wife and children; he had what seemed to be a great life, and a super business of, what I believe to be at the time, six shops and a manufacturing business.

Now his wife was left to look after their business all on her own, with two young children, which must have been an impossible task, and then, after about a two-year struggle, the business folded. And, as our business was no different, it made us think - what if...?

The two of us played many parts, we wore lots of hats, and so, if one of us were to go, that would mean 50% of the key staff would go from the business and the other 50% would crack under the pressure.

At that time we were the only ones who knew everything about the business; the managers had their areas of responsibility, and Elaine and Jo were too busy with the advertising and promoting of the business, and all of the customers to deal with. That left little time to learn the boring bit of how to run a business. At that time neither was interested, as the other stuff was far too exciting for them.

I did not want them to be left in the same position as our friend's family, thinking that if one of us died, it would be awful for them to be left with a huge debt that I had happened to accumulate in both of our businesses due to expanding them. The answer was to play a game that I heard on one of my motivational tapes, called "Dad's dead"! The game went like this: "Dad's dead; what do we do now?" Then Marilyn, Elaine and Jo had to decide what to do.

Would they keep the business? And if so, how? Would they sell? And then do what? Some very interesting questions; and a lot of answers were needed. One answer I got was that we would carry on as normal, so I said, "OK, I will be dead today - run the business." Within five minutes of that, someone started asking me questions; "Have we got enough money to buy this property?" I said, "I'm dead, ask someone else," then more questions followed; "Have we got enough space for surplus stock? Who is our estate agent? What bank do we use? What is our plan for the business in the future," etc., etc.

The game of "Dad's dead" went on for a bit when we realised that we needed to do something; that game alone makes you aware of the need for key staff, and for partners to know more about the business that they rely on for their living. I urge everybody I talk to to play that game before it's not a game any more; you too should try this in your business, or just in your life in general.

We wanted to pay off the £1,075,000 because of what we had seen with our friend, so I made a plan to pay off this debt within three years out of profits. When I said this we hadn't got a chance, but what the mind can conceive and believe, you can achieve and, in fact, we paid the debt off in 2 years 9 months. This was due to Marilyn, Elaine, Jo and me all strictly overseeing every financial thing that went on in the business.

Although Jo was only about thirteen at the time, she had been in the business since the day she was born; she knew what was going on, just like Elaine; their eyes and ears didn't miss a thing. We tried to get them into the office work but, to them, opening the mail, doing the invoice payments and seeing the bank manager were too boring for them at that time.

We needed to clear the debt at this stage of the business, if only to prove to ourselves that we were in control and we weren't getting out of our depth with borrowing. It was a very good exercise but, unfortunately, I was so stubborn over it that I lost out on a couple of good deals that, with hindsight, would have paid the debt off with the profit. Also, with inflation, the debt would have been much smaller after the three years but, at the time, the exercise was for today, not assuming for three years' time.

Another thing, too; if we had bought another million pounds' worth of property during those three years, that also would have increased in value at that time. I tried to find someone to give me advice, but I didn't know anyone who had made any amount of money who could advise me on what we should do. I think I panicked, not looking at all of the ways out of the situation that we were in; after all, it was just a scenario in our heads and not a problem, as our assets would always cover the debt three times over.

## I Found Nine Pensions

In doing this exercise to get rid of the borrowing, I found out that we had some insurance policies that we had taken out each time we got a bank loan, and we did not understand that we could have cancelled the insurance when each loan was paid off, or the insurance could have covered the next loan. Having not had this understanding, we were pleasantly surprised when I cancelled them; the premiums went towards paying off the loan and also, we got back £75,000.

The other thing I found was that we had both got nine pensions each, which had been taken out over the years, starting in 1976 at £20 a month, apparently to save tax and to provide a pension we could draw when we retired. I amalgamated them, and found that we could put this into a property. I hadn't realised any of this before because, when you are new to business, all you care about is the loan you need, not what they're saying to you, and when you are signing paperwork or saving tax, you are not really thinking about the pension in 60 years' time. Looking back now, it just seems amazing that we did these things on trust of other people dealing with our finances; it all comes back to **"You don't know what you don't know."**

## The Art of Understanding Money

Watching every penny in the 2 years 9 months, Elaine bought what we could sell in a month, which was very hard when you get offered clearance stock, but she would negotiate taking the stock over so many months. Invariably, suppliers would send it in to us in one go and invoice every month, because we had told them what we were doing and they understood that we weren't short of money, it was just self-imposed; and honesty paid off.

The other thing I came up with, that was a first in the trade and has probably never been done since, was that we would pay in a day. We normally got between 2% and 5% off if we paid in 30 days, and we then negotiated 7% to 10% settlement discount. So if suppliers sent £1,000 of goods in every month, we would get £240 settlement in that year but, on the new scheme, we got £1,200 settlement discount; so in 1997, if we persuaded every supplier to take our offer up, we would save £200,000.

Marilyn and Elaine were doing the buying; they got the majority on board and got an extra £160,000 on the bottom line, which proved to work for us as, between 1995 and 1996, our profits rose from £323,000 to £484,000 making £161,000 extra profit without having to put up our prices to the customer.

Every week that went by, we had less interest to pay on our loan for those three years. We were paying an average of 12% interest on the loan, which meant I divided the £1,075,000 into 156 weeks, paying off £6,891 a week. In doing this each week we would save £15.90 interest, equivalent to £827 pa; and then, after 144 weeks, we had paid the debt off by paying only £992,000 out of profits and the remaining £83,000 from the interest that we saved.

# Free of Debt at Last

BACK

My goal for the last 3 years had come true. I had promised myself that, if we had paid off our debts within the time, I would take all the family to America to stay at Disney and visit Cape Canaveral along with the other attractions. As soon as we had achieved our goal we booked a £10,000 holiday, which seemed a fortune then; we took the girls, Scott, Sophie, who was two, Dad and Marilyn's Mum and Dad.

# Push the Boundaries

## *"Can we get people to buy without demonstrations?"*

## Another Name Change

In the July of 1997 we had taken Jo, Elaine, Scott and Sophie on holiday to Tenerife. At the time, the hotel was supposed to be the best there. As we were sitting around the pool, chatting about the business, I was going over the past when I got an idea for the future.

About twelve years earlier, around 1985, I saw a computer sitting on Marilyn's desk, one she was having installed. I thought that I would never be able to use one of those things because of my dyslexia, but I knew they could do incredible things. New challenges were ahead of us, so we needed to embrace them and not be afraid.

SIDETRACKED

When I met Marilyn in 1966 I was also introduced to her uncle, Des Green, who was a pig farmer. I had something in common with him. Then, in 1967-8, I worked for him each Saturday. At the time, his wife, Norma, was expecting a baby; they had already got five children. I remember that when she was 8 months pregnant she was holding a sheet of corrugated tin, herding the pigs from one pen into another.

Des and Norma not only had my total respect, they were great role models for us; they weren't afraid of what life had to throw at them. The new baby arrived; they called him Robert and, as Bob grew up into the 80s, Des would say that Bob was into computers.

Des would tell me that they were the future in business and, although I couldn't see how I personally could make money out of them, it didn't take long for Des to convince me that this new technology would change the world. By 1985 we had already been using the technology of mobile phones for years, which proved to be invaluable; even then, the majority of people thought anybody using one of these was either a yuppie or a show-off. I would have to make computers work for us; Marilyn was the first person in our business to embrace this technology, and then all we had to do was employ others to do the same.

Obviously, in those days, people didn't know how much money you could make if you had a computer in your business; incredibly, in 2014 there are still people and businesses that make life so hard for themselves by not using technology to their advantage.

BACK

I was now 47 years old, my back was the best it had ever been since I was seventeen, and I had found a new lease of life. I wanted to keep moving the business along every day, implementing new ideas to keep it evolving. I had to come up with things that others in our trade weren't doing; I didn't want to sell every pram, just the next one that would be sold within a 2-hour driving radius of the shop. I had thought that Scott, our son-in-law, was wasting his time working on his own; I knew that the more heads you put together, the better outcome it is for everyone.

I had read Sam Walton's Wal-Mart's book and lots of other books too; they were written by normal people who had just created enormous businesses, and this confirmed that we were heading along the right track. We had pushed the boundaries every day, even though we didn't know where those boundaries were taking us, but it felt good.

I imagined that all the owners of any family business were the same as us; Marilyn and I had constantly eaten, slept and breathed Marville and Kiddicare, which took up all of our time, and our girls were no different, either. We knew that we would always find good people to fill any job that we created to expand the business and, when I came up with a new idea to expand again, what better way for Elaine and Scott to work together? So I said,

**"I reckon this thing called the Internet will take off; then, in five years' time, our customers will be buying their prams from us in that way if we had a website, instead of coming to the shop."**

I said to Scott, **"You could do that for us, as you know about this kind of stuff."**

I asked Scott to register kiddicare.com for us, this being the first of many names to protect and also to expand the business in the future

# The Changing World of Retail

I knew the retail business had to keep changing for us, if we wanted to bring in all of our growing family in the future, and survive going forward in the ever-changing retail world.

Most of the independent shops in the industry were still putting goods away for people on a deposit. This could not carry on, because profit margins were getting smaller and space was getting dearer, products were changing more quickly and the law was on the consumer's side, thus destroying business practices that have tried to help the customers.

It was a problem when customers changed their minds after keeping the products for 6 months, leaving the shopkeeper with old stock. Luckily, we had disposed of this unprofitable system ten years previously, but I could see others getting into trouble if they didn't change and embrace new ways faster than ever before.

Elaine, and then Joanne, came into the business naturally; well, they were brought up in it, and had been paid for every hour that they had worked since they were 10 years old. Maybe that's what would motivate any child, or perhaps it wasn't about the money.

And now our dream was to continue with the business in whatever form it was to take, until the day we wanted to hand it down to the two of them, if that's what they wanted; then, for us, seeing the third generation come in was the dream. Computer technology was here to stay, no matter how much competitors and suppliers tried to ignore it; some were involved with the problems that the Internet caused whilst we, on the other hand, were embracing the way forward.

*"If you don't embrace new things your business will die."*

Neville Wright

# The Customer Is Still King

The businesses had got 23 years of our philosophy of wanting happy customers; we loved the nursery business much more than the property business, as all of the people involved were so nice and we had everything we wanted - happy staff, suppliers and customers. What else could we wish for now, after all those years?

I read a book called *Raving Fans*, written by Ken Blanchard, as I wanted to turn happy customers into "raving fans" instead of just customers, and the only way to do that was to solve their problems. A major problem was that people would ring us every day to tell us that their friends had visited us and that they themselves wanted the same products, but our store was too far away, and they would give all of the reasons why they could not get to us.

This problem had started four years earlier, when I had already invented the free petrol give-away. We advertised this in the hospital maternity books within a two-hour drive of Peterborough, the book that ladies get when they have their first doctor's visit in pregnancy. The advert said that we would pay for their petrol to come to us and they didn't have to buy anything. Some people asked if it was a joke, others asked whether it applied to diesel cars, and most people thought that we had a petrol station on site.

## We Will Pay For Your Petrol

I was the first and only person in the industry to do this; it was a phenomenal success, and something that hasn't been repeated since in the nursery industry, or in any other, for that matter.

John Thompson, our service manager, made a calculation on the average fuel consumption and came up with so much money per mile, over all the miles for up to four hours away. Well, it didn't really matter how far they came, we paid them. All the customers had to do was produce their driving licences; we would calculate the miles from their address and then we would pay them the money. They didn't need to purchase anything, so it persuaded them to come to the shop free, with no obligations.

When devising this scheme, I had put myself into the customer's shoes. I knew the objections the men would have: one would be the cost of fuel and the other would be having to buy something. Customers would come up to us with the maternity book and shyly say, "Um, I've got..." They would be holding the book; we would interrupt, saying, "That's great; have you got your licence? I will get your money."

If we saw someone hovering around with the book in their hand, we would go up to them and ask if they had been given their petrol money. Some would reply that they hadn't bought anything yet, and we would say that they didn't have to buy; then we would give them the money.

We knew that, with the expertise of our staff, they would not be going out empty-handed; in fact, lots of customers asked if we were on a bonus because they had never seen such motivated staff before. When we said no, they were hooked on promoting us to everyone they knew.

## It Was All About Reverse Psychology

We had taken the cost of travelling to us away from the man. I say "man" as I'm talking about over 20 years ago, although it feels like yesterday; as we keep saying, every day changes just a bit. It was then up to the ladies to explain that they were only coming for a look.

They were our secret sales staff, selling the idea of just looking to persuade their partners to travel all that way. When they entered the shop, instead of getting pounced on by a salesperson, they were offered a cup of free tea and a biscuit. Talk about disarming someone; this was total reverse psychology and, after the shock of this being real, invariably the man would say, after a two-hour drive to get here and another two hours of demonstrations from our staff, "I've not come all this way to go home empty-handed," a win-win situation.

We did have a few sharp people coming in, who worked in Peterborough but lived an hour or so away; they would come in every day to claim the petrol money but our staff were just a bit sharper than they were, as we kept records; so off they went with a flea in their ear. In cases like this, our motto was: "Don't 'f' with this cat, matey."

## More Complaints

It was great; however, the more customers we had through the door, the more people complained that they wanted us to deliver. Nothing much happened for 18 months; we used to talk about it, but Scott was working for himself, commuting to London doing IT work for people. He had got the ball rolling by getting us the website name, etc. and formulating everything that we wanted.

This project was unknown territory for him; with him working part-time, trying to create something was always going to be slow. We were all too busy to concentrate on things that were alien to us, although we all knew by now that if we didn't push this, someone else would, and we would be left high and dry.

In September 1998 we had put an advert in the Job Centre for a general warehouse person, because I needed someone to flatten cardboard boxes and put them in a skip as I was too busy taking in deliveries to do it myself, and everybody was running around like headless chickens. We used to tell customers, when they rang wanting to know something, not to come to the store on a Saturday as we were too busy and the chances were that they wouldn't get served. Customers have said to me, "I thought that when you said don't come in it was to encourage us to come, but I see you were telling the truth." *It was manic*

## The Gadget Man Arrived

It was Tuesday afternoon; I was in the yard as usual, sorting deliveries, when a lad went into the office. I knew he was there for an interview. Within ten minutes he had come out and gone. I opened the office door and shouted, "When does he start?" Marilyn and Rosie, our secretary, said, "He's not." I said, "Why?" They said, "He didn't speak." I said, "I don't want him to bloody speak, I just need him to dispose of the fcuking boxes; ring him now and tell him to start tomorrow." I was totally knackered and just needed some help.

Very often we would book lorries in at 6.00 pm, when the shop was closed, so some of us could unload 2,000 highchairs all by hand, as we didn't have a forklift truck at the time. There would be Marilyn, Rosie, John, Elaine, Jo and anyone who had the time, all unloading the truck. The lad turned up on 3rd September 1998; his name was Barrie Ainsworth. He helped me with the deliveries and, when we got chatting, he told me that he had left his last job as a storeman because he had been bullied. I said that he wouldn't have any problems now and, if he did, I would sort it at once, as there was no time allocated for that in our environment. The lads in the service department started to call him "Gadget" because he had always got a tool to do any job, so he immediately fitted in with all of the staff.

## Everyone Has Opportunities

One day, about four weeks after arriving, Barrie was collecting the girls' waste bins from the office when one of them said, "Oh no, my computer has gone wrong." He looked over her shoulder and pressed a few keys - problem solved. Everyone was amazed; although computers had been in our office for years, there were very few people who could use them to their full extent. I said, "Barrie, how did you know what the problem was?" He said, in his quiet and unassuming voice, "It's my hobby." I said, "Put the bins down, Barrie; you are now our IT manager." He smiled, and carried on emptying the bins, saying, "I'll just finish this, and then I will be back."

The next day I hired another person to break down cardboard boxes. The next week I was speaking to Barrie about my dreams of taking our business online, and asking whether he had any knowledge about the Internet; he told me that he had already created a website for himself.

For me, Christmas had come early. Scott could communicate and organise the new site with Barrie; Scott knew what we wanted, but hadn't enough time to do it, whereas Barrie was full-time, and was technically capable of doing the work. Marilyn, Elaine and I could tell Scott what we wanted, and he could put it in order of build; it would take all of us to do it.

I knew that the market for us would be enormous and, although a few other shops had started to go online, I could see that they were under-funded and there was no passion or expertise that was needed in the building of their websites. Maybe they lacked the staff with the skills; a lot of success is down to luck in finding the right people, then recognising what you have, and then doing something about it. After all the time we had spent working on the shop floor we could put ourselves into the minds of our customers, so we knew what had to be done.

## Just a Single Thought

All businesses start with a single thought, a single seed that can be either left in suspension, or sown and nurtured. Normally, with a new business it's hard work, but with this I thought it would be easy. Well we had, by this time, an already very successful and profitable business, and this was going to be just an extension of our business, so customers wouldn't have to take their goods home in their cars - a delivery service.

Ideas get more valuable if they affect more people. It all came back to developing the cogs in a new wheel; we had all the ingredients that we would need to take us to the next level. We had by this time been in the trade for 23 years; we knew the business inside out, we had the stock all paid for, we had the premises all paid for, we had the trained staff, and we had the spirit and enthusiasm to push the business further.

We had the key people in place who could make it happen. The lists of work got longer, and things were getting exciting; we could see the website coming together. The buying office would be turned into a photography studio within minutes of any rep leaving, enabling Barrie to take photos of the new products that were to go online. This was a new era, and one that was very exciting, this now becoming the reality of that "tech moment" I had had two years before.

# How Wrong Could I Be?

I thought that I just knew we had the customers that would be so happy to give us their details through their computer. **I was wrong.** We had a village Post Office that would take the parcels for delivery to the customer for us; I just knew, too, that the Post Office would be so grateful for the extra business that our local shop would bring to them. **I was wrong on that one, too.**

Our suppliers, too, would be happy; they would be eternally grateful to us as we were enabling people from John O' Groats to Land's End and not living near shops, to be able to get their products within a few days. Well that's what I thought, anyway; how wrong could I have been?

# Get Your Recipe Right

You have just a moment in time to get your recipe right, and then you should make your cake. To be in business reminds me of when I was working for the Co-op bakery when I was 17 years old, with the world at my feet. All the business did was to make bread and cakes; people ate them, and they made some more; simple, day after day.

Get the ingredients right and you have success; get it wrong and you fail. You're saying, "I know that, everybody knows that." Well, if everybody knows that, why do so many people fail? It's because they have not thought about just how many ingredients go into making the cake. It would have been impossible to start an Internet business from nothing at that time in the history of the Internet, and propel it to the number-one independent nursery retailer in Europe, without having all the ingredients that we had stored up over the years.

What we were doing was going to turn the nursery industry on its head; nobody, not even us, knew this at the time. Unbeknown to everybody, we were at the start of the UK's biggest retail shake-up of all time.

# Why Have a Pension?

SIDETRACKED

When I first realised we had had got about £200,000 in the nine pensions, I was annoyed, as we had still got another 17 years before we could start drawing the money as a pension. I didn't want to waste any of it through erosion, sitting in some bank account just going down in value over those 17 years. Now we were thinking of expanding again, we could transfer all of the pensions into one, which was called a self-invested personal pension, or SIPP, and that meant we could control it ourselves under some very strict rules. I didn't mind that; as long as I was able to make the money work for us, it would be great.

The rules were that you could buy commercial property in this SIPP, and get a 50% mortgage but, with only £200,000 it wouldn't get us very far and, if we saved up in the normal way, it would take us years to accumulate enough, after paying tax, to buy anything substantial like we needed.

Now, after three years of strict financial constraints, around 1998 we suddenly found we had over £430,000 extra profit that year. I had the mind set needed to manipulate money; I may have been dyslexic, but I knew how to put money to good use, and Marilyn trusted me implicitly with every penny, like I trusted her with the decision-making in relation to the rest of the business. So we put the £430,000 into our pensions as, in those days, you could go back six years and reclaim your tax that had been paid, consequently getting a £215,000 tax refund. We did that again in 1999, reclaiming around £240,000 of tax, so we did benefit from paying our taxes. It was **"a window of opportunity"** at the time, not to be missed.

# The First Car-Seat Fitter

BACK

We were not only short of retail space, we were short of car-parking too. We also needed six dedicated parking bays for baby-car-seat fitting, something that I had done since starting the business; a company called Securon had just brought out the first child's car seats that needed to be bolted into the car, and I am pretty sure that I was the first person in the UK to fit them.

The customers would park their car in the bus stop in front of the shop. By then, most cars had holes under the back seats; if not, drilling would take place, bolts would go through the holes and I would lie under the car while Marilyn would be in the car, holding the bolt while keeping an eye on the shop as I tightened the nut up. All this would be done for free.

We made all of our customers aware, right from the 70s, that every child had to be in an appropriate restraint for their age, years before any legislation came in, but it was an uphill struggle to persuade mothers not to put their babies in between themselves and their seatbelts, as a baby could be killed in an accident by doing this.

We also told people to put restraints on the baby in the carry-cot when in the car as, in an accident, the baby would fly out of the carry-cot and go through the window. Sadly, some people thought that we were just trying to make an extra £2.99 sale. In the end, we put the harness in with the product and told them it was a free gift from us.

## The Second Stand-Alone Warehouse

I never liked stand-alone warehouses - they were a waste of time for me; all that time spent travelling back and forth. We needed to utilise the time to the maximum, and time & motion was always a part of our success.

In 1999 we bought a 15,000 sq ft warehouse on 1.5 acres of land for £500k. In 1992 it was for sale at £240k but, at that time, it was too much money for us. If we had taken a mortgage out it would have paid for itself; maybe I couldn't get a mortgage on it, or perhaps I didn't think - who knows? The same day, we exchanged on three acres of land next to the warehouse for £150,000; this was from the pension money and, over the next three years, we put virtually all of the profits into the pension to not only get tax relief, but to also build a new store sometime in the future.

With the purchase of this building we were set up for the future forever, as we had already purchased, in 1992, a 2,500 sq ft warehouse on the industrial park near the village when we were re-building the shop. Within months, we had doubled the size and, by 1994, had bought the two adjacent buildings, making 15,000 sq ft in total. All of these buildings were stocked to the roofs, all tidy and well-organised, with date stamps on boxes. Every single box was sold in strict rotation as we had seen, early on in the Orton shop, that when we had hundreds of pushchairs returned, it was best not to mix stock up as it would prolong any product recalls that might occur in the future.

## December 1999. The Internet Went Live

Scott and Barrie had been working to open up the website ready for Christmas Day. Scott was still doing this while working in London; I am sure that, at the time, he didn't think there would ever be enough work for it to be a full-time job for him. When we got the first order of a Maclaren pushchair, wow, what a great feeling for everybody after so much time and money had been spent on it. This was an extra to our everyday business; it reminded me of my window-cleaning days, when I could get another house in before it got too dark to see.

This was a whole lot different, though; this system would work 1440 minutes a day for us with no hassle, no sales people, no sickness, no lighting or heating at nights when the orders were coming in; in fact, no extra overheads. Again, we had two businesses for the price of one; fantastic, so easy, and so simple.

Once you have a working business that is successful, all you have to do is bolt another allied business to it, using the infrastructure that you have already; therefore, all of the profit drops to the bottom line; well, in theory anyway.

*Christmas party for 150 people; staff, their partners and our friends. From the left: me, Scott, Gadget, Dad, Barry, head of Security, and Marilyn. On the table behind Gadget were Sandra and Clive Kent, the people who looked after us at home. Elaine took the picture.*

# Money for Nothing

So we were off on another exciting roller-coaster journey. The orders were coming in, and gradually going up from three or four a day, to ten, then twenty. Over the first three months, each day we would walk down the road to our tiny village Post Office to send the parcels off. Then we started to send our van; one day the van came back with the parcels still inside - the post person had thrown their rattle out of their pram, which I can't blame them for as we had filled their shop completely with our parcels, which included large prams, and cots too; now no one could enter their shop, so we had no option but to take our parcels to the main sorting office.

# Don't Accept Road Blocks

Then, every day, we had to take the van to the main post office; then two trips, until we got to the point of employing a carrier. That's when we realised there were more unforeseen cogs to this wheel as, in 2000, there were very few carriers that took parcels direct to customers' houses, and the ones that did were either very expensive or wouldn't take large products like ours. So with us being so small, all we were left with were companies that couldn't do the job properly, so we then started to get items broken during transit, which were then returned to us at our expense. We didn't think this was right.

# A Massive Learning Curve

Six months into this we were sending out fifty orders a day, which could be anything up to two hundred items. Carriers would turn up in a mini-van then, in desperation, they would send a 40ft lorry. One day in October of 2000, they had sent us an extra lorry as we had so much stock to send out; this lorry had been delivering waste oil. We didn't see the oil that had leaked, as it was dark when it turned up, but we knew about it two days later, when calls from the customers, together with the bills for compensation, started to roll in; the oil had got on their clothes and in their homes - a nightmare.

Eleven months had now passed, the shop was busy, and the Internet was attracting more customers; lots of people in those days were starting to look on the Internet, but no way would most people trust giving their credit card number online. Nevertheless, the Internet was a great advertising tool for us, as it attracted more people into the store.

The Internet at that time was just a sideline that became an irritation, because 99% of our problems were to do with that; we were fire-fighters when it came to that part of the business, which looked so easy on that first day.

The new 15,000 sq ft building we had bought by using the pension money was now full of stock; it was packed to bursting point, which meant we needed another floor or some racking put in. We chose a floor, because racking would be too time-consuming to pick goods from. We were using the warehouse as a 'just in time' facility for the main shop, which worked perfectly for us; we had been perfecting this type of operation since 1992, when we got our first real stand-alone warehouse as a temporary measure while we were re-building the shop.

## Could Anything Else Go Wrong?

Every day we would come up against new problems, as this was all new to us; in fact, it was new to the world, too, and we were part of it, pioneering in something that would change retailing forever.

We had new staff members who helped pick and pack the goods; they had no supervision, as we were extremely busy and, inevitably, they sometimes picked the wrong products. The mistakes were causing big problems and chaos, as we had to uplift incorrect items or, if the cost to us was less than £10, we would just tell the customer to keep it, as it would cost us more to get it back. We then had to send the right product out; these errors alone were costing us thousands each week.

One day I went into the service department when I saw about twenty cots that had come back from customers they were broken, and I could clearly see the footprints where the carriers had walked over the boxes. At this point we were getting about 70% of the goods back, either because of our mistakes or because the goods were being damaged due to inadequate packaging or damage by the careless carriers.

## In 2000 This New Internet Was Rubbish

This could not carry on so, one day, when Scott had come back from his job in London we had a meeting, Marilyn, Elaine, Joanne, Scott and I, to discuss the situation. Then, after discussing every problem the Internet had caused, we decided that we should close it and just keep going with the shop; after all, shops were the normal way of retailing, although we were not normal.

None of us could see a way out of this situation, so we each took a vote; the answer from all of us was to close it down. The mood was one of despair, and cutting our losses seemed to be the only way out. Then I had second thoughts, because there had been so much effort put into the project from everybody, especially Scott as he was still working in London, and I had said "You can do this for us," nearly 3 years before.

I said, "Give me one week to turn it around and turn it from a loss into a profit." Everybody agreed. I think they were just being nice, letting me prove the Internet was not a profitable business; if I had said a month, it would have fallen on deaf ears, but a week was OK - then we would shut it down. The reason I was doing this was that I had remembered that we had been through a similar situation one year after we had started the business, with virtually the same scenario as this, so we had got a bit of experience. I knew deep down they all wanted it to survive, but only with a profit.

## Take a Step Back

Having agreement from everybody, and our backs against the wall, there was not a single minute to spare; time was of the essence so, with that, we left the meeting and went straight to Barrie, who was sitting at his desk. I explained the situation which, to be quite honest, everybody knew already. I asked how many products we had on the site, and Barrie said around 500. How many had we had any problems with, no matter what they were? The reply was about 350. I said they had to be taken off-line now. How many products were in multiple boxes and had to be re-boxed? The answer was around 60. I said to take them off-line. So, after the first hour, there were only around 90 products out of 500 left online. As we were going through this process I began to think nothing would be left and, if that happened, there would be no business.

## Throw the Products Down the Stairs

Elaine, Jo, John and I examined samples of the 90 products we had left online, checking to see that all of the packaging was good. Just to make sure, I threw them down the two flights of concrete stairs to see if they broke. I did that because I was so paranoid that customers should receive the product in perfect condition.

I thought that if the samples survived that treatment, then we could put the product on the Internet and it would get to the customer intact. That packaging became the standard for all the packaging on every product that we have sent out ever since then.

Every single product that went out that week had come in from the manufacturer in a single box that was in virtually damage-proof packaging, and, on top of that, Jo, Elaine, and John picked and double-checked every order before it went out.

Within a week there were no returns, and what we had sent out, we made a profit on.

Wow!! So, in just one week, we had turned a loss-making part of the business into profit. Looking back, it was so easy to do, but it's just a case of standing still and asking yourself where you are right now, and where you want to be. I had done that in seconds sitting in the meeting, and then taken the first step to get it going. We had now created a standard that was reliable to build upon.

## *"First do a risk assessment, and then do a method statement"*

### *This only takes minutes.*

## Stand Still, Look! Don't Panic, Then Act

We had got carried away, thinking that everything we sold would be treated with care when it came to be delivered. This caused us problems and aggravated customers and, consequently, we lost money. As soon as we stood still, looked at what was going wrong and acted upon it, we started to make money again.

Every day after that we were fanatical about quality of product packaging, and the partner to deliver the goods; this was really the first time I had thought of another company as being a partner, whether when delivering products or when manufacturing for us, and even to how it was packaged. This was so important after that.

We had now been in business 25 years, and we had implemented great standards, but this was the first time I had considered the importance of working in partnership with our suppliers of goods and services; this is probably one of the things that saved us in the recession that was to hit us eight years later.

From that day, we would ask reps to have products like pushchairs and car seats packed in single boxes instead of in 4s, and to put products into thicker boxes. When we were told it would cost more, we said it was cheaper than getting it broken. I think that, over the next few years, it was us that changed the way nursery products were packaged within the industry, which was to benefit everyone.

## A Rejection Can Be Great

There was at first a lot of opposition to putting products into new packaging, because we were the only ones asking for it. They couldn't do it just for us, so, in those situations, we had our own new boxes made and just put one box inside the other. One good thing came out of this - we were able to have them printed with our name and what Kiddicare did, advertising the website and the shop to everyone who handled or saw the box all over the country.

It was a blessing in disguise when some companies refused to make better packaging for us. We weren't going to accept this, and it made us even more determined to run our business without them.

## Property and Retail, Same Principles

It was a very similar situation to that which we had in the property business in the 1970s, when we realised that it would be better to just work on our own property and not do other people's work, as there would be a limit to what we could charge.

We needed to be in total control of our Kiddicare business, only choosing to do business with the people who could see where we were going in this trade, and being in control ourselves by manufacturing and selling our own brands, enabling our profit margins to rise.

## We Just Re-boxed Their Products

In the meantime, we would just re-box their products ourselves, knowing that their other customers were nowhere near us and would have to go through the same obstacles as us if they were to follow this path which, by then, we knew they would have to because we could see that retail businesses were definitely going in one direction, and that was down the drain.

## We Were Leading the Field

From that first hour of changing the way we did business on the Internet we knew that we were in the lead of the nursery Internet field. Manufacturers would say to us, "You are the only company that is asking for this change, or having these problems." We knew that if others were doing what we were, they would eventually be asking for and saying the same thing as us.

Every day we would be adding product online but, with the setback that we had, we were so cautious not to go back, so consequently we had an uphill struggle because every conversation we had with a manufacturer was the same - get the packaging better. ***"simple"***

If they took notice of us, the changes would take at least 4-6 months to implement and, in the meantime, we got used to repackaging stuff ourselves. The wonderful thing was that we all believed that this was now the future in retailing - for the masses to have access to products that, before, they could only dream of.

We constantly looked at not only what our business was doing today, but also what we wanted it to look like in five years' time, transporting our minds into the future. Getting the recipe right was crucial; then, tweaking the ingredients to suit the customer tastes, we found success. If we then repeated the things that worked every day, and stopped the things that didn't work, every day, and then trained the right people to help, we then could be the best independent nursery business in the world.

We were the first to deliver the next day, the first to text-message our customer to say the goods were on the van and on the way to their house, and I was the first to give a 365-day money-back guarantee. We were the first to give timed delivery slots, and lots more to make the customer's experience memorable.

I was able to put myself into our customers' shoes and so make a system that would answer any of their questions with a "yes"; now if we couldn't do that, then I knew what to work on. Sometimes this was difficult, which was good because it meant I needed to think outside the box and train staff in the art of selling only our own-brand goods.

Most of the time it worked, but some got away, very often to return after having thought about our offering, in many cases due to the sheer facts that the staff were outstanding in their knowledge of the products and their seamless customer service between every department was so well-driven by the managers' and staff's loyalty and dedication to us.

# The Retail Environment

The 80s and 90s Saturdays in our shop were equivalent to what a Black Friday is nowadays, but we just took it in our stride, not knowing that this way of life was not the "norm" in all of the other nursery retailers. We didn't open on a Sunday or a Monday, so the customers were restricted to when they could come to us, consequently filling the shop when open and causing a buying frenzy as, when customers saw the products that they were looking at being marked down on the product ticket, the fear of loss kicked in, forcing them to buy but always knowing they could get their money back.

# An Industry Going Into Turmoil

## *"The traditional way was about to go for ever"*

By 2001 our business was going crazy; we had vans and staff flying backwards and forwards moving stock around our 55,000 sq ft of warehouses and shop, which were all packed to the rafters. We needed to expand again and the building Marilyn & I had purchased in the pension was ideal to build a 50,000 sq ft shop and warehouse combined. So off we went to the planners and, as you know by now what I am going to say, yes, they didn't want to grant permission; again we were up against bureaucracy. All our efforts to build a business employing lots of people seemed to hit a brick wall.

So I put my thinking-cap back on; what could we do to persuade them that we were a special case? At the time there was a big thing about not giving planning permission to out-of-town retail; well, I say that - maybe all of the big stores had got their permissions before the ban came in. I tried to tell the planners that we were already an out-of-town retailer and we just wanted to go a few hundred metres down the road, but I forgot to tell them the new building would be ten times larger.

The Council told us to find a retail unit in Peterborough centre; there were no 50,000 sq ft units anywhere in town, so that was out of the question. Then they said we should work from several sites, which we were doing already anyway; this was proving to be impractical and uneconomical and, by then, we needed a much larger building for efficiency and economy.

Our deliveries each day were going to our main warehouse, from where we would ferry the stock into the village with our small vans; this was to keep the 40-foot-container lorries out of the village, as we were mindful of keeping the peace with the residents. So, with the Council's reluctance to let us move, we were stuck. Then, one day, a delivery truck did not turn up from the docks and someone had wasted their time waiting for it at the warehouse.

I had the bright idea of making all of our deliveries come into the village store, then go on to one of our warehouses to unload; that made it up to 20 lorries now coming in and out of the village each day. We informed the Council of the lorry movements in the hope that they would recognise a health and safety issue and grant us permission, but guess what? They didn't.

# Things Had Come To a Head

One day, I booked five lorries in at 3pm and started to unload them all. We took photos of lorries reversing out of our car park onto the main road; it was at the same time as lots of children were coming out of the school opposite, and going over the crossing. We had asked the police to be there too, and make a case for us having a need to move.

We sent all of the photos off to the Council with a very long letter which came from my heart, telling the story and history of Marilyn and myself starting the business in that terraced house and how far we had come, and our dreams for the future. This went to the head of the Council, explaining that we were a local family business and that we deserved the same as the nationals.

## A New World for the Nursery Industry

*Marilyn had her office over the entrance. In 2002, to have built a baby store of 55,000 sq ft was incredible; in 2003 we added another 20,000 sq ft warehouse then, in 2004, we added another 20,000 on to that.*

Something worked. We must have touched a nerve somewhere with planning, as we were assigned a person to deal with the application; we started building six months later, which took another year to complete. We moved in on 10<sup>th</sup> December 2002; this was another milestone in our lives never to be forgotten.

We just couldn't believe how far we had come in such a short time. Life was really great and we couldn't wish for anything better. We became friends with one of the site contractors, who had done a million pounds of work on the site's foundations and roads; he asked if we had ever been on a cruise. Since then, in the last 12 years, we have travelled the world with Roy and Sue.

*Just some of the people celebrating with us at the party*

On 8th December 2002 the move to the new store went well, with a brilliant opening party inside a marquee inside the new warehouse for all the staff, suppliers and friends on the Sunday night.

SIDETRACKED

In a complete contrast to Roy, the builders I hired to do the fit-out had everything except their horses; they were cowboys who cost us £160,000 that we could ill afford to lose, but it would have been twice as much if my friend Jon Nugent, who is a quantity surveyor and disputes arbitrator, hadn't have stepped in and helped. I felt hurt when this happened, as I trusted that they would do what was agreed and were paid for. We had two choices: go to court, wasting lots of time and losing more money by not focusing on the business, or just carry on focusing and working on the business.

# Another Lot of Bullshitters

At the end of the day they were just another lot of bullshitters, and it was my fault for hiring them. I was in a hurry to get the job done, and I gave them the benefit of doubt that I had when I saw one of the jobs that they had done. It was appalling, but they said that someone else had come in after they had finished the job and messed it up, and I wanted to believe them. This type of thing just made us more determined to succeed so, with focusing on the things that counted we not only made that money up in what seemed to be no time, we also had our best year ever to that point.

BACK

As for me, I didn't need a desk; there were so many exciting things for me to do. I liked being everywhere and, as long as I was working with my girls, Elaine and Jo, then I was happy. I had worked with Jo over the last year building the store, and now she would be working in every department from forklift-truck driving to serving customers. There wasn't a thing she wouldn't do when it came to running the physical side of the business, helping the managers with their everyday situations, whether it was to do with goods in or out, service, or the shop floor.

The shop floor was where Jo excelled, especially with the customers. I had so many wonderful comments from customers about Jo, how she had served them, and they would say, "Your company should hang on to her, because she is so good." I used to be thinking, "I know, she's my daughter and I am so lucky - I've got two of them." When they both got on the shop floor selling, there was no stopping them, the place just rocked. Between them they created a buying frenzy; customers would be waiting for each of the staff to finish serving so they could get the chance of buying something, and the staff, in turn, would be interrupting Jo and Elaine to get a special price. All of this was pure theatre.

All of the staff would ask for a bit more discount for their customer, which gave the customer an extra experience that they could take away to tell their friends. In turn, the customers became our very own dedicated sales people, by telling the story of how extraordinarily they were treated in such a busy environment; and at the heart of it were our two wonderful girls.

# Creating Space Like a Magic Trick

Making room for stock was a daily occurrence for us, but there were always unexpected deliveries of ten 40-ft containers that were in the docks, which some big company or other had cancelled from their supplier. That supplier then unfortunately had to get rid of these goods fast, and this is where Elaine helped them out by buying the stock. By doing so, she very often would get it for half price on the terms that it had to go into our full and overflowing warehouse the very next day.

I always knew when she was about to buy an enormous quantity of something; she would ring me and say, "Have we got any money? Like £120,000 to spare, and can you make room for between six and ten containers?"

Another thing that she would say was, "You need to come into the office and see this," which meant, "I'm not telling you unless you are sitting down." She knew the answer would always be "yes", and that I could always magic the room and the money where there wasn't any, providing the deal was right for everyone concerned.

Within minutes of doing the deal, Elaine, Jo and I would be in the warehouse with a team that we had gathered from other areas of the business to help make room; these were special people like Christine, Sharon, Mia, Lynne and Jackie, plus Barry Security and Barrie Gadget; they were never afraid of hard work.

I am so proud of my girls because they would, at the drop of a hat, come and help me; they weren't afraid of hard work, and time meant nothing to them - they would do the job no matter how long it took, and with unbelievable pride and enthusiasm. It was not only our lives that the business consumed; it was so for the girls and boys of Kiddicare too.

Around 2002 Scott's work in London came to an end and he was realising that working in Kiddicare would be better than in London. He had said that he didn't like travelling on the Underground in the summer. Elaine had always said that she wanted to work with him, but she didn't like the type of work he was doing. She thrived in the retail world, alongside Jo; they had the freedom in the business to make a difference. With all four of us pushing in the same direction, it made the business a success, and now there would be five heads.

Halfway through the build I decided to build another 20,000 sq ft unit at the end of the car park to rent out as an investment but, by the time we had moved into the main building it was full, so we started to use the other building, but only temporarily, for only a week or so; but of course that never happened - over the next year, we filled that as well.

By now we had spent £2,250,000 on the building; we had a £750,000 mortgage on this through our pension. If we had bought this building like we had the previous ones, we would have had to have earned £3,000,000 instead of the £1,500,000 tax free, as we were in the 50% tax bracket due to us being sole traders and not having a limited company.

There were some advantages to having a pension, especially this one that we hadn't known about because, without those nine pensions Marilyn and I had paid into at £20 or £30 a month, we would never have had the idea of making a self-invested personal pension (SIPP) that we were able to put hundreds of thousands of tax-free profits into, and also at the same time reclaim six years of back tax; like a loan, really.

Because we employed more people and made more profit, this in turn attracted far more tax than before; the system worked for us at that time - it was a window of opportunity that isn't around now.

This was all legal because the government makes the rules; we just have to see the opportunity when the time is right, seizing the moment before it, or the opportunity disappears forever and you are left saying, "I should have."

# A Job for Jackie

BACK

There's a job for everyone in the world, it's just a matter of finding it. Just after we moved we had been taking on more staff. A girl came in and said she had been made redundant from the factory next door and had we got any warehouse jobs? I said there were none in the warehouse, so I gave her a job on the shop floor. In those days we just had men in the warehouse, although Elaine, Jo, Marilyn and all the long-serving staff had no problem working in there but, as it was getting busy, I didn't want to put new staff in the warehouse as it was such hard and often dirty work, so it wasn't conducive with sending staff on to serve people in the shop as well as working in the warehouse.

After two weeks, Jackie came to see me to give in her notice. She said that there was no way she could work in a shop, and she was going to look for a job in a warehouse. There was something about her that told me not to accept her notice, so I asked her why. She said that she was used to a production line managing forty people, so she could work on picking and packing products. I said we had not picked and packed anything for a year.

I couldn't bear to think that the customer would get the wrong products ever again, and that we would lose money again. People would have to wait until such time as we got a foolproof system, but that was just another thing on the IT to-do list. There were now eight people in that department, who were producing probably the same amount of work as forty people in a large organisation. We had now perfected the picking system, which was one product per box as it had come in from the manufacturer; the only downfall was that we had to have staff who knew every one of the 1000 products by eye as, again, bar-coding was on the to-do list, which would take another few years to implement. Luckily, we had by now some very good staff who knew what they were doing.

I wanted to keep this girl; I could see in her eyes that she had the will and determination to succeed.

So, I had Jackie standing in front of me intimating that she could do the job blindfolded, standing on her head, and I believed her. There were about 3000 items to go at but, with so many different sizes and types of things, I said I would choose six items like rain covers and pram mattresses that go with prams and pushchairs that customers had repeatedly asked us to send over the last twelve months; we would try it for one week.

## The Internet Took Off

One week passed and the six items had gone up to eighteen, and she was still there. I was worried that Jackie would leave through boredom, and I would be back to square one, so, each day, Barrie Gadget would put more small stuff online which just flew out of the door. Jackie then needed an assistant, and then another; within a year she had six staff, and I could see that she was happy. She became our Warehouse Manager in 2008 and, in 2010 she was responsible for £35 million worth of stock coming in and £40 million going out.

I had found out years ago that to have and keep happy staff it was all about fitting people to the things they liked; then they excelled, like the vast amount of staff who worked in Kiddicare.

Newcomers generally applied for a job that was advertised but, once they had been there for a while, we found out what they were interested in and capable of doing. They then stayed, just like Barry Herbert; he applied for a job in the warehouse but, after he caught a thief, he told us he had worked in Oxford Street as a security officer. From that moment on he was our Security Manager, and has been so for 17 years. He took recordings from 56 cameras that showed a thief entering the car park, stealing from the store and going out, putting them on to one disc for the police to prosecute them.

## Suddenly the Industry Mood Changed

In 2003, the mood changed in the industry; it seemed to come overnight - all of a sudden, the people who were running the independent shops in the UK had woken up to the Internet, while we had been working away silently at perfecting our systems.

I made Gadget a photography studio; now I wanted him to make videos of products, as some prams were complicated to fold and having a video demo would stop accidental breakage. My mind was racing; I had always put myself into the shoes of our customers, but now this was a bit different from before, when we were standing in front of the customer having given them a cup of tea, then transferring our feeling for a product on to them.

We needed to do exactly the same thing with the Internet, but now we had to do this remotely; a picture and just a price were not good enough - some sites never even had a picture in those days, which was appalling. I was the customer, so I knew what to do, but transferring it to the Internet was down to the team.

## My Wish List

As a customer I wanted to see the product as a picture with a full description, a price not only for one but a discount for buying more. I wanted to see six accessories or related products on the same page, to remind me of what I also needed to buy. I wanted to see not only if it was in stock, but how many were in stock. I wanted to know, if I bought it now, exactly when it would arrive. I needed an easy returns procedure, and my money putting back into my bank immediately. I wanted to contact someone if I had a query or a problem, and I wanted the phone to be answered within three rings; plus, I wanted the person on the end of the line to be knowledgeable about not only the product but also the business. I wanted them to be able to make a decision regarding my call immediately, whatever it was, and I wanted my question answered with a "yes".

That was the basis of the wish list, which went on and on; the list was huge when we put all of the wants in, such as advertising, credit cards, and fraud. All the integration that was needed for what we all wanted meant the team would have to build a new website, as we had outgrown the first one, just like all of the buildings that we had grown out of along the way.

All of this information came from Marilyn, Elaine, Joanne, and me, all as buyers on the ground with more experience of the nursery trade than all the nationals put together. We then fed all of it to Scott to implement with his IT department.

## Please Take My Customers

The more we did, the more other retailers complained to the suppliers about us supposedly taking their sales; but when we looked into this, most of the people who were complaining hadn't got the stock and didn't understand, even if they had been in the trade for 30 years, that the retail environment was changing, and fast. It was the customer who made the choice of where to buy, and the Internet opened up a whole new avenue once they had made up their minds to buy; they wanted it now, not in three months' time and, as we had the stock to deliver the next day, we got the sale.

It was the KISS principle - keep it simple, buy the stock, advertise it, sell it; don't demo something and let the customer go elsewhere. The shops that did this were just giving their customers away to us. I even told some of them that if they didn't want to stock the products, they could order from our website, have us deliver to their customer the next day and we would give them half the profit, but no one took up the offer. I think they were afraid we would steal that customer. I was looking for a win for them by us sharing their customer, but they couldn't see they would lose them anyway.

I told our suppliers that complained to us many times about undercutting prices, to sell more products into the complaining shops; I believed that, if they had the stock, their customers would buy from them and not from us, but they said the other shops would not put money into stock before they had got an order. And besides, they said that their profit margins were being eroded and they didn't see why they should sell for less. Arthur should have told them, like he told me at the age of thirteen, to "Speculate to accumulate."

## Don't Bury Your Heads

Most of the independent retailers saw what was happening but buried their heads in the sand, preferring to keep things as they had been in the past; they wanted to keep tradition alive, with usually one nursery shop in each town with very little competition.

We, on the other hand, knew that wasn't going to happen. We were looking to the future and what was going to happen and, if we were to ignore progress, we would fail. This was a major turning point for the whole of the retail industry.

This reminded me of the conversation with Mr Smeeton in the 1970s, when there was about to be a shift in the housing markets in the UK; although we stood together that day having that conversation, his mind was just at the end of an era, and mine was just before the beginning of the new one. I have always thought that if you get accused enough of something, you might as well do it, and we were accused of undercutting everyone.

Again, most of the trade were just waking up to this. They thought that the Internet was new, but we had already been working on this by now for seven years, and now we were working on our second-generation website and planning the third in our minds. We had been quietly working, doing our own thing, going forward one day at a time, making sure that our business was a little different, on leaving each night, from what it was when we entered it in the morning. We did this every day, day in and day out.

## Kiddicare Sunblinds Travelled the World

My mind never stopped thinking of how we could leverage whatever we were doing. One day, I saw some sun-blinds in a car, advertising Boots, which didn't tell me anything. I had always known Mothercare had the same thing too, but again, it lacked a call to buy. Also, everybody sold these things and, at that time, we were selling sun-blinds advertising our suppliers.

Then the penny dropped that we were crazy to sell sun-blinds advertising another business; why not advertise our own? The KISS principle comes to mind; this was at just the right time for us as, by now, we had thousands of customers with cars all over the country.

Not only that, we decided that we would be the only company to give them away with every car seat that we sold.

## National Mobile Advertising for Pennies

Another first: we designed our own sun-blind with *Kiddicare.com* at the top. Elaine made the "com" into a funky pushchair; I wanted a matchstick family below, so Jo designed a dad, mum, and two kids with a dog, and Elaine came up with a tag-line saying, "Big savings for little people," all perfectly positioned so the words were all visible. We had 5,000 made at a cost of £2.50 each, with a retail price of £7.99, the same price that others were selling at. One small difference - I had decided to give these away with each car seat, which cost us £12,500. They lasted just two months, and that's when we realised just how many car seats we were now selling.

The next order was for 20,000, and we halved the cost price. Very soon, new customers were telling us that they had seen the blinds, and that's how they found us. This was great. Another thing we did was advertise our name on all of the thousands of boxes that Jackie sent out; we also gave a free Kiddicare car-seat bag away with every car seat, which would pop up all over the world on the airport conveyer-belts. We had so many people saying they had seen our name in all parts of the world.

One day it was time to put another order in for more sun-blinds; we knew they brought in customers, but they had to see the side of the car, mostly when they were in car parks. I wanted them to be seen on the road, and the only way to do that was to make one for the back window. Rodney Cottrell, a supplier of ours for many years, found a manufacturer that would do a set of three with a minimum quantity of 60,000 sets. Nobody was doing a set of three. Now we could have an advert in another 60,000 cars, but this time the cost had come down to an incredible 60p. We had mugs printed with "I love Kiddicare.com," that we gave away; we wanted a reminder of where to get nursery equipment from at every touch and turn.

We were still acting like a mum-and-dad local nursery shop in a national arena; there was no way that we were competing with the majority of the independent shops, they just got stuck in a bad place between us and the nationals. The nationals could compete only on price, as the content on their websites fell well behind ours. I remember at that time that we were amazed at how many major companies, not just in our sector, were so far behind; more disturbing to me was that they were non-existent when it came to the Internet.

# We Were Doing Our Own Thing

Twenty years before this, when John Lewis came in to Peterborough in 1980, they seemed to be always looking for trouble by undercutting us; but we could run rings around them by always putting packages together like "buy a pram and get a cot free." This they could not get their heads around and, by the time they did, we would be on to the next offer; they could only follow as we made up new multiple offers that totally confused them. But we won the customers because we had a secret weapon - our sales staff - which were way more educated in what they were selling compared to any of the national stores.

In 2003 the same game was being played, only this time it wasn't like behind closed doors in one town, one shop competing against another; it was the Internet. The Internet was for the whole world to see, that's what made the difference. Everybody got tangled up because there are very few nursery brand suppliers, so most shops stocked most brands and, with the big players not being able to think outside of the box or be creative, they had only one option, which was to compete on prices, dragging all of the industry into a massive playground scrap. Looking back, this was nothing to what was in waiting for the nursery industry over the following eight years.

## Don't Fight It; Do Your Own Thing or Die

Accept the things you cannot change, have the courage to change the things you can, and have the wisdom to know the difference. I spent years trying to change things that were impossible in a lot of cases, but I did change a lot, especially in myself. By this time in life, however, I was becoming wise to the difference in what was going on around me. We were being told what to do by some of our suppliers; if you have got this far, I think you will know what my thoughts are on this matter - they could go and play with themselves.

Dictators were coming into the industry, mostly, I think, from the supermarket arena. They would become the sales manager or the CEO of a company that we had done business with for years without problems, and then this person who knew nothing about the nursery industry would tell us what they were going to do, whether we liked it or not. They wanted to fix the prices or, we were told, we would lose the brand; normally we would have two options, lose the brand, or lose the sales if you fixed the price. Bullying springs to mind.

For us, there was a third option not normally open to most businesses, which was to create a new brand and manufacture the products ourselves, a completely new direction, for we had seen inexperienced people like us going down that route only to go bust through having been stitched-up by unscrupulous manufacturers, who cut costs by using soft rivets, cheap material and bad stitching. For a moment in time we didn't know which way to turn, but we knew that if we didn't act fast and make decisions, we would end up being dictated to, and eventually lose our independence.

## Dammed If You Do or Don't

Everything was moving so fast in the trade. We had burned our fingers so many times with buying crap product, or product that just wouldn't sell because we had similar stuff that was so much cheaper. I traded with an old Jewish guy once, buying just a few bits because I liked him. When his sons took over, I found it a job to buy because of the quality and consequently I told their rep the truth.

I think it became twisted by the time it got back to them, that they needed to get some quality stuff in their range. Well, they got a new brand, called "I Candy", which he presented to us, but instead of trying it, I said that I would wait until they had got over the inevitable teething troubles that they would have. This product became the industry must-have, literally overnight and, when we asked for it, they were delighted, reading between the lines, to tell us to go and \*\*\*\* ourselves. ***I do hope that whatever I said about their products in the early days spurred them on to get their business right. Sometimes it sounds like criticism, and then the messenger who should get a thank-you is shot.***

# We Accepted What Was

## *"We each have our own agenda - some are a win-win, some are stupid"*

We needed to find an easier way, and we needed to find it fast, as Marilyn and I were not going to be dictated to over what we could and could not do with our own business. With hindsight, the people who were dictating to us saved us; they were the best thing that could have happened at that time, and doing this to us was really great - it gave us no choice but to go ahead and create our own brands.

There is a saying that when a butterfly flaps its wings on one side of the world it has an effect on the other; well, these butterflies were a lot nearer to home. I think that they were stupid; they should have invested in our business instead of trying to make us lie down and conform. If any of them had just stopped for a minute and looked at the past, they would have known that we were the future and that they could have been part of it.

## The Nursery Industry Battle Had Begun

We had dabbled for a few years, from the late 1980s, with own-brand Kiddicare baby goods and then, after 1999, *Kiddicare.com* goods too. However, we kept it to soft goods like bedding, and things that didn't go wrong. A few years earlier, when we had a disaster with the disposable pushchair which had been imported from some dubious Chinese manufacturer, we had our fingers burned, but now it was getting to a crisis point, with suppliers refusing to supply us unless we had the highest prices and, as a consequence of this, other shops were undercutting us and even very often the ones that didn't have any stock, too. Once again, bullying tactics; the big boys against the independents. My brain went into chess mode; now to figure the moves - what would happen if, and then what to do to come up with a win–win answer.

The answer was easy - all we had to do was manufacture our own brand; but how? So, back with some CTT - creative thinking time - that really worked, as normal. We had now been in the business for 30 years; we had never been to China and wouldn't know where to start and, besides, we were retailers so didn't want the responsibility of looking for the best manufacturers and then having the hassle that goes with it. We wanted someone in between us and them. I knew we had no choice but to go down that road. ***"Easy".***

The next day, when a rep came in, there was only one conversation to be had. As with all of them, it was about prices, because we had put our prices up in line with their recommendation and we had stopped selling any of their products. I asked him who was now selling their goods, and he said no one; and yet, our overall sales were on the increase every week. This led me to believe that if we put a price up, the majority of customers would buy a different product. We looked at this with other suppliers and found the same; their sales had gone down with us, yet our overall sales on other products had gone up. So, this affected the suppliers more than the retailers - customers were generally buying a cheaper product in the same category.

So with that in mind, we asked one supplier if they would like to manufacture for us a product that was pretty much identical to their own brand, but with our name on it. I said that, in that way, they would keep their product on our shop floor without having the hassle from the rest of the trade about us cutting prices and, at the same time, they would also sell thousands of products that they had made for us. They agreed, and that opened the floodgates for us to expand our own brand.

We would get product that had been tried and tested from reputable factories, ones that other people had found and had done their due diligence on, all without us setting a foot into China. We did this with lots of suppliers and it worked incredibly well for both parties.

Our sales rocketed. Everyone was happy except for the brands that refused to manufacture for us, as their sales went down and, of course, the other retailers that had been complaining about us were now back in a price war against all the other retailers, undercutting prices on branded products, something they couldn't do on our own-brand products and, consequently, shops were now going bust.

## The Race to Change the Business Was On

We had been working for a few years with a guy called John Cotter, an agent for David Lowe, Ireland, who had been supplying us with a nursing chair that we had continually improved each time that we sold a container-load, which had 307 chairs in it. I knew that this was a win-win partnership; they wanted as much as us to get the best product to the customer, with no problems and at the best price and, like us, would do anything to ensure that happened. We all went to Ireland to meet David.

SIDETRACKED

Marilyn and I went over in our motor-home. Our friends Roy and Sue, who also had a motor-home, went as well. We travelled around the coast of Ireland for 30, mostly wet, days, and loved every minute of it, going to the local pubs each night, where there would be people turning up with their instruments and playing music; we would sing and dance the nights away.

We hired a boat and went fishing at dawn, an experience I had never had before - the mist rising from the water, the silence and then the geese taking off from the lake and just missing our heads. What a contrast to the crazy world that we lived in, where every second counted in a world where you were either going forward or going backwards; and backwards wasn't the place to be.

We caught trout and barbecued them for our supper. What a fantastic month, but any more and I would have been climbing the walls to get out; the peace was nice, but the excitement of business was better. And now, with our batteries charged, we were ready.

BACK

We had arranged to get to David in Dublin, have some Guinness, play a round of golf at Powerscourt, go out that evening to a place called Jonny Foxes in the hills outside of Dublin, and have a great time. The next day we would have a breakfast meeting at 8 am in a five-star hotel where Elaine, Scott and Jo would stay, as they were flying in early for the meeting; then we would go to David's showrooms, where their offices and warehouse were.

# The Day I Was Silent

We left Roy and Sue at the campsite where we were staying, and I drove the camper to the hotel. I parked on the busy forecourt, where there were three lanes of taxis and limousines. Doormen with top hats were greeting people. I can't remember getting there, but I can remember saying to Marilyn that I couldn't go in to the meeting, I felt so ill. She went in, and the doorman beckoned me to leave the forecourt; needless to say, I didn't. I put my hood over my head and lent across the steering wheel. The man knocked on my window and said, "Move". I locked the door and ignored his repeated requests as I could not speak to him. Marilyn then drove to David's showroom through Dublin in this 30-ft camper, telling me in a loud voice to never ever mix drinking Guinness and whiskey ever again. I really appreciated her wise words. Marilyn obviously thought that I was deaf when she conveyed to me the errors of my ways that I had already learned from the night before.

## A New Chapter

They discussed a vast range of product, while I sat there quietly with many cups of coffee. His company could oversee the manufacturing for us so, when we left two days later we had a range designed with the colours and quantity ordered for shipment in three months time under the *Kiddicare.com* brand. Then, after three months, right on time as planned, the stock came in as good as we had hoped for; this was the start of a continuous, never-ending cycle of expanding product ranges, making improvements along with dropping things that didn't work, e.g. whiskey and Guinness.

By 2004 things were going really well; a new website had been built and we were churning the products out of the main warehouse. We had once again changed our carriers to a company called DPD Interlink, which had a depot in Peterborough. Clive was the boss there and, once again, we had a real partner in him. As I have said before, it's people who make or break businesses in general.

The 20,000 sq ft warehouse that we had built with a view to renting out was now also full, as was the original 15,000 sq ft of buildings we had accumulated as temporary storage since 1992. We had a great system; most of the nursery equipment came through suppliers from China in 40ft containers and we would then unload them, usually getting forty pallets of stock. We then put two pallets of each product into the main warehouse; we had someone transferring eight assorted pallets of stock on a trailer pulled by a forklift truck from one warehouse to the 50,000 sq ft shop all day long, an unbelievably laborious job. We used to change staff around on that job each day until, one day, a ghost from my past appeared.

## Karma

SIDETRACKED

In the first chapter I spoke about teachers, bullies and bullshitters. Well, a new forklift-truck driver/warehouse man started and, as I was doing my daily inspection with the manager of that warehouse, I recognised this chap as a school bully, one who had stood outside my house with a gang when I was 13. He had a piece of twine and they said that they would hang me that afternoon. I was petrified that they would kill me, so I missed school, but I still feared that the teachers would cane me if I got caught. Well, how he stayed for two years I don't know; it was hot in the summer and cold in the winter. Backwards and forwards from one warehouse to another, all day every day, hour after hour, which I thought was a complete waste of life; well it would be for me, unless I could be utilising my time for another purpose as well as earning £8 an hour.

I remember one day I was in the warehouse, when the manager said who was off on holiday the next week, and guess who it was - him. So I went to him and asked where he was going; he said, "Nowhere; I am getting a garden shed instead of going on holiday, because I can't afford both." My thoughts were, "If only you had been nice with me, your life would have been far better," because it's not what you know, it's who you know and, in a lot of cases, like so many people in Kiddicare, he could have had the opportunity to have done what he liked doing - if he liked sheds, we could have had a shed division, as most families have sheds full of toys. But there we are; I should thank him for making my life hell at school, which motivated me.

BACK

Another person would be running around getting the next eight pallets onto the next trailer. Even though it was great to think that we were selling sixteen pallets of stock an hour, at the same time this frustrated me, but what could I do? I never expected we would ever need that space and, if I had, I would have built one larger building, although you don't know what you don't know. What we did know was that we would have struggled with the money, so we were right taking it one step at a time, even though the steps seemed to be rather quick.

The property side of the business was still very busy; as normal, we were always on the lookout for property deals. There was a new township going up on the south side of Peterborough; it was on the reclamation land that I had worked on from 1968 to 1971. There was a sports field that the London Brick Company had used for its workers that had not been excavated for clay; it lay alongside the main ring road of Peterborough.

I had tried to buy it in 2000, a site to put a new shop and warehouse on, but we were rejected as the owners wanted the best companies there, not independent mum-and-dad outfits like us. Some four years later, when I was talking to an agent about another piece of land, he suggested this site. He said the owners had changed their minds and they would allow us to buy it. Wow! They had come down in the world, or had we gone up? Having already built the new Kiddicare store on a site in Werrington, we decided to go ahead and buy six acres to build two warehouses as an investment to rent out, one to a pharmaceutical company, the other an information storage business.

## The Biggest Shop in the World

Then, when Elaine and Joanne saw where it was, they both said, "Will you build a new shop for us?" I thought long and hard about it for at least ten seconds before deciding to build a new shop. I wanted to do that, but hadn't mentioned it because I thought that Marilyn would say no, as we had just gone through another year of building, but she was as enthusiastic as everyone else. Besides, by then we thought it would be fun to build the biggest and the best baby nursery equipment business in the world.

It was there to be done; no one had done it before. I, fortunately, was given another chance in life, so to build this was just to say to myself, and others in the same position that I had been in, that, **"You can do it,"** and in the end we were there to share the journey.

We then had another two years of disruption with the building work on top of the day-to-day running of the business, but by now we were used to this - it was all part of growing a massive business.

Doing this every day for years and years inevitably puts a strain on you, everybody around you, and everybody wanting the best for the business. Now differing opinions were starting to emerge. When business is good you can ride over the day-to-day problems that you constantly get, but one day there will come a time when the tipping point kicks in and things all change.

By 2005 we had completely run out of space; all of the new warehouses were now full because we were buying more and more clearance stock. We were desperate for more space, and we needed it immediately, but we found it to be impossible to get another building in time as the deliveries were coming all day, every day.

The day came when we literally ran out of space; the lorry driver wanted to unload and the yard was full of stock that we couldn't get in the store, so I asked the supplier if he could leave the container lorry for a few days, so we could put it in the customers' car park.

They refused, saying that it was not their trailer and it now had a six-hour time limit to get back to the docks.

## Why Not Use 40-ft Lorry Trailers?

I had a thought - why not buy an old 40-ft lorry trailer? With that, I went to a local haulier just outside the village and bought a worn-out but dry trailer for £400; the guy delivered it that afternoon. The minute we positioned it in the car park, we drove the full container up to the back and transferred the stock into it. The next day we had the same problem, so I went back to buy some more, but he had only roadworthy ones at £2,000 each, which was too dear, so I set about looking for some.

I went on the Internet and came across a company which sold lorry trailers that had finished their lives on the road; they were for £700 a time, so I bought four and had them put in the car park. The next four container deliveries that day were transferred into the trailers, so I bought some more until we had filled the space with 35.

Normally, we got around 1400 items in a container, like pushchairs or travel-cots, so I figured that if we were to put another 50p on an item, that one product would pay for the trailer. Those trailers had no rates on them and, after about one month, each one had paid for itself. That's not a bad return, and we sold them three years later and got our money back because, by then, we had built another 20,000 sq ft extension. Never before or since have we had such low-cost storage.

## Space Drove Our Sales

When we looked for space to accommodate deliveries, if we saw only a few products left on a pallet and they were not coming back into stock again, we would reduce the price online and on the shop floor. Invariably, they would start to sell straight away, literally in a few minutes, leaving space for a new, full pallet. It annoyed some other retailers, as they thought we were discounting against them but we weren't, we were just making space, although, in turn, it increased sales, which were mostly on discontinued items.

# The Golden Goose

***"Our business was the goose that just kept on laying golden eggs"***

## We Were At the Top of the Market

Early in 2006, plans were being prepared for the new Kiddicare building in Hampton; at the same time, another much smaller building of 8,000 sq ft just across the road that was being built had just been completed by another developer. We bought it as an office for the Internet department and an office for Jo and me, as we would be overseeing the building project across the road.

We bought it for £710,000; then, no sooner had we bought it, than agent Jones had a tenant interested for £50,000 pa on a 10-year lease, so we abandoned our office plans and took the tenant. I thought that we had bought it at the top of the property market but, within a few days, we had an offer of £1,000,000, which was definitely at the very top of the market. What a dick I was not to sell as it's not worth that now.

We refused to sell, as we thought that we might want it in years to come for the future expansion of Kiddicare, although I had designed the Kiddicare building 33% bigger than the biggest-ever building I thought we would ever need, only because I did not want to be moving again in a few years.

We knew that there was only one way for property prices to go! And that had got to be down, but I had been thinking that for about the last four years, so what the hell did I know? By now we had been on the property scene, watching and learning, from 1966. I am now glad we didn't sell that property, because we were able to put it into our pension a few years later giving us £700,000 to put into the business when we needed it, in the depth of the recession.

## People Started to Notice Our Business

At about this time I received a phone call from a guy called Mike Hughes, who worked for a company called Grant Thornton. He asked if we could meet, as he had someone who wanted to buy our business. There was no way we would ever sell, why would we?!

The third generation would be entering the business soon and, if I could teach them to respect and look after the golden goose that had been our priority in the past, the business could last forever. Nevertheless, I still needed to know what was going on in the market so we could steer the business in the right direction and not to just react to it, so I agreed a meeting with Mike.

# Bringing Children Up and Businesses

SIDTRACKED

Many times, when I have been talking to people about business in general and, to be fair, I might come across as so focused that there is nothing in my life that comes before business, people have just come out with a statement from nowhere, "My children come first before our business." Obviously, whatever I have said touches a nerve with a lot of people. I also hold that same thought dear to my heart; that's why I can be so focused. My children do come first, and that's why I am so focused in my mind and saying the business comes first, because without that, the children would not have such a good life overall.

I have found with our family that our children have adapted to any situation and condition we have met, and even thrived. I believe I was actually giving them more real-life experience in educating them in the business, and they loved getting a pay packet each week; that's if they had worked. And if they didn't, that was all right, but they still had to come to work with us, so they soon made up their own minds to help because they knew that each hour they worked they got paid for. It taught them the value of money and the value of wasted time.

BACK

Mike came to see Marilyn and me, saying he had a company that had been watching our progress over a few years and wanted to buy us. Although we had a nice chat, I said that we had just started the new project so, even if we wanted to sell, we could not. He said that would be no problem; they would still buy and carry on with the build. We refused, as the project was too exciting to walk away from and besides, our thoughts at that time were just to carry on until we dropped, when the next generation would carry on. He respected our decision and asked to stay in touch so, to be polite, I agreed.

The latest building started in August 2006 on Hampton, what was to end up being the biggest independent baby nursery business building in the UK and, from what suppliers said, in Europe too. I had committed to a contract to build the shell and the surrounding areas, car parks and fencing, etc. for £5 million, and then stop if we wanted to, or in case we ran out of money. But from the day we started, I knew we would never stop. It would be down to me to find the money; the estimate was £12 million, which this time was going to prove my most difficult task ever.

I was amassing money for the build by selling some of our properties. Richard (agent Jones) rang to say that *Deutsche Bank* wanted to buy a warehouse that we owned, as they had just bought the freehold of the estate that it was on, and now they wanted to buy all of the leaseholds back. Two years beforehand, we had paid £250,000 for the 10,000 sq ft. They offered £300,000, which I rejected. Richard just kept on ringing with offers; on the one hand, we were getting a 12% return on the rent but, on the other, we eventually would need £12,000,000 to build the new shop. In the end I said £500,000, which was way too much, but times were crazy in March 2006, and they bought it. Now, in 2014, the value is only £300,000 maximum - my decision proved to be right.

## We Were Invincible

It seemed that we were invincible; everything that we did went right - the type of stock we bought, the colours, the quantities, the price we paid and the price that we sold it for was right, suppliers were piling stock into us, never worrying if we had gone over our limit. Going through the accounts one day, I saw that one company had given us £300,000 worth of goods when our credit limit was around just £30,000; these were mad times - nothing could go wrong. Every business has its ups and downs; whether it's going up or down, in the long run the ups get bigger and the downs get smaller, and vice-versa. I had a saying I had heard somewhere that I quoted regularly if things seemed too good:

*"If there haven't been any problems for 48 hours, you have either just come out of, or you are just going into a crisis."*

Banks were climbing over themselves to give us, and anybody by the look of it, unbelievable amounts of money at ridiculous margins, providing the borrowers had a pulse. Even then, I would say they erred on the side of lend it; the way that I saw it they were giving it away - it was free money to some, as there was no way they could ever pay it back as long as they had got a hole in their arse.

# The Recession Was On Its Way

I started to have concerns in June 2006 that we were about to enter another recession, just when I had agreed to buy six new buildings from agent Jones for £2.9 million in the April for Marville Properties. But, by June, we hadn't had any interest in leasing them at all, which was so different from what we had been used to seeing since 1997.

On the face of it, everything was booming; property prices were still going crazy, and it seemed that nobody was feeling the squeeze except for me. Or was it because I had embarked on spending £12,000,000 that I hadn't got? Or was it because we had seen the signs before in other recessions and I was starting to realise that there was too much being built to cater for the number of businesses looking to expand? Maybe the Internet was just starting to affect every sector of the market and not just the nursery industry.

SIDETRACKED

My mind was spinning, thinking, "What's happening, and what shall I do?" By the way, we pulled out of that deal; well I say "pulled out", not actually, because we don't like doing that. We resubmitted our offer for the property at £2,100,000, which was what we thought the market price was by the June as the property prices started falling. The vendors told us where to go and then, unfortunately, they went bust a couple years later. A company bought their stock and, in 2012, we picked up that same property, plus 5 acres of building land adjacent, for £2,500,000 from that company. Now, in Jan 2015, it's still empty, but I think we could sell it for double now as things are today.

# The Suppliers Were Making Decisions

BACK

A lot of our suppliers were making their decisions of, "Do we go along with the Internet and Kiddicare, and then probably lose lots of small customers, or do we just supply shops without the Internet." Some chose to ignore the Internet, giving us less choice for our customers; that just made me more determined to get through the recession.

## Some Did, Some Didn't

There were so many brilliant suppliers that came along with us; they had confidence in what we were doing and, with no hesitation, they poured money into their areas that we had given them. Many spent £100,000 in building stands for their products; we were amazed and humbled by their gestures towards us, for which we will be forever grateful, as they had all become family friends.

*From left: Dave Welsh, Joiebaby.com, Eric and Gloria White, East Coast Plastics with Marilyn. I could fill the book with photos of friends from the industry, but sadly, the book would be too thick to read.*

## Thank You All

While I am on this bit about suppliers, I really would like to thank every one of you. Although you may not have been named, you know who you are. Thanks also for the wonderful, heartfelt and sincere comments that you put in our leaving book, we shall treasure this forever. Thanks especially Mike Chapman (East Coast Ltd), Mike Lukins (Rochingham), Jonathan Feingold, Clare Adamson (Playgro), Rodney Cottrell and family, Jan and Rob Mann, Mark Waldron, Luke Burns, Warren, Steve, David, Simon & Selina, Daniel, Andrew, Chris, Andy, Mandy Thomson (East Coast), Sue, Deb, Adam, Martyn, Jeremy, Anne, Karen, Falu & Samir (Trend Tidy), Phil Ludlow-Smith (Little Acorns), Helen, Ian and Georgina Elmes, Kevin, Bradley, Magnus, Guy Schanscieff (Bambino Mio), John Cotter, David Lowe (Babylo), Peter & Andy Crane, Alan Halsall, Ben, Nick Paxton of Silver Cross, Alan Maton (Tomy), Karl (O'Baby), Paul, Jane & Tris, Stephen Whitley, Magnus, Kevin Golding, Jonathan Golding, Brother Max, Miles (BabyDan), Roger (Clippasafe), Peter Archer, and all from the toy and other trades. Sorry - I have run out of space.

# The Internet; Leap That Changed All Our Worlds

I said people make businesses, and I know that we would all like a crystal ball, but we haven't. What amazes me is that, in those days, most people who owned or managed the businesses that supplied us never seemed to understand the Internet and how it would affect their business, or how it could benefit their business by them embracing it.

There was mass hysteria from probably 200 small shops complaining, and the majority of our suppliers never stood still to look at where their business would be in five years time; they seemed to be looking back and hoping that, if they ignored the Internet, it might just disappear. It's great when this happens with anything new, as you get a head start on something that is inevitable in the progress of future business technology.

When the suppliers came in to complain about what we were doing, I used to say to them, "How do you buy your holidays,  or pay for your airfares, gas, rates, electric, or move money about?

Then I used to say, "Do you buy any goods from the Internet?" Most used to say they did, but they still couldn't see, or didn't want to come to terms with, the changing way the industry was going; they just wanted to stop us selling that way, but it wasn't going to happen - can you stop the tide?

Most of the small shops hadn't seen this coming and, by the time they did, it was too late; they, unfortunately, went the same way as the other small shops that the supermarkets had taken out some years earlier. This was a really horrible time for all of us, as the nursery industry had always been such a friendly one.

**The new building - summer 2007**

As the build was progressing, Jo and I started to create a floor plan of where all of our suppliers would go in the new shop; there were three floors, each with 20,000 sq ft of space. We drew a walkway on each floor about one third from the outer walls, and divided the floor into sections of around 500 sq ft each. We then gave the suppliers the option of where they could display their stock.

We had the criterion that all the suppliers of wood products had the top floor, all the pram and pushchair suppliers had the first floor, and the rest went on the ground floor. This worked extremely well; some wanted more, and some wanted less, but everybody was happy. They all said that this would be their flagship store, where they would bring their manufacturers to see what the UK's new market was like.

We put a 70-seat café on the ground floor, which would feed the 130 staff three times a day; all of the reps would eat there and, of course, the customers would use it. The kitchen equipment cost us £250,000, and six staff would work in there.

# We Had To Let Our Biggest Supplier Go

Everybody was happy except one who used to be our main supplier for twenty years, with 12% of our turnover. For this bit I have to go back to May 1981. Mike Turner, who had been supplying us from day one, came into the Orton shop selling his Harrington range of clothing as normal, only this time he had something else to show us; it was two pushchairs and a playpen. They were stunning, and nothing like the UK stuff; these were from Italy. The brand was called *Mamas & Papas*. Now, to get this into perspective, a Harrington's rep was so far up the food chain with what he sold that you would take notice.

### *If Mike had come in with a bucket of horseshit and said it was the next big seller, you would order a lorry-load.*

Mike told us he had been into one of his customers' shops who sold his clothes. He had seen a pushchair belonging to the owner, Luisa Scacchetti. She had just had a baby and had bought the pushchair from Italy, where her family lived. Mike discussed selling it in the UK, and said he would get all of the 10 Harrington reps involved in selling it.

We gave Mike the very first order that Mamas & Papas had taken: 6 Chip pushchairs, 6 Piperette Lusso pushchairs, 6 playpens and 6 rain covers. Mamas & Papas was an instant success. The business was owned by David & Luisa Scacchetti and Margaret Simm; they were all really nice people, with whom we had a very successful relationship for many years.

After being established for about five years, they became the most sought-after nursery-product supplier ever, and the UK's top nursery brand for something like 15 years. We went on to be their top independent retailer for about 20 years. As they got bigger, they got more demanding and dictated the amount of product retailers should put on their shop floor; if the retailers complied, there would be little room for any other supplier's stock on their shop floor, so, unfortunately, from about 2003 their policies were no longer compatible with our way of business. When we were in the process of allocating shop-floor space in the new shop they did come to see us but, by that time, we had let virtually all of the space go, so we had only around 2,000 sq ft left out of 60,000.

*Harrogate Pram Show, 9<sup>th</sup> April 1991. Richard Faulkner from M&P presented us with a copy of our first order we had given Mike 10 years before, a £1000 holiday to Italy, and a tour around the M&P factory. That never happened, as Mike said they had second thoughts as we could buy direct. However, it would have been silly of us to do that.*

## Can You Please Everybody? No

They wanted the 20,000 sq ft on the middle floor, where all of the other pram and pushchair brands were going, so it was impossible to accommodate them. They were not happy, although this was the last thing that we wanted to happen, but, by then, we had allocated the space to some really good friends in the industry, and there was no way we would let them down.

As a reseller you have to be careful that you don't have one supplier who has too much of your sales. We couldn't rely on one brand to make our nursery business work and, by then, I had thoughts in the back of my head of taking lots of new brands in a different direction.

# I Told Him Where to Go

The next week, their new sales manager visited us. I got the impression from him that he came into the nursery industry after selling baked beans or something like that. Anyway, he came to the new site, and told me in no uncertain terms that, if I didn't give him the space that he wanted, he would go to, in his words "your biggest competitor." Wow, and I had been telling people for years that we never had any.

There were lots of great independents that weren't competition; they helped us, and there was John Lewis and Mothercare that helped us too - they weren't competition. There were people like Asda; the suppliers said they sold goods below cost, but that got them nowhere, did it? So they weren't competitors either.

When he told me who this competitor was, I said, "I don't compete with them, because they take the customers' money and don't send the goods to them; if you want to supply them, go to the roundabout, turn right, then left, and you will find them in 40 minutes. And when they go bust, you will lose money and get aggravation from your customers."

He said, "They are not our customers, they are the shop's customers." I told him he was doing a disservice to his employers, whom I greatly admired, and said that it was the nursery industry we were in; the customers needed and deserved our help, and it started with the manufacturer, then the supplier, which he was, then us, the shopkeeper. We all had the same responsibility. He then left.

## Tell Me What To Do?

Other nursery retailers that I didn't know would ring me about suppliers that were not honouring their guarantees and, basically, not taking responsibility for their faulty goods. They would ask me if I was getting the same troubles, and what I was doing about it. Invariably, I would say either that I didn't, or I was not going to deal with these particular companies again because of their bad attitude towards the customers, and their arrogant nature in doing business.

They would go on and tell me, in great detail, how it would affect their business if they stopped dealing with these awful people, and how they were trapped. All I could say was that our business thrived on doing business with nice people, and if they thought that their business wouldn't survive if they stopped dealing with those suppliers that they were complaining about, then they hadn't got any confidence in themselves and they would go bust alongside their arrogant suppliers.

This was a prime reason in my mind when making decisions to have our own brands when expanding the business; I could foresee conflict in the nursery trade that would inevitably be on its way. So early on, when the Internet was getting established, we wanted to work only with people who were compatible with our philosophy of just "keep it simple," leading to a win-win for everyone concerned.

We would not be dictated to by anyone who was being unfair to either their retailers or the end-user, even though we complied sometimes for a while until we had got alternative products in place, or until all of the guarantee periods had run out. We looked for suppliers with a win-win attitude to a situation, or we would walk away; and as for the money, that was immaterial.

So as to avoid price competition, we made our own brands through people we trusted, rapidly getting up to 39% of our turnover, securing any business vulnerability from other suppliers that could go off in other directions, so we did not follow the crowds, and we always watched our ever-changing market on a daily basis, in what was going to be the worst time in the history of retail.

## 12 Brands

I had it in my head that we would be different; we would stop all the nonsense around price-matching and undercutting. We had plans to introduce 12 brands into the business over the next 3 years; these would be displayed prominently, with the mainstream brands taking a back stage with no discounts. That would sort out everybody's problems with us once and for all, and then we could leave members of the trade to squabble between themselves.

After all, we had only ourselves to please, no shareholders looking over our shoulders. Then, once again, our business would be unique in the customers' eyes, and we could get back to having fun once more. Well, that was the plan, but when a window of opportunity appears, sometimes it's prudent to take it.

# Losing Control

## *"My hero died on 7<sup>th</sup> August 2007"*

Dad had been ill for six weeks when he decided to leave us. There's not a day goes by when I don't wonder whether I could have done more for him in those last few days. We were called at 4am by one of the nurses to say he was going; my brother, Terry, and his wife, Judy, were there with Marilyn and me by his side from about 4.30 am.

Elaine and Scott were away on holiday, I think in the Maldives. Scott rang me at about 5pm. I hadn't called them; I thought that I shouldn't disturb them on holiday, as they were having enough to cope with in the business and needed to take some time to think.

After he had told me that I had caused some problems in his department, he asked how my father was. At that precise second, Marilyn appeared from Dad's room and said with her lips, as she couldn't speak, "He's gone." Then she quietly said, "You should have been with him, not on that bloody phone."

I said to Scott, "He's just...," and couldn't get the word "died" out of my mouth, so I handed the phone to Marilyn and I think she told him as I went back into Dad's room.

SIDETRACKED

I had made all the business decisions over the 36 years by myself, then with Marilyn, then with the girls, but, at the end of the day, I was responsible for the finances and ultimately carried the responsibility for our business; however, there was always my dad there in the background whom I could talk to. At this point, I found that I started to re-evaluate what I wanted in life; what had driven us before had now changed, and I felt it was time to go.

## What Could I Do?

BACK

I went into the shop the next day and painted the service reception area; why, I don't know. I wasn't in control of keeping Dad alive, but I was in control of doing something. My dad hated painting; when we worked together, he did the carpentry and I did the painting. Ever since that day I have thought, "Could I have done more to prolong his life?" He was nearly 92 years old; the doctor had asked when he became ill about six weeks before, did we want him to be kept out of pain? What was he saying? Was it, "He is going to die, so this will take away the pain"?

I don't know; I never asked, but I wish I had. Then maybe I could have prolonged his time, but then would he have been in pain? With the right treatment, could he have had another ten good years? It bugs me to think that I never asked enough questions, as I was too busy wrapped up in my own world. I was focused on hundreds of things that make up an ever-expanding business, always thinking that Dad would be there forever and that, once the business calmed down, I would spend more time with him.

## The Funeral

### *15ᵗʰ January 1916 - 7ᵗʰ August 2007*

Terry organised everything. I wanted Dad to go with his dancing shoes on, as he just loved dancing every week, but the vicar said no, as they were toxic. What a load of old baloney. Well, when it came to the eulogy I started off by saying, "If you hear a tapping noise, it's only Dad; he's got his dancing shoes on. Everyone laughed, except the vicar.

I had also organised that we would give out a leaflet with Dad's favourite song on - *We'll Meet Again*. Again, the vicar refused the request to sing it in church. Two of the staff who were coming to the funeral were to hand them out; I had told them which village the church was in, and they said that they knew it well; "It's near Stamford," they said. I said, "Yes, that's the one," but they stood waiting outside Ufford church, which is also near Stamford, not Uffington, where we were.

## Looking Back

It's the kind of thing that you see on a comedy sketch, but at the time I found myself saying, "I should have," a sentence I had heard my dad say a thousand times, and here I was, saying the same thing that I said I would never say. I spent the rest of the day reprimanding myself for not getting it right. Looking back, I think that we all beat ourselves up over things that are not within our control.

## No Choice but to Carry On

By the beginning of 2008, sales had gone flat for the first time ever in the history of the business; even in previous recessions, we had managed increased sales. I thought it was because I had taken my eye off the ball with building the new shop.

We were all working on getting the new project up and running, the building, the website, and all of the systems that were needed. This took our focus off the normal business. It's very hard when a team splits up, even for a very short time; I have always said that two people focused on one thing are better than five people working separately, and five people focused together on a project can equal as many as fifty people working on their own.

By this time we had 70 staff who were preparing for the move, and there was a serious problem. It was with the economy; what we had predicted was emerging like a hurricane. On the other hand, we were surprised to find that we had made £3,494,965 net profit in both of the businesses that year, but it wasn't easy, and things were about to change dramatically.

## Finally, the Superstore Was Ready

The move took place on 14th April 2008 with no fanfare, unlike the opening of the previous shop in 2002, when there was an abundance of money. Joanne, Marilyn & I, along with security Barry, and Ginger the Kiddicare maintenance man, were all there laying the entrance carpet at midnight on Sunday 13th. After Jo had run the london Marathon, she came back to help finish off, as did Elaine & Scott, as everybody wanted everything to be perfect.

The building looked fabulous, inside and out. I had designed and overseen every aspect of the project, a building that shouts out to people coming into Peterborough from the A1 motorway that Peterborough is the place to be for business; a baby shop that's the biggest in Europe and, to top it all, a Peterborough boy and girl did it from nothing. At the time, we never gave this a thought; we were far too busy trying to learn and to build a business and a better life for so many people. Yet I never would tell them, just in case we failed.

I was determined not to have the same problems with this build as we had with the last one, so I employed my friend Jon Nugent who has a company called Arbicon to oversee all of the work.

## Just Another Problem, But At 12 Metres High

Joanne had become our forklift-truck trainer; she had taken all the appropriate courses and now she had bought eight new forklift trucks, one red, four blue and three pink, to go with our two million pounds worth of 12-metre-high racking. The pink ones cost about £50,000 each, so we could have whatever colour we wanted. Jo chose the colours. The trucks went up to 12 metres high, and had cameras on the forks so the driver could see where he was placing the pallet.

On the first day of training in February 2008, we realised that, at 12 metres high, the mast of the forklift truck swayed backwards and forwards 150 cm, and the racking bars were only 5 cm. Consequently, the first pallet with half a ton on missed the bar by 2 or 3 cm and toppled over, wedging it between the racking; it then took three forklift trucks with seven people at 12 metres off the ground to sort it out. I was with Jo, Barry security and Steve, our General Manager, sorting it.

All of us needed to be involved in any type of thing like this, so that we could document them for health-and-safety training, something we took really seriously. Then we would do a risk assessment and method statement which, in this case, was done to retrieve the contents, which went into our knowledge bank of "Don't panic, we know what to do." Each department had the same system so, if anything happened, they would know what to do.

That incident led to Jo, Barry, Ginger and I going in every morning between 6am and 9am for about six weeks, in the freezing cold, fixing metal struts across 2,000 pallet-spaces, each one having to be drilled out and riveted. Jo was then 26 years old, working on open steelwork 12 metres high, drilling holes and handling heavy, cold metal; she just took this on as her responsibility.

At the time, we just got on with it. Now, looking back, I think how proud I am of both of my girls - they just got on and did what needed to be done, immediately and without any fuss. By the way, when I referred to Barry as "security", it's because there were two Barrys; they were Barry security and Barrie gadget. Anyone who had the same name got different titles, like big and little Claire; this went on throughout the business, just as you would do in a family.

At the time of opening, and for the next year, I should have felt proud, but I didn't feel anything. My dad had gone, and I hadn't realised just how much I had talked to him, always asking for his advice, even though I acted like I took no notice of him. He used to say, "Your business is too big for me to understand," and yet at the same time he would ask if I was happy doing whatever or going in a certain way in the business, which always made me come up with the right answer. He could see things in a very simple way and he asked simple questions like, "Is that what you want?"

## Show Us How You Do It

Literally hundreds of people from all over the world came to look around our new warehouse, storage, pick-and-pack systems, Internet process and the store, visitors who were connected to the nursery trade, either manufacturing or distributors, and retailers too. I would show them round and go through all of our processes.

Doing this, I was playing chess; the more people that I could show around, the more they would talk to other people about us. The advantages were then that some competitors would think it would not be worth competing against us and, if they did, we knew they would have an uphill struggle and it would cost a fortune in doing so. The upside was people talking about us - whether it was trade or customers, it would all bring in more business and offers. I knew the sacrifice you had to make to get this far, and most wouldn't do this, or couldn't and, in a lot of instances, shouldn't.

## To Say the Least, Mike Was Persistent

Mike Hughes kept in touch every six months or so, asking how things were going and, of course, the usual conversation that led to saying, "I have someone who will buy your business when you want to sell," but this time I said that we hadn't got a business to sell at the moment because, if we were to sell, everything had got to be working, and proven, and the new pick-and-pack operation had not yet been implemented, so we would never sell if there weren't lots of upside for the buyer to take it to the next level.

## Customers Were Feeling the Effect

In 2008, I could see by the type of prams we were selling that something was wrong. In July it started to gradually change; every week we were selling out of prams that were costing £399 or less, when normally we sold prams that cost between £400 and £1,200; this was an indication of what was to come. I was warning everybody involved in buying to be very careful, and not to go crazy on anything they bought, as one, we were coming into a bad recession, and two, there would be some bargains in the trade as retailers went out of business.

Everybody took this on board, but there was friction in the business. I put it down to the uncertainty of the economy; people got stressed as technically, things never went to plan as we were always in the forefront when it came to inventing new ways to retail our goods, way ahead of any others on the Internet.

I knew that if we didn't all pull together, we would go down like so many others in business would, and unfortunately did, over the next few years. I found it very frustrating to tell others what was likely to happen in the future based on my experiences from the past but, if people have been brought up in relatively affluent times, they can't imagine or believe what is about to happen, and in 2008 we were going rapidly into the same sort of recession as we had been through in the 70s, which was horrendous.

Financially, things were getting serious in the business; news had started to appear each night about the possibility of a recession, or that a large company was in trouble. Having been through these cycles a few times before, I was able to understand what was going on; but putting it right was a different matter.

# Falling Like a Pack of Cards

We had always leveraged whatever we did to make sure that, if one thing went wrong, another part of the business would compensate for it, making it right. So, in the Kiddicare business, we leveraged by selling what could be a business of its own - toys, clothes, nursery equipment, and furniture, all in-store, and all online; that's four different product ranges and two ways to sell. On top of that, we cross-leveraged in our minds with the property business- having rents coming in each month and building, buying and selling mostly commercial buildings, so we were covered in the event of some of these areas of business going into meltdown; it would be unthinkable for all to go down at once.

But the recession was progressing at a rapid pace, even though some people were still burying their heads in the sand. At that time we had about 40 tenants in mostly industrial buildings; a few came to us and said that things were tight and could they have their rents reduced? At first we said no because, on the face of it, the businesses looked great; we would only consider if they produced accounts proving that what they said was right.

Consequently, we reduced some rents but, gradually, even after doing that we still had lots of tenants who went to the wall, leaving us with no income on those properties and little hope of finding new tenants. On top of this problem, as of 1$^{st}$ April 2008, the government stopped rate relief on empty buildings; that meant we lost rents, and were now having to pay the rates on the empty building, too.

A double whammy, so, over the worst recession, we lost around £1,000,000 because of this, just at a time we could ill afford to. We, like every other builder, stopped building speculative commercial projects as the business rates would cripple us if no purchasers or tenants could be found; if the government ever wanted to stop spec commercial building in its tracks, this was the time, and they did an excellent job of it.

I am sure that none of the decision-makers in the government were builders; we were all being made to pay because of the greed of a few bankers!! Now, did I get that spelling right?

# Losing £250,000 a Month

SIDETRACKED

Lawrence David - where had I heard that name before? Then I realised the name was only engraved into every other 40ft trailer seen on the UK roads. Andrew Leech, our long-time friend and commercial agent, rang me just after we moved in and asked if I would let 20,000 sq ft of the warehouse; Lawrence wanted the space to set up a production line to make haulage trailers to transport potatoes but, unfortunately, after manufacturing only around 200, his overall business went from having 3 years of orders for 90 staff to 3 months, literally overnight; that's a recession.

*Lawrence and I having just done a deal on 5 acres of storage land 10<sup>th</sup> November 2015*

Now, 8 years later, he is making over 100 trailers a week and we have just done another deal. Lawrence asked what I was up to nowadays, and I said that I had just finished a book on our lives in business. He wanted to get a mention, so I asked him to justify why I should re-open the book and add a page, as there should be a story. His reply was, "Don't you remember? In the depths of the recession we were both losing ¼ million pounds a month." I said, "That's good enough; how could I have forgotten?" It just shows you that, once you get through something, you forget the pain. So here we go.

## *"Lawrence David builds what I think are probably the best haulage trailers in the world"* Neville Wright

# 2008 Was the Longest Summer

BACK

This was the longest summer on record for me, with too much day left at the end of the money; we had always made plenty of money each year. Every day I would spend an hour in the accounts department juggling with the money that we had received in the last 24 hours; we had about a million pounds' worth of bills which were about two months overdue. I could never, ever remember being that late before. We were up to our overdraft limit; we would only pay out what money we got in on a day-to-day basis.

One day I got a call from the RBS bank saying we had breached their terms by £40,000 and we had until 5pm to pay. We had done our calculations, but forgot to add the £40,000 direct debit going out that day to the local Council, for rates that month. "Shit." They could, by rights, call in the £6,000,000 loan, even though we had always kept all of the payments up; we would be bust. I had to negotiate a further loan so, with tongue in cheek, I asked for an extra £1,000,000 to cover extra stock that we wanted. They agreed, but they wanted £20,000 for the privilege. I managed to get them down to £10,000 and, the next day, we paid all of the outstanding invoices for the stock we already had in the warehouse.

## Now How Do I Just Magic 4 Million Pounds?

I was very much aware that 70% of the assets that Marilyn & I had accumulated over the last 30 years were in the hands of the RBS bank, as collateral against the loans of around £7,000,000 we had got on the new building. On top of that, we still owed about £4,000,000 for extra stock, overheads and the internal fit-out of the building, that I had calculated would be paid off out of cash flow from the two businesses which, in normal circumstances would have been OK; but this was a completely unexpected situation.

Back in 2004, when the idea of this project was conceived, the economy was booming. We were increasing sales by around 25% year on year, and this was on high-price, high-margin stock which would have paid off the £4 million in just one year. Now, four years later, the world had changed; our sales were still going up, but the margins had come down and, with that, we needed more staff to cater for the higher volume going through the system.

# A New Type of Worker Started

To fill the vacancies we used agency workers; then, when we knew the workload was consistent, we took them on permanently, as full-time employees were what we were used to. Workers on the agency got paid every month, including their holidays; we, on the other hand, used the method from the 1970s, when workers accrued their holidays over one year to use the next. So, at that time, everyone got 5 weeks' holiday allocated in April, to be used in the year but accumulated from the previous year.

As soon as we gave the temporary workers full-time jobs, some said they thought we were cheating them as they wanted their holidays every month; so I thought that I would just give it each month and not accumulate it for them. But, of course, I also had to alter the system for our seventy staff who were on the old system; most didn't want that, but we weren't going to be called cheats. Consequently, around fifty of the most experienced staff got ten weeks' holiday that year, at an extra cost of £90,000.

Although it made cash flow more difficult for a while I was pleased, because if anything did go wrong with the business, at least the staff wouldn't lose their five weeks' holiday. I then realised we also held around £40,000 of wages where staff had worked up to 4 weeks before getting paid when first joining us, called "in-hand money," and also a scheme from the 1970s; so I paid this to the staff over the following three months. After making these changes, I was now happy that nobody would lose out if things did take a turn for the worse, as I had a real fear that this could happen.

I contacted Barclays Bank and asked for a loan, as RBS wouldn't extend theirs. Barclays said that they couldn't give a loan on the property as there was one in place already and all of our other property was held as collateral; but they sent someone from another division, who gave us £2 million against all the equipment in the building, if anything had happened!! How would the two banks sort that out? Knowing banks, they probably wouldn't care; they would just sell the assets for a pittance to some subsidiary, who would make a fortune for themselves. I think there should be a law that the original owners should get part of the proceeds, but pigs will fly before that ever happens.

## Only 2 Million to Go

Still owing about £2 million, increasing by something like £250,000 a month because staff numbers had gone from 70 to 100, plus outside contractors were creating the new systems at huge costs, I decided to finance the cars; but that money lasted just a few days. I even got a new camping car. The staff thought that things must be good, but I had sold a really nice one for a really cheap one, and come away with £10k in cash to put into the business, which lasted about 1 hour. The first time that we went out in the camper we hated it, but it could be our new home if the worst should happen.

Then I looked at our personal pensions; we had £2,800,000 sitting there. By this time I really thought there might be a big chance of going bust before we got over the hill, so our dilemma was: do we try and get this money out and put it into the business, which was devouring money fast with no sign of ever stopping, or do we keep it for ourselves? Marilyn and I talked about this in great detail, well, for no more than one minute; we thought about the prospects of going back to live in a caravan; we thought about having the £2,800,000 pension pot for ourselves, living a comfortable life for evermore, and we thought about the wonderful staff who had got us through all of the good years. Guess who won? As for us, we would just start again with nothing, apart from each other.

## Start Small and Speculate

Without first starting and speculating 72p a day on pensions in 1976 (that's all we could afford), we would never have had that £2,800,000 sitting there in 2008. I looked at the pensions in more detail and realised that, if you were over 55, you could draw down 25% tax-free, so I did that and put around £728,000 into the business; then I immediately drew down our pensions of £140,000 for that year but, with a 50% tax bill, we got only half, £70,000 - that went straight into the business.

With £2,000,000 left locked up in the pension, I looked at our portfolio of properties that was collateral for the now £7,500,000 loan. I found five properties that had tenants who were either just about to go bust or were leaving, so I had a meeting with the bank and told them that they would be in a much better position if I swapped them as collateral with a piece of land that I had purchased a few months earlier for £380,000, which was on the market for £1,700,000. To my astonishment, they agreed to swap without any fees.

## Fire-Fighting on an Unexpected Level

I immediately got an independent valuer to value them with their existing leases in place. The value came out at £1,800,000, so we immediately sold them to the pension; that money, too, went back into the business, leaving us with five crap properties that, if the tenants went bust at this time, would be worth very little. What's more, we would be liable for the rates and, on top of that, there wasn't much left in the pension. This was a situation where we were sorting out problems just for today, juggling money again.

It didn't matter which way we turned, there were fires to put out in the form of money, or rather lack of it. On one hand we were selling more stock but, on the other, it was the cheaper products that were selling fast leaving the higher-priced stuff in the warehouse; this normally sold well, but now it had almost stopped.

Within a month we had run out of our low-priced stock, and now we had to reduce the higher-priced stock to bring in some money while we were waiting for the new stock to be manufactured, which takes three months. At the same time, we were spending like crazy on getting the Internet systems sorted out; we knew exactly what we wanted, but Scott could not find the companies that were capable of doing it right first time, as it was the first time anyone had attempted what we were doing.

We all had our backs against the wall, literally working every hour of the day and night to overcome this unique situation. Scott's job was to get the Internet working on a new level that had never been seen before. Elaine and Marilyn had the task of creating more of our own brands, and Jo's job was to create more sales by getting rid of stock that was not going to be bought again. We could not get all this done quickly enough, as it felt like everyone else in the industry was blaming Kiddicare for their problems.

The main problem with the recession for us was that, at first, we were made a scapegoat with the price war scenarios, which was not very nice, but proved a blessing as we had to overcome the problem; making our own products was the answer, and then no one could say that we were undercutting their prices.

Unfortunately, that made things even worse for some people in the trade who had been upset with us, as our own products immediately started to sell against other brands; then others hadn't got a comparison to compete against us. This kept us going, but we still needed more money to feed the ever-growing business that now was fighting the recession.

# Liquidate Our Assets Fast

Looking around at what assets were left to liquidate was easy - there weren't any. Well, other than one - our house. But who would tell Marilyn? Yes, me. I knew that Marilyn was not going to be happy, and I was right for once; but it was Marilyn's business, and we were only doing what we had done time and time again to build the business in the past. But this wasn't the past; we weren't kids any more, ducking and diving, having adventures, risking it all while laughing at the things we did to get through.

**_Park House, Stamford_**

This time we weren't growing the business, we were saving it; we were no different from thousands of other businesses and business people who were caught in the middle of expansion when this financial tsunami hit the UK. Here we were, after 35 years in the business, multi-millionaires, risking every penny we had simply because we were responsible for what we had done in the past. But the past had not put us in this position; this was beyond our control.

# Remember the Past

If you don't remember the past, you will make the same mistake in the future; are you listening, bankers? I always thought that if we worked really hard and put virtually all of the profit back into the business, it could not fail; "shit". For once I was right, but only by the skin of our teeth. Now, at this point, I could get into conspiracy theories about the government and, indeed, the people that are above it, but I am sure that, if I did, the book would never get finished, and not because it would be too long, either.

# Burning Our Bridges Once Again

It was like being in a horror movie. The directors of our film were the government and the banks that disrupted our business, and now our lives; not only ours, but the whole of the UK's. Our film was still being shot. Running away and playing safe could have been an ending; well, not one that we would have written or lived with.

This was our last stand. This was, for us, a do-or-die situation. We could have wriggled out of this mess and lived a very nice life financially, but doing that would make me feel like a shit; I knew that if it all went wrong I could get another business going as a window-cleaner, and I would be the best at it.

On the other hand, I could advise in the red-tape department for the government, but cleaning windows would be doing something useful for the country. Obviously I'm joking; I could now live for very little by taking my luck as it comes, and starting a business again from nothing tomorrow would be no problem.

## Someone Needed To Tell Her

For 26 years we had entertained people from all over the world in our house when they were visiting the shop on business; so just by chance, when I designed the new building I had incorporated a visitors' suite on the top floor, a fantastic entertainments area with 20ft-high curved ceilings, an open kitchen with bar and lounge area, and two guest bedrooms; it would have been great for putting people up for one night or entertaining them in the day.

I suggested to Marilyn that, if we lived in the shop, we could put another million pounds into the business and save the overheads of the house, plus we would save £150 a week on fuel and, on top of that, we would be able to spend more time in the office to overcome the crisis. I said to Marilyn, "Would this not be a fantastic opportunity?" She just looked at me with tears in her eyes and said nothing.

## Could We Have Anticipated This Earlier?

Marilyn knew we had no choice, and I knew that we should have done this at least a year earlier, but anticipation can be fraught with dangers and I didn't want to be wrong. Twenty-six years earlier, when we bought the house in a recession, the people who had owned it had gone bust by waiting too long before selling, and now I realised that we should have sold six months before, as we would have got about £500,000 more for it. But I also knew that, if we left it any longer, we could end up with £500,000 less than it was worth at this time, as the property market was dropping like a stone, and we didn't want to end up in the same situation as the people whom we had bought it from in 1982.

After spending £5,000 on resurfacing the drive (speculate to accumulate), we put the house on the market the next week and sold it. I had priced it to sell to the first person to come in the door. We weren't there when people came looking, but I understand there were three lots of nosey people, someone who wanted it for a care home, and the ones who bought it.

They then sold their house the next week to a person who had to move house that week; so we all moved, but all we took were our clothes, a few personal, sentimental belongings, and left everything else - hundreds of thousands of pounds' worth of stuff we could not accommodate. But there you go, the decision was made.

This had been no ordinary house, and neither were the contents that we left behind. Our minds couldn't think what to do with this stuff as there were much more important things on our minds to sort out in the business, so we left everything. All of the beds were made with fresh linen; it must have been like walking into a hotel for the new owners - all of the beautiful furniture, the oil paintings, 7ft-tall vases, life-size wooden Chinese statues and some bespoke stuff that just wouldn't fit into your normal property. Things were moving so fast, we hadn't got time to think; we were too busy saving the business.

We left all of the things for the garden - thousands of pounds' worth of tools and equipment, garden furniture, an accumulation of twenty-six years of good stuff including the girls toys collected over the years. They said that they didn't want them, then, when Jo had her babies, she realised that we should have saved them but, at the time, our minds just could not cope with things like that, and besides, where would we have stored all of this stuff?

# Leveraging Was Just a Part of Our Lives

SIDETRACKED

As soon as we sold the house, we had to pay off a £750,000 mortgage that we had taken out on it two years before. We had taken this out because we had found an industrial unit for £3,000,000, but we had got only £250,000 in cash. We had leveraged our house for £750,000 to make a million-pound deposit. We could get another £2,000,000 mortgage on the property; that's leveraging £3,000,000 out of £250,000 cash. The site was a 6-acre plot with 100,000 sq ft of building; I was thinking we would need this at sometime in the future for Kiddicare, as it was just down the road from the new Kiddicare site.

## A Real Fire That Made Us 1.5 Million

I was not going to be caught out again over space; in the meantime, we let it to Hotpoint, an electrical goods manufacturer, for £280,000 a year, which paid the loans at 7%, leaving a 35% profit on the £250,000 we had put down; not bad for a dyslexic.

On 25th February 2008 there was a fire in some warehouse a few miles away that destroyed it. Within days, we had an offer for these warehouses of £4,500,000; it was one of those moments when you don't have to think. I just said yes. That made £1,700,000, including £200,000 profit on the rent, which is just good luck in the depth of despair. So, just to recap, we invested £250,000 and, within 3 years, made £1,700,000 putting in the same amount of man-hours it took in 1974 cleaning enough windows to make us £20; but, had I not done one thing, I couldn't have got the other.

BACK

The remaining million went into the business. We left our fabulous home on 10th October 2008, after 26 years; we moved on, never talking about it, as there was no point in loading our minds with regret; we were too numb to even shed a tear, as it was a business transaction made to inject some cash. ***"Go back, to eventually go forward"***

A month later we had one of our regular meetings with one of our banks, when the person from the bank said that, with a business of our size, we should take on a Financial Director in preparation if we ever wanted to sell, which I was immediately against; but then, after thinking about our future, I agreed to it.

Although I agreed that we should hire someone else in the business, there was no way he was going to change the way I juggled money for the good of the businesses; but we all needed some more sophisticated systems in every part of the business, and someone who understood big business, which we were entering into, could now be an asset.

# Stuart Spink Arrived In November 2008

I took to him immediately; he showed me that he was there for the business and not just for himself, like I had thought he would be. He immediately employed a new in-house accountant who had worked for Paul Temple, our accountant, before he sold his business.

Andrea had been overseeing that department along with the HR department, plus being our personal assistant; this is how everybody in the business was in the early days, we all were very good at spinning plates but, by 2008, most managers had increased their workload and at the same time decreased their areas of responsibility. Andrea spent more of her time working as our personal assistant.

Then Stuart taught everyone how to incorporate pivot tables into the business. For me this was a godsend and worth every penny of his £1,000-a-day-fee, but that was only one of many plates that he was spinning, as there was a much bigger agenda that had got to be sorted out.

# First You Must Understand

Within weeks we could see at the touch of a button what stock we had, the margins, how many we were selling and when we should re-order; it put us into a new league. He also chaired and refereed partner meetings each week, generally calming things down so we all got a feeling for where each of the others was heading.

Although he could never persuade me to alter our terms of payment from a "pay-in-a-day system" with most suppliers, he would say that nobody pays so quickly. Marilyn would say, "No they don't, do they? But, at the same time, nobody else gets such good prices, do they?" I felt that, with employing him, I could see more clearly what was going on with the political agendas that come up in family businesses; then, and only then, would I be able to help.

Stuart wanted to understand the history of the business so that he could get a better understanding of what a first generation had been through, and what our expectations were for the future; this made us really think of all the options there could be for the family's future.

He also spoke to numerous staff, plus Elaine, Jo and Scott, getting their thoughts and ambitions, whether it be with our business or someone else's, and reporting back his findings to us so we had a better understanding on where we were, like a snapshot in time, which I would recommend to everyone in business to do every 1-2 years.

Stuart asked us, if we were to pass the business down, how it would be done and, if not, would we issue shares? I said that once we were ready to take a back seat, we would hand over the reins and eventually, when we popped our clogs, our businesses would pass down equally to the girls to hold or to do with what suited them.

We told him that we had already made the three of them partners with no liability for debt, nevertheless all that he said went into the thinking pot enabling us to make an easy decision when a window of opportunity came along.

## The De Minimus Limit Saga

Just because you own a business doesn't mean that you can do whatever you like. We found this out when we handed out the title of Associate Partner to Scott in 2002, when he joined us full-time; we made him an Associate Partner because Elaine and Jo were already on those same terms.

The deminimus limit was all to do with reclaiming VAT as our businesses were still classed as one for VAT purposes, just red tape that doesn't help. In fact these things actually deter owners from business expansion. We just wanted them to be partners without any liabilities.

But, once again, we found we had fallen foul of bureaucracy. Because we had made Elaine and Jo Associate Partners of both of our businesses, we now found bureaucracy was forcing us to make Scott an Associate Partner in both of our businesses also. This was purely to comply with the rules & regulations of HMRC but, fortunately, this did not make him liable for any debts, like Jo and Elaine would be.

# 2009 – The Worst Recession Ever

## *"This time was not like any other recession that we had seen"*

We felt helpless; we didn't know which way to turn. Something was happening to the business and it was not of our own doing, it was totally beyond our control - the world was in recession, taking everyone down including us, although I am always saying:

## *"You are where you are because of what you have done in your past; that's up until this point in your life."*

So I accepted that it was my problem, no one else's. I thought that, with our backs against the wall, we had a fighting chance to succeed and, if not, we would go out knowing that we had put everything into the fight; but, unbeknown to me, our backs weren't against the wall, and you know what that means - someone can stab you. Usually, you cannot legislate for what others are thinking, or for their agendas but, if you thought of that all of the time, you would not do anything.

## Fresh Air for Sale

The industry was awash with businesses folding; every day, it seemed that another great pram shop had disappeared off the face of the earth. It seemed like everyone in the world was fighting for survival; we were up against traders who were selling fresh air, they would be advertising product that we knew they could never supply, but they still took the customers' money.

This was hurting everyone's business and giving the trade a bad name; we knew that traders like this would eventually go out of business, but when? It took 2 years for one of them to go bust.

In the meantime, it hurt us; customers would ask us to price-match against their advertised lower prices. If we did that to keep the customer, we would lose money and, if we didn't, the customer would lose out when the products never arrived; a very frustrating time, as every week we were expecting that this would be the week they would go bust but, as I say, it took 2 years. Every week we would have customers crying on the phone, telling us their story and that they wished that they had taken notice of what we had told them.

At the time, it was a double blow for the trade; first, there was the Internet that changed the face of retailing and started hitting unsuspecting retailers who thought it might be a passing phase. Then there was the recession, which crippled the economy. One of these things on its own would have been bad enough, but the two together were devastating, a totally unforeseen set of circumstances.

The only sure thing in a recession is that one day it will be over, but which day will that be? Would the system that Scott's team were working on ever be finished? It felt like I was feeding a giant one-armed bandit every minute of every day; I knew that there was a jackpot in there, but how much money had we got to put in before our numbers came up? Or would we run out of money first? We had now got to the point of no return.

*I was in despair; I was feeling ill because of the 35 years of hard work that were now slipping away in front of our eyes. It felt like putting money into a one-armed bandit.*

# The Game Is "A Fear of Loss"

I was playing the game called "The fear of loss." Most people play this by not putting their money into the business, house, investment, or maybe a fruit machine but, once you do this in any area of life there comes a tipping point, when you have invested so much money, time, or effort into the project that you cannot stop. So, for Marilyn & I, after sacrificing everything, it was make or break. We all knew Scott and his team would get there eventually, but would our money run out before that? Whatever the outcome, decisions would have to be made, as I couldn't go on like this any more.

# One Day the Combination Will Be Right.

We had always had a fantastic business that made lots of money every year, but that wasn't enough; at this point we needed to invest more. We had normally taken this in our stride over the years, but this had come in the middle of the worst recession in recent history.

# A Slap in the Face

By this time, the planned expansion would normally have been completed, and paid for out of cash flow. We should have been sipping our gin and tonics, and sailing around the world while our golden goose continued to lay another golden egg for us every day.

A sense of despair was with us; everything was going down a black hole. The recession we could cope with, the building of the new website we could cope with; it was the underlying tension, coupled with the fact that we were potentially going to have multiple court cases that could be very damaging.

One thing was that other businesses were using our brand name, which we would have to stop them doing, and the other was that the Environment Agency was taking us to court for not filling in a fcuking form that no one knew about; bureaucracy gone mad.

From 26th September 1974, when my first potential customer rejected me and closed their door on me, it had felt like I had been verbally slapped in the face. This just drove me on, and then, when my best customer, Mrs Corton, went into a rage and told me in no uncertain terms what my obligations were to her if I was to have any more work, again it was a verbal slap in the face.

This situation went on for the next 35 years, with customers and some suppliers telling me what to do, keeping me on the straight and narrow; building on all of this information was very valuable knowledge to us.

I had learned very early on that, if we were to succeed, we had to take each and every one of these verbal slaps and learn from them, every day turning negative into positive. This is all right when you have a dream and you are making a contribution to other peoples' lives, your family, staff, customers, your industry, and the country; then there is a tipping point, when you feel the rewards - not money, I hasten to add - have gone, yet the mental slapping still carries on.

# My Diet Mainly Consisted of Alcohol

By 2009, my diet once again mainly consisted of alcohol; we were prepared, after 35 years, to go back to living in a caravan. Well, we had a motor-home now, which was parked in the warehouse; even after living in a mansion for 26 years, we still didn't worry about having a standard.

What we did worry about was our family and the hard-working, loyal staff who had become our dear friends; they didn't deserve to lose out - the buck stopped with us, not them. We had taken our chance and gambled, all or nothing, but we would never do it at the expense of others.

Marilyn would sit at her desk, working away, with tears streaming down her face; she was worried about the staff and their families, and she was worried about our girls and the grandchildren. There was not a thing I could do to ease the pain that I could see she was in.

SIDETRACKED

In my mind I could still picture Marilyn standing in that first shop, wearing a tabard smock and looking really young, pretty, innocent, smart and happy. I remember her being so helpful and proud, serving customers with their baby clothes.

Elaine would be standing next to her, this little 6-year-old girl in the same sized smock as her mum, her head barely showing above the counter, taking in everything her mum was saying when selling the stock. Marilyn would then add up the items on a piece of paper, and Elaine would take the money from the customer and give them change, thanking them in her squeaky, high-pitched voice.

Marilyn has not done a bad thing in her life, but now she found she was the owner of the business that had not filled in a form to say we were recycling cardboard, something I had been doing from the very first day of going into this business. I was fanatical about it, as all of our staff members were aware. Apparently, this was an offence punishable by a minimum of a £30,000 fine, a regulation that businesses are not made aware of, just expected to know. The thought of going to court was making her ill, to the point where she told me that she wouldn't go because of the humiliation. It really scared me to think what she would do to get out of it.

Today, 16<sup>th</sup> April 2015, I have just read an article from *Business for Britain*, of which I am a member. It says that, since David Cameron has been prime minister, there have been 4,700 new business regulations introduced; that's 20 million words, and they expect all businesses to understand them. At the present time we have in our business 112 commercial tenants; a few cannot read or write, but they can mend your car, earning a living for their family by helping people, and I am sure the others who can read wouldn't have the time; I know I haven't. I just hope they don't meet a jobsworth like we did.

## We Put Our Heads Above the Parapet

BACK

Unbeknown to me, Scott had put Kiddicare forward for some awards in the industry, something that we had never done before, although I had always promoted the shop in the Peterborough area and on the Internet, which was aimed directly at the customer.

The sort of awards that Scott had put us up for were, in my opinion, just showing-off awards, saying to our industry, "Look at us, we are better than you;" in other words, rubbing each others' noses in it. I was wrong; I wasn't looking at the big picture, and I had never had the time or the people to go down such a lucrative route.

This awards thing just came at the right time for us, as we had built a very strong business; but could we weather the onslaught of the competition if we stole their thunder?

In the past, I used to see who had got the awards each year; I would then scrutinise their business to see what we could do differently in ours. I used the awards to set our standards even higher but, at the same time, keeping under the radar as other people would copy us. I knew in the past that, if I were to get awards, someone in the industry would interrupt our supply lines.

On 23rd June 2009, we won the multi-channel award and the retail website of the year award, beating all of the big boys, who had probably never heard of us before.

As soon as I was told the next day that we had won the awards, I loved it, but it scared me. I said that now we had to work our socks off, and get all the awards that were going, because we would have put some noses out of joint and they would try to destroy us. on one hand I wouldn't have done it, but as soon as it was done I was just as excited as everyone else and raring to show the world who we were and what we could do.

So our plan was set; we would go and put ourselves forward for awards, and everyone in Kiddicare would make sure that we were the very best in that field to get every award that was going in our industry, whether it be retail or technology. Everyone knew the categories we were aiming for. Please don't get me wrong, I loved the awards along with everyone else in the business; I was just concerned for everyone, as now we had got to work our socks off whether we wanted to or not. Up to this point we had a choice, but now we hadn't.

## Awards Came From All Directions

Awards started to come from all directions; after all, we had all been involved in working on the Internet now for some eleven years and, in that time, had implemented an in-house department and had now been working with specialist subcontractors of services which were creating our vision of the customer having the same experience online as they would in-store.

So now, after being under the parapet wall and not showing ourselves for twenty-three years, it was so easy to get the awards when competing with businesses that were new to it; we were miles ahead of the majority of businesses. We were mainly up against large players, like Tesco, Boots, Asda, etc; they seemed to lack the ability to connect with their customers, something that we had done from the first day that Marilyn had opened her first shop.

We went on to win the Mother & Baby 2009, 2010 and 2011, *Evening Telegraph* Business 2009, Baby Products association 2009, the E-Commerce 2009, Retail Systems 2009, *Kiddicare.com* Best online shop which 2010, Experian Hitwise 2010, E-consultancy Innovation 2010, Mother & Baby best Nursery Retailer, best Nursery

Product 2010, Practical Parenting 2010, IMRG E-commerce 2010, and Prima Baby 2010.

Then, in 2011, Retail Systems Jan 2011, Retail Week Jan 2011, Call Centre and Customer Jan 2011, Online Retail Jan 2011, Golden Chariots Customer Service Jan 2011 and, to top this off, the winner out of 75 leading websites Jan 2011. What an achievement for all of the loyal team, who all had a part to play in this success.

## It Takes Only 1% Extra Effort to Win

Marilyn had empathy with her customer, something that seems to be a gift with small shopkeepers. It does not matter how brainy you are or whatever sophisticated systems you invent, they cannot replicate a Marilyn, Elaine, Joanne, or all the other girls and boys who they taught with Marilyn's natural secrets of success.

## Sponsored By Kiddicare

We would have meetings to see if we had enough money to incorporate any new technology that Scott thought we needed and, up to this time, he had been allowed a free hand to spend whatever he liked from the time he joined us full-time around 2002.

Every time we met I would always be eager to find out what the project was, because I knew that we needed to keep ahead in perfecting a new experience for the customer, which by now was becoming an obsession with us; we all wanted to be at the cutting edge of technology but, at the same time, not all new things worked.

One question I would ask is, "How long before we will get our money back and make a profit?" But I would always spend more than we had originally wanted to, that's if I could see that it would keep us in the forefront. Sellers of tech would come up with an ingenious statement; when I asked how much, they would say, "Nothing. It's free; free to install, free to test, free to integrate." Then I would say, "For how long?" They would say it was for three months or six months, so you would have to watch them.

## I Could Only Imagine the Price

This particular day, when Scott came in I said we could only spend money if we could convert it into a profit within a month, as this was how bad things were getting. Up until that time, the payback on any project was about two years and then, sometimes because technology was moving so fast, it was obsolete.

This time it wasn't tech stuff. We had been approached by a TV advertising company, and my first thought was, "No, no way, it will cost a fortune," although my mind was saying, "Yes, I want to do this, but we can't afford it." I then I realised I had said the word that I never, ever used, and couldn't describe: "CAN'T". This was not in my vocabulary, so I then altered my thinking and said, "How much?" Because when I said no, I could only imagine the price.

***Marilyn, Katie, Peter, Joanne and me***

## Stateside

On 14th April 2009 we went to the exclusive screening of the first episode of *Katie and Peter: The Next Chapter Stateside* at the *Soho Hotel* in London. This was the start of our many TV advertising campaigns. We sponsored Katie Price and Peter Andre for something like six weeks of programmes. I was told that a sponsor had pulled out at the last minute; they were paying around £400,000, and it was up for grabs at £150,000 if we had the advert done in something like three days. I think we got it for £70,000. I was in my element, and it was as good as getting all of those radio ads in the 1980s for two quid a time.

The rumours were that the original sponsor got scared off with all of the controversial publicity that Katie was getting at the time and, as it was a very high-class diamond retailer, it could be bad for its image; that's if you can believe rumours.

It was great; after the first commercial break, our site nearly crashed with getting so many new visitors. We got 173,569 extra page views in that next 24 hours, and the money just rolled in. It was a great success, and established us with the UK public; we now had our minds on other programmes, like *Coronation Street* and *X-Factor*.

## Lots of Adverse Comments

Lots of people who knew us asked why on earth we had sponsored Katie Price, or Jordan, as she was known, as in the press she had got mixed reviews to say the least; they thought this would damage Kiddicare's reputation, but we were coming from a different angle - everybody liked Peter; well, the girls did, and they were our target audience.

Katie had her problems, which most people couldn't quite get their heads around. Yet a woman could understand in a way, if she were a parent, and the men all knew her, like it or not. So, all in all, we had got a couple who were a bit different, and this fitted in with our business model of being in the forefront, doing the unexpected and pushing the boundaries.

Like everybody who didn't know them, we had an image in our heads of what they would be like - brash, cocky, arrogant, uncaring, all the things you see on TV. Well, what a shock! They were the nicest people you could meet, none of those things that we thought. Katie is such a caring mother to Harvey and a really nice, considerate person, and Peter is just a down-to-earth, normal bloke who you would want as a mate.

When we met them they had just gone through what looked like a normal daily photo-shoot, with 50 photographers all screaming at them to look their way, and then being bundled from one room to another for interviews, being treated like a commodity. It was awful but, when Jo asked for a photo, although they were exhausted, they had time for us. Peter and Jo talked about their marathon-running, which they had in common, before they were whisked away, late for another interview. ***"And we thought our lives were crazy"***

## The Apprentice

Another thing that gave us a massive boost was being on *The Apprentice*. We went down in the history of the programme for giving the winning team the biggest order that any sales team had ever got; again, the money just rolled in when we needed it most.

The next day we made the news in a national paper, with someone saying something like it was a con but, of course, we heard that this allegation came from a disgruntled retailer. Our buyer just looked back on her records on a nearly identical product which we had been selling, and ordered the same quantity of 30,000 pieces. I told her that, if the product was good, not to mess about with buying a few samples but do a proper order; after all, we had wasted an afternoon with the bloody film crew disrupting everything, so why not win the challenge and get the advertising that came with it?

Although it was the year when I think the recession was the worst time for us, I was in my element juggling the money; it was what I did best, although I felt sick in the stomach most of the time because of the constant fear of the banks starting to call in their loans all over the place. Each day I would wonder if it would be us today, that those scared, incompetent vultures would be after, clawing in the money from good businesses to prop up their past mistakes. This put a huge strain on me as they, in theory, owned our business.

There was Marilyn always in the background, watching and listening, always a steady influence, a constant, to be there for everyone, guiding with her knowledge of the business and her wisdom of the past, yet knowing where she wanted the business to go in the future. She was the spokesperson for the staff, although they never knew it; she knew the value of every one of them being with their children, so no Sunday working, no Easter Monday, no Christmas Eve, no Christmas Day, no Boxing Day, no New Year's Day, plus a subsidised restaurant. Everything they got came from Marilyn and, when I questioned her about her working on those days, she would say, "I have a choice; the staff wouldn't have." ***"So don't question me."***

## Twenty People Needed To Go

A review of all the overheads was carried out by Stuart to see what we could cut down on; this went from stationery to lighting, everything was looked at, but there was virtually nothing as we already ran a tight ship anyway, apart from being over-staffed. There needed to be a reduction of twenty people, but we knew that when things turned around we could make that in just a few months, so Marilyn said, "No, we will find another way," because she couldn't sack anyone as they were all good people.

Everyone had to cut their hours to save the jobs. Also, lots of staff close to us did far more hours than they normally did, just to help out; thankfully, this was for only a few months, before things were back to normal.

## The Day We Got Reported

One day, in all of this mayhem, I had a phone call from the reception on the ground floor saying that there was someone from the Council here to inspect the premises because they had been informed that there were people living on the premises. I saw the lady and took her to the apartment, where she said that we could not live there.

I proceeded to tell her of our circumstances - the struggle in trying to save our business along with the livelihood of 130 families, but I knew that I would only be p***ing in the wind, because she was a jobsworth with no common sense or feelings for other people. She, along with her bosses, who are public servants, hadn't got a clue when it came to our occupancy of that part of the building.

I did find out who reported us, though. She also told me that we had a motor-home in the warehouse and said that, when we moved out of the building within 21 days, I could not live in the motor-home on the premises. Thank you to the person for doing that to us and putting 130 jobs at risk.

## *I also wish them diarrhoea for the rest of their life.*

I said to her that we didn't sleep there all the time, maybe just three or four times a week. She asked where we spent the rest of the week and I said, "Here in the office; we have a £14 million debt and we are trying to get through this recession, and besides, should you not be concentrating on people selling drugs on the street, like they do every night outside here, instead of trying to put me on the streets with them?" But of course, that was not on her tick sheet, was it?

## Common Sense Was In Short Supply

Anyone with a bit of common sense and records would have known that a couple who had lived in probably the most prestigious house in the area would not be stopping there in that tin box any longer than necessary. I said that we were no different from our fire-fighting and security teams that were on call 24/7, and the 24-hour callout tech people like Gadget.

We were here all of the time and, if we went away, others would cover. It was frustrating for me. I think that I suggested they get hearing-aids and guide-dogs; did they not know we were now one of the biggest employers in Peterborough? Did they really think that this situation was wrong? I said that the business would need a 24/7 shift system with security, so that there would be people there when we left in the future.

## John Dadge to the Rescue

Luckily we had John Dadge, a city planner, to tell them that they were wrong. For a start, there was no private access to the property, only through the main car park, and we could access the apartment only through the inside of the shop, which would have made it impossible to rent out.

We stayed, living there for nearly three years; Marilyn said that if we stayed in there for the third Christmas she would divorce me, as I had promised her that we would be out the Christmas before. We moved out on Christmas Eve. The funny thing was, Marilyn took some presents to her mum and dad's house after work, and then went back to the shop. She rang me to ask where I was, forgetting that we had moved that day, as we had left the apartment just as if we were living there.

Two years before we moved out, the building society that we had used rang me and said that, in the terms of our old mortgage, they had to offer us another mortgage, so would I like one? I asked how much, and they said .04% over base rate, which was .05%. I could not believe it; here we were in the middle of a recession, and they were offering me a 90% mortgage at only .04% interest for 10 years; I had to ask the lady to repeat what she had told me four times, because I thought that I was hearing things. Well, I couldn't say no - we still have it.

## Pure Greed Went Through the System

It seemed like bankers were struck with panic, running around like headless chickens, unable to make any kind of sense for sending good, profitable businesses bankrupt just when they needed support; or, in most cases, like us, they should have left well alone, enabling businesses to come through the recession with the banks' assets intact and more valuable for themselves in the long run.

One of our banks, RBS, decided at the height of the panic to call in around £6 million of loans. Their excuse was that we had breached our covenant, yet this was a load of rubbish. We knew that they were doing this because we were getting an interest rate of .80% over base; we had paid the interest every month without fail.

They referred to a clause that was buried in jargon; it was extremely complicated for our lawyers and accountants to interpret. These were the same crazy people who, just a few years earlier, offered us £36 million to do whatever we wanted to do with it; nobody can understand that they were prepared to lend this amount then, four years later want it all back, even though we had never defaulted and had a business that was worth a lot more than the loan.

*Throughout this turmoil, our best friends Roy and Sue were there for us, turning negative into positive, lifting our spirits by seeing beyond the present crises, showing even in our darkest days that we should never lose our sense of humour.*

# Free Umbrellas When the Sun Shines

We thought at that time that we might lose the business; I said that if I, the customer and our lawyers and accountants couldn't understand the small print, a judge would have to decide. However, it didn't come to that; we called their bluff and they realised that they hadn't got a leg to stand on, so they left us alone to go on to easier prey.

Can you imagine that any bank in their right mind would have made this offer of 36 million? I thought that they couldn't be right in the head, but I wasn't right in mine, either, or I would have taken them up on it. All I was thinking was, what on earth could I do with that amount of money? Well, I knew that the prices of property were too high, so I couldn't buy anything without getting stung; but I wasn't thinking clearly. What I could have done at the time was taken the money and re-lent it back to a bank or building society at 6% for a 5-year fixed term, making a profit with no effort at all - but I didn't!

# Red Tape Can Kill Mind, Body and Soul

## *"If there is a constant bombardment of it"*

2010 was a horrendous year for us all; I had always prided myself, right from the first day of business, by recycling our cardboard and plastic, etc. By 2010 we were having a 40ft trailer packed full every week, collected by PMK Recycling Ltd, our friends Roy and Sue Pumpr who, by now, owned a recycling business.

I was at my desk at 9am when the post landed on it, and I opened it immediately. This morning is one I will never forget. I was totally shocked, as the letter came from the Environment Agency telling us that they thought we had not complied with the packaging regulations and that they had already fined someone £280,000. I rang them immediately to tell them that whatever we owed we would pay, as we had no idea that there were such regulations.

They said that they were going to make an example of us by taking us to court. I just could not understand this action, but they wouldn't listen to me, I literally pleaded with them, saying how it could damage our company and hurt every member of staff, as all of the staff took pride in recycling everything that they could.

Apparently the recycling wasn't an issue - but the paperwork was. they said they would take us to court and make an example of us on three counts: one, because we hadn't applied for an application form; two, we hadn't filled in an application form and three, we hadn't sent it back and they hadn't approved it. For a minute I thought this was a wind-up, and someone was going to say it was an April Fools' joke.

Going to court would be such an embarrassment to us personally, and for no reason, apart from not filling in a form when we already had given them the evidence of the recycling paperwork from back over the years. These were issued to us each week by the recycling plant where we had sent it. We kept thinking that even criminals don't go to court for major things. We asked why they had not told us about the regulations; they said that it was on their website for all to see. I said that I didn't know that there was a website and, if I did, what would make me look at it? What had my voluntary 36 years of recycling been all about? Were they not going to take that into consideration? "No," was the answer.

# How Do You Know What You Don't Know?

I rang our solicitor about the regulation, and he had never heard of it; our accountants hadn't, the local town hall hadn't got a clue, the Nursery Association hadn't, the recyclers hadn't, our suppliers hadn't, and even our cardboard manufacturers hadn't. What a bloody farce.

There was no one who could help. We had to tell them how much packaging that we had had going through our business over the previous six years; we had to get all of the suppliers involved. We put two people on to this, which took months to do, just at the time that we were fighting for survival along with the rest of the UK businesses.

After all that it appeared that we owed £29,129, which I said we would pay, but they were having nothing but blood and setting an example of what other businesses could expect for non-compliance with this regulation, one that they had never told businesses about. I think that politicians should have run their own business before trying to run Business UK. Maybe I have already said this, but I think that most of the things that they do are a waste of time and money, and this is just another example.

## Just a Nightmare

With no way out, and the court case fast approaching, they gave us an option; Marilyn & I, the owners, and Elaine, Scott & Jo, as partners, were all implicated. We could have five in court, or we could elect one of us. Well, this was too much for Marilyn; she was feeling really ill at the thought and the humiliation of going to court.

Joanne and Scott hadn't got the full history of the business to answer the questions, so that left Elaine and me. The financial crisis had already affected me over the months, on top of all the other things that were going on; then Elaine said she would do it, and we would represent ourselves as money was so tight.

A couple of days before the case I was at a friend's house, where I got chatting to another guest about the case. He seemed to know about court procedure, and said that we needed a barrister to represent us; so, the next day we went to a local solicitor, who got a barrister from London to come to Peterborough the next day. We met in the solicitor's office about an hour before the case, just Elaine and I; Marilyn was sick with worry, and Jo and Scott were in the shop fighting fires.

# The Farce Began Tuesday 5<sup>th</sup> October 2010

The barrister said, "You have ten minutes to tell me your life story." I poured my heart out; how we started the business and the struggles over the years, how proud we were to have accomplished this with our family and how we were so proud of employing so many people in Peterborough and now, through red tape and the fault of the system, we felt failures. To top it all, we were in debt to the tune of £14 million, this now being the straw that was mentally breaking the camel's back.

## A Mental Meltdown Was About To Happen

We got into the court. There was a coffee shop, so we sat down at a table with a lady whom the solicitor recognised; she was the solicitor for the Environment Agency. They started to talk, and I sat next to a young girl. I asked who she was; this was the person who had instigated all of this fiasco in the first place.

I asked how this all came about, and she said that she was passing the new building and just thought that we might not be complying with the regulations. I said, "Why take people to court? Why not just let them know, so they can then comply?" She said that they had no money for their department, and the only way that they could get it was to prosecute.

I told our solicitor that these people hadn't got a clue how they were affecting peoples' lives and how damaging it was to businesses; he said that I must not say anything in court - I must remain silent at all costs.

The prosecution, as I understood, was that we hadn't complied on three counts of the regulations: one, we hadn't applied for a form; two, we hadn't filled it in and three, we hadn't sent it back. All three had a minimum fine of £10,000 each, so the fine would be £30,000. They were also saying that we owed £29,129 in back duties for what we had sent for recycling.

Our barrister told our story virtually word for word, with such compassion; listening to that brought back the memories of the hardship and the continuous fight that we had been through. To then end up in court was too much for me; I could feel myself cracking, wanting to shout out that this was an injustice, but I had been told to stay silent.

Then it was Elaine's turn. They asked her how she wanted to take the oath; well, she didn't know what they were talking about. I was urging her in my mind to swear on the Bible, as there were three middle-aged and, I assumed, English people on the bench, and I just had a feeling that if she didn't, it would go against her. I am sure that in not understanding, she just took an oath without the Bible.

# I Had Never Known What "Beside Yourself" Meant

At that point my whole life flashed before me, going back to when we first started the window-cleaning business when I was freezing cold, my hands red-raw, and the excruciating back pain; then Marilyn on her first week having the ladder fall on her, nearly breaking her leg, and the time when I walked off a three-storey, flat-roof building with no man-safe system like there is nowadays, only to cheat certain death by catching hold of a TV aerial on the side of the building. Sitting there in court, I started crying. I was beside myself; I was here because I hadn't filled out a fcuking form, one that I, and everyone that I knew, didn't know even existed.

### *Red tape*

I was, and had been for some time, in tears; I hadn't wanted to bring attention to myself, as there was a reporter a few seats away looking and furiously taking notes. By now, the front of my shirt was soaked. I had no choice but to get my handkerchief out, I think to my solicitor's despair. He was sitting next to me, and shuffled around so that he sat sideways with his back to me; but I just couldn't help it - I had lost control and couldn't contain the gulping noise that comes out of you when feeling distraught and trying to keep it in.

The man who had been intimating that Elaine should know all of the hundreds of regulations, and that she was really incapable of running a business, was now looking at me and saying, "Is there anybody else who wants to say anything?" Was he talking to me? Or was he talking to the solicitors on both sides? Although I thought he was looking at me, I could hardly see through my tears. I really think that I was having a breakdown and, besides, I didn't want to jeopardise our case or be reprimanded once again. (Shitworld) I said nothing, although my mind was screaming inside to stand up and shout out my thoughts on the farce that was going on.

# The Crazy Outcome, and What a Waste

The three of them went off into a back office. After a couple of minutes, I overheard the court clerk saying to the solicitors that it was unusual for them to go out, as they normally made up their minds there and then. After ten minutes, she went in to see them; apparently there were a lot of cases that day. She came out and said, "Go and have a coffee, and I will call you when they are ready." Then she added a comment that this was not normal.

We waited; everywhere I looked, it was full of people waiting - in the café, in the corridors; the cases were backing up. Then, after forty minutes, we were called back; the man summed up by saying that they didn't think we were guilty of any wrongdoing but, at the same time, they were responsible for upholding the law.

They obviously had a real problem with this, as he was trying to justify what they were doing, saying their hands were tied; he repeated himself, and then he said, "Although we don't think you are guilty, and the minimum fine is £10,000 on each charge, we are going to impose a £2,000 fine on each charge, £6,000, plus the back payments of £29,129.

Immediately the solicitor for the prosecution stood up and said they couldn't do that. I thought, "Shit, we are going to have to pay £60,000; how am I going to get that?" The judge asked the prosecution why not. The prosecution replied, "In law, you have just fined them, so you can't now impose the outstanding back payments on them."

They ended up getting nothing from us, not even their costs, which I had offered them, or whatever they had wanted from day one, which was the £29,000. I have sometimes since wondered if the girl from the Environment Agency ever realised what her actions could have done to our business, our family, and all of the people who worked there, obviously not thinking that the consequences could have been catastrophic and changed peoples' lives for ever.

# A Flying Cow

Throughout my life I have fought cynicism. I used to joke and say that when I died I would come back as a bird and I would shit on all of the people who had shit on me. Now, after this fiasco, my mind has changed - I would now come back as a flying cow.

# Is This The Business We Chose?

## *"We only wanted to sell a few prams"*

Before the court case, we had been through the Kiddicare name cases with several businesses that had decided to either piggyback on our name or hadn't done their due-diligence when naming their business. This all took up valuable time, mainly for Scott and me, as we dealt with this over a few months, and cost a great deal of money. We could have well done without it all.

## The Venture Capitalist (VC) Saga

Now the business was churning out thousands of products a day but, as everybody knows, this does not go unnoticed. We were attracting attention; a sight to behold was seeing sixteen double-decker 40ft lorries leaving our premises full of stock, making money on every item, yet we were still spending more getting our systems to perfection.

We got everybody's attention whether we liked it or not, and we now got the attention of VCs. Scott came in one day all excited; he had met someone at a tech show in London, and said that they wanted to buy part of the business for £40 million, and did we want to sell? For a start, I said that we really hadn't got a business to sell, even if we wanted to. It wasn't working to my satisfaction, and had Scott told them where we were with this, as I wouldn't want them to get down the line and then find out that we hadn't perfected our new systems? He thought it didn't really matter to them.

I said that if I were to sell the business, it should be working properly to our satisfaction and ready with the potential to double or treble the turnover, something I had already been through when Marilyn & I had sold other businesses. I knew that if it wasn't right, it wouldn't sell for the right price, so the next question was how long and how much will it take to get the warehouse and pick and pack systems working to our satisfaction?

The answer was that I didn't know; it might take a month or it could be two years the way things were going. So, we took a vote, to sell or not and, if we were to decide to sell, this would not stop us carrying on getting the systems working while the selling process was going on.

Marilyn asked what everyone thought because, although it was her business, she would not do anything that the girls didn't agree to; so, in about one minute, we all voted to sell, as the strain on all of us at this time was obvious and wouldn't get any better soon.

The decision to sell at that point in time was really a knee-jerk reaction to save, and also to grow the business; it was no different from us making any other business decision from the first day in 1974, when Marilyn and I had started our first business together. Then, when the girls were old enough, they had joined and were involved in the decision-making process also.

This offer had come out of the blue and took us by surprise, as we were still in the middle of the expansion. We couldn't see ourselves coming out of this recession in a hurry, as it wasn't like any another that we had experienced, and carrying on harvesting those golden eggs every day, together with the costs, was getting much harder.

Were we all saying now let's kill the golden goose? And, if we did, what would we all do? While the girls were talking, Scott asked what I would do with my share. I ignored that comment and suggested to him that we could just start another business, as we were used to doing that, but he didn't seem as keen as I was; he just said that he wanted to create a much bigger business than I would want.

When I said we could just start again, I was putting all of the proceeds into what was going to be the next generation's business, but the impression I got was that he wanted Elaine to get her share early so they could go off and do something themselves. But of course, Marilyn and I had still got a lot of life left in us and would have needed the proceeds to develop the next thing; this gave me the impression that he wanted out so that he could do his own thing, which can be normal thinking for some.

I could understand his frustrations; there he was, in no-man's land, working in a business that he hadn't built. Some people can, and others desperately need to, do it for themselves like I had, and he obviously had the ability to do the same. One of the things that didn't help was the fact that he said he was constantly being offered a million-pound salary to work in America that he kept refusing. He said to me that he knew it would break Marilyn's heart if Elaine and the grandchildren were to go, so he said to me that he would stay to help the family, which I appreciated, because I had loved working with him. I also knew that the more heads that you put together, all focused in the same direction, the better the outcome, but I wasn't going to restrict anyone so that went into the thinking pot when making my final decision.

# A Strange World

I never told Marilyn about this conversation, as she was on the edge anyway with all that was going on, and living in that shop didn't help; it wasn't like living above a traditional shop in town, which could have been nice - this was 160,000 sq ft, a tin box, a massive warehouse on an industrial estate. At night, we could see the drug dealers just outside, opposite our main gates, in the shadow of the Mercedes car dealership on the other side of the street; cars would pass every few minutes, hands would be outstretched between cars and the deal would be done in a second. She hated it.

# Just a Regular Night

SIDETRACKED

We worked until 11pm, and I would then cook something in our 70-seat restaurant located in the showroom; sitting there in this massive shop, all in darkness except for a few dim security lights, was spooky. At around midnight we would take the dog around the building, doing a security check on all of the doors, fences and gates. I would always be carrying a gun, just in case I saw any vermin.

We would get some fresh air to clear our heads so that we could think straight then, very often, we would just go back and carry on in the office; why not? We did not sleep anyway. I would be out again at 3am. Each week a foreign car transporter would appear and then, within minutes, lots of cars and motorbikes would be loaded on and in seconds it had gone. Some of the staff thought that we didn't get out of bed too early, because they could hear the water from our shower running through the pipes in the ceilings above their desks, but we probably had been there for only two hours, or we would have a shower and a change of clothes because we had been working throughout the night.

BACK

We had meetings with these VC people and, to be quite honest, I didn't want to sell something that in my opinion wasn't working to my satisfaction. Maybe I was too wrapped up in it, not seeing the wood from the trees because, at the end of the day, it worked perfectly and, looking back, always had done. It was just a lot of manual work that could, and occasionally did, go wrong when picking orders; even one order being sent out wrong was too much for me. I used to focus on that, and not on the 10,000 that had gone out that week without any problems.

It came to light that they just wanted to dangle a carrot in front of us; although they valued the business at £65 million, the £40 million price-tag was the value of the part we were selling. They said we had to leave about £25 million in the business, but it was just a paper exercise with no money involved, and we would still be left working in the business too. We would get the money out only when they sold the business on to someone else. The other thing was that the business would borrow the £15 million that we would get, so this is how you can get a £40 million share in a business for nothing.

I asked what the VC's intention was in the long run; they said that they would like to sell it in three years' time, by which time the turnover would have gone from £40 million to £120 million.

I asked how they were going to do that. They said that they were not going to do it, I was. I immediately thought, "Sod off; if that's the case, why do we need a VC?", and, if we carried on and did it ourselves, it would be better than having someone on our backs all of the time; I wasn't going to be answerable to anyone apart from our customers.

Within a few days we asked Stuart to inform the VC that we had decided to withdraw from the sale; we were pulling out after doing our own due-diligence in general on VCs. It didn't matter to Marilyn and me, or the girls, whether we sold the business or not, and certainly not after that encounter. If we were to sell at any time, we would only sell the lot, as we were not staying in a business where we could not do things that we wanted to do, and we certainly wouldn't be asking permission from anyone.

## Back to Work

We hadn't perfected the automation in the warehouse, which the contractors couldn't get right; it was very time-consuming and difficult, coordinating all of the outside contractors who were working on it. The fees for these people were astronomical, and they had a completely different attitude to the problems from the one that we had. Luckily, Stuart was there to intervene and help Scott, and then they finally got it all working, to everyone's relief; however, by this time, it had taken its toll on all of us.

The integration of the warehouse and order processing was done, after around two years of incredibly hard work, and of fixing and re-fixing hundreds of bugs in the system. A crowd of us went to the local pizza restaurant to celebrate; every two minutes the "happy birthday" song blared out, interrupting our conversation of ecstatic euphoria; but I didn't care, I just joined in the singing and must have sung "happy birthday" fifty times, accompanied by as much wine. Everyone had contributed so much, and now it was done.

We had probably done what was impossible for most businesses to do at that time; even some of the biggest household names in retail, with thousands of staff and with all of their resources, could not achieve what we did. This now meant that the ordering process was seamless.

***A moment in time, a very rare day***

I like this photo, taken on a very rare day in 2008 when we were all together for a minute for a photo, leaving the Werrington shop we had built five years before. This photo should have been in the chapter "Losing Control" but it would have been too near to my dad's funeral picture, so anybody flicking through the book would not realise that just over one page was 8 months apart, and the smiles would convey the wrong image there.

I wanted to put this photo in because so much in the ending chapters can be construed as negative when, in fact, our lives overall have been so positive. What I am trying to convey to you, the reader, is that the negative was a very small part but unfortunately, from my prospective, a very big stimulant to killing our Golden Goose.

# The Final Days of the Golden Goose

### *"Time was running out but I didn't know it"*

I now had a plan in my head, one that would be so unique to the nursery industry that we would exceed the £200 million we had predicted with the new warehouse and systems that we had just put together; this would work in no time at all, and I could not understand why nobody had thought about it before.

Having said that, we had been in the industry for 30-odd years, eating, sleeping and breathing it, and I had not thought about it myself up until now. The new project would mean a 24-hour-a-day operation, and we would probably need larger premises in the long run, but the really good thing was that it was all UK customers, so we could deliver within just hours. But before I presented this new, unconventional way of selling baby goods to the masses, things dramatically changed so, to this day, the plan is still inside my head.

## Micro-Management

There are times when you leave people to just get on with things and take responsibility for their actions but, as a business owner, you are ultimately responsible financially, and this was not the time to let anything go by chance. Micro-management was rife at that time, because getting everything right at this stage was crucial.

All five of us micro-managed every aspect of our respective responsibilities that we had in that last 4 years as we slid deeper into the recession; each of us would overlap the other four to seamlessly integrate everything together. This caused friction, but nobody can possibly see every aspect of the whole business in minute detail.

Life for those last few years seemed like we were in a pressure cooker, "our business"; we were cooking the food to absolute perfection but, to do that, the pressure inevitably has to build up and you know that in time that pressure-valve will blow; but will it blow before the food is ready? Will it blow when it's perfect? Or will it blow after the food is absolutely fcuked? Every one of us micro-managed that baby to its perfection; then, and only then, did it blow.

# Years to Build, Weeks to Copy

Immediately this goal was achieved, the next one would need to be set and implemented. We would be looking at what the business needed to be like in five years' time. Well, I could see tremendous changes in the retail and Internet environment coming along, so we would have to start on the new website now; we were already miles ahead, but what takes years to create takes only weeks to copy.

In business, as in life, changes take place all of the time. Were we all hungry enough to start the next project, a new revolutionary way of selling? Did we want to put ourselves through building another website where the technology had not yet been invented? And what was the motivation to do it? I couldn't answer the questions; then, as with all businesses, everyone has to be on the same wavelength and gel to make the project work - that is probably the most important thing in any business to making it a success.

## Preparation plus Opportunity Equals Success

### *The story of the Chinese bamboo tree springs to mind; does the tree grow to 30 metres in 6 weeks or 5 years?*

Year 1) water and fertilise it, nothing happened
Year 2)    "    "    "    "    "        "
Year 3)    "    "    "    "    "        "
Year 3)    "    "    "    "    "        "
Year 4)    "    "    "    "    "        "
Year 5) the tree grows to 30 metres in 6 weeks

Metaphorically speaking, Marilyn had constantly fed and watered our tree, "the shop", since she planted the seed all those years ago and, although I had changed the name three times to reflect the trends, the last being "dot com" on the end of Kiddicare in 2008 when we moved location, as it was more conducive to the whole retail market at that time, it didn't change the business owners, Marilyn and myself, or our desires.

It had been such an amazing time; if anyone connected with the business takes a moment to step back in time and look at what we achieved, I think they would agree that we did more in that period than in the history of the nursery industry in the radical transformation, helping and changing the public's culture of buying nursery goods, all the way through from the 70s up until we sold in 2011 that will never be seen again, well, not in my lifetime.

SIDETRACKED

Mike Hughes from Grant Thornton had kept in touch with me over the last five years. He had been to the new shop and was aware of the Venture Capital people who had been interested around April time; he knew then that I was not going to do anything with the business until I was 100% satisfied that we had completed what we had started out to do when we had moved. I didn't want another fiasco like the one we had with the VC.

Looking back now, I think he probably knew more than I did about where the business was eventually going, as he had been gauging not only my thoughts and perceptions, but that of others in the business, too; he could see the strain that the recession was causing, and he also could see that the business would be a very valuable asset for other people to bolt on to their businesses, not only to get rid of a competitor, but to get into the forefront in their market with our technological development, or to instantly capture another segment of the market if they weren't already in nursery.

# A Great Set of Circumstances

BACK

The way things were panning out on the High Street, anyone could see there were going to be lots of casualties before the recession was over. Marilyn and I just had a feeling that we were going to be on the same treadmill that we were on for a very long time to come.

Panic set in with the major retailers; businesses were looking for ways out by adding acquisitions to their portfolios by way of buying-up competitors or new types of business to make themselves stronger, or developing new technology to keep ahead of other competition, which would take forever.

We could stay the same as we were, or follow the panic on the High Street by trying to acquire some competitor, but that would be crazy; or we could do what we were used to doing, which is to think outside of the box, and not go down the route of being the hunter of expansion any more, but for us to become the hunted. The time was right to cash in, just like we had with all the other businesses we had sold along the way.

I really knew in my heart what we should do, but I couldn't make a decision because of Marilyn and our girls, and also the staff; but, for everyone's sake I should, however hard it was going to be, because I knew that all things in life have a life cycle and, for us, being in this business was nearing the end. We also knew, however, that the business itself could be another person's Golden Goose.

## At the End of the Day

Over the last few years I had come across situations that I had not experienced before. I wanted other opinions, but it was me that needed to make the final decisions on the business, and I knew that the natural cycle of cells were dividing and then re-forming. I was out of my comfort zone, and it showed. Throughout our lives we knew that there was no gain without pain but, at this time, I didn't want either; I wanted things to stay the same.

Once again, with all of the stresses that were still going on in the business, I saw Marilyn crying, and finally realised that this was not what I had wanted for my family all those years ago. I had already come to the conclusion that there was too much stress on everyone to get the business to the next level for the rewards, and it was Marilyn and I who had the financial responsibility, so it wasn't a good time. Over the next three days I felt ill, trying to keep composed; Marilyn, the girls, Scott, the grandchildren and now Andrew, were my life, and I didn't want to upset or lose any of them. Furthermore, whatever I did, I was going to be wrong.

I took my blood pressure and found that my monitor had gone wrong - it said 260/150 - so I went to Boots to get a new one. The lady started to tell me how to use it. I said that I already knew, as I had one that was faulty. She said that she doubted it so, when I told her the reading, she insisted on taking it again; she then told me to immediately go to my doctor, because I could be in serious trouble.

Blood-pressure tablets were prescribed and re-prescribed over the weeks, until they got it right. The cause was apparently stress, something that I thought over the years I had thrived on, but there is a tipping point for everything. There is also yin and yang to every event, too, because ever since taking blood pressure tablets, I have never had a hangover!

# Who Will Take Care of The Golden Goose?

## *"We didn't want to go"*

## One Phone Call That Changed Our World

Thursday, 29th July 2010; I was in my office, it was 2.00 pm and there were lots of things going on, with staff coming in and out of our office. Andrea was having a meeting with Marilyn, and I was feeling very light-headed as though I should be in bed. I had decided to start to sort out 36 years' worth of accumulated paperwork and stacks of rubbish, like old computer cables, ones that we all kept thinking that one day someone will come in and I would have just what they wanted. Well, I had decided it all had to go, because I was going. Well, everybody gets those days!

Mike happened to ring with all of his usual shit; "How's the family? How's the business? Are you going on holiday?" And so on. I went through the motions of being polite, hoping he would get off the phone, because I was feeling drained and really felt too ill to talk; then he said, "Well, don't forget: if you ever want to sell, just call me."

## The Tipping Point

When the tipping point was at the right angle, meaning that we couldn't stand the stress any more, and walking away wouldn't hurt as much as staying, then a window of opportunity was created which we took, knowing that there was great potential for a new owner to both take and make the business into a major player in the world.

## Ready For £200 Million Turnover

I had heard all this stuff from Mike for five years now, and didn't want to hear it any more, so I said, "Actually, Mike, we have a business to sell now; it has been working without any problems at all for six months, and I am sure that if we keep it we can take it to £200 million turnover with a good profit." I think that, after so long, it took Mike somewhat by surprise as he said, "Are you sure you want to sell?"

With hearing that I thought, "Do I want to sell?" In the next second I had made up my mind, so I said, "I don't want to take it to that level; I want to sell." I thought that would shut him up and we would never hear from him again or, if we did, then I had taken the agony from Marilyn, being responsible and trying to make a decision that would be impossible for her to make.

I knew that Marilyn wanted to just get back to being happy, and would only agree to a sale if her girls were happy too, which was rather like getting blood out of a stone; when we had a meeting to discuss this, all they would say was, "You must do what's best for you," which wasn't a straight answer. That really said to me that they didn't want the business to go out of the family as, eventually, it would have been passed on to them; but if we sold it, they would just get a great deal of money, and the business would be gone forever. Did they think like that, or was that just my thinking?

## Decision Made

Mike came in the next week, on 3$^{rd}$ August 2010, with the paperwork to sign, and to sort out with Stuart the due-diligence work that had to be done, which he estimated would take at least three months. We obviously would sell it as a going concern, complete with all of the staff; the business could be run without us anyway because, in the last six years, we had gradually put systems into place, even in the chaos, as we had decided that when things got better we would take a lot more time off travelling around the world.

We had a whole team of people working on this, both inside and outside; lawyers, solicitors and accountants crawling over every detail of the business. I was told there were equivalent to 150,000 sheets of information in the cloud for prospective buyers to look at; they went over the business from day one with a fine toothcomb.

We left the due-diligence work to the staff; Marilyn and I just kept out of the way, just answering any questions that we were asked. I accepted the situation that we were out of the team but, just because I accepted it, I can't say that it didn't hurt.

Our minds weren't in that zone at the time, but that's why you employ others who have the skills to do the things that you personally don't want to do. It was nice to see Scott in his element, getting involved with every aspect of the process and seeing all of those people who were interested in buying the business. He said that a very large company would pay £79½ million for us but he thought that they would then close us down, only incorporating bits of the business. This was not on my wish list, and I doubted that they would keep any of the staff, so I dismissed them without a thought.

## Ready to Go to Market

After all of the preparation, Marilyn and I had to answer dozens of questions, which the lawyers said we must answer honestly. I thought, "What other way is there? Who wants to get down the line, just to find out that someone is not happy?" We had been there before. We told it as it was, warts and all, and then left it to the prospective purchasers to make their own minds up.

Once I had made up my mind to sell, a great weight was lifted from me and, after that, I didn't care if we sold it or not; part of us was praying that it wouldn't happen, so we told them every problem encountered over the years, such as people copying our name, our website problems, problems with planning, faulty products, etc.

The list went on and on, which was a big deal to us but seemed to be irrelevant to all of the interested parties; this was interesting to me, as I had been on the shop floor selling to the customers literally all my life. I knew what made a raving fan of a business, and yet the people in charge of buying our business once again were only looking at figures; but I can't knock them, as all the businesses that were interested in us were the biggest and appeared to be the most successful in the High Street.

## Please Find Something Wrong

In my heart, and I think Marilyn would say the same, I was "willing" that someone would find a problem and the whole process would collapse, leaving us just to carry on as we were. As I have said, we disclosed every problem that we had ever had in the business, but it still didn't put off prospective purchasers; I suppose those things are nothing compared to what big businesses have to deal with.

At this point Scott was in his element; because everybody wanting to acquire the business had said that they would want management to stay and I would say with the brilliant IT team that he had, together with Stuart and all of our management team and the staff, there would be no problem at all in achieving what had been our goals going forward.

# The Dilemma in Telling the Staff

The due-diligence was done; everybody knew everything about Marilyn and me. We had been through the wringer so many times it had become normal and we were now getting immune to anything, except the thought of worrying the staff. By law, we had to tell the staff that we were putting the business on the market; we thought that this would cause unnecessary distress for some of them and, if we didn't sell, the stress would have been for nothing.

By the end of November 2010 everything was ready, and Mike went out to the market two weeks later. We had about thirty interested parties; 11 were VCs, which I dismissed immediately. By the third week there were something like eighteen offers; it was approaching Christmas, so most companies would be shutting down, or so I thought.

By the New Year we had got it down to eight serious buyers who were in our price range; they were rapidly going through the due-diligence process, which was rumoured to be costing them £2 million each and, by 31$^{st}$ January 2011, the third round of bids was in. Everybody had worked over the weekend, except us, and then, on the Monday morning, we were presented with the offers at 9am.

That was the one and only Monday morning in the last 37 years on which I was not eager to get up; I wanted to put my head under the covers. Our office was full of people - lawyers, accountants, Sally Winham, Paul Hughes, our accountants, Mike and his crew, advisers and bloody Tom Cobley and all.

I didn't want to be there; I wanted to go back upstairs to bed and then wake up realising it had all been a bad dream, but I couldn't escape. Mike read out all of the 8 offers, which were basically all pretty much the same and, by the time that he had come to the end, I had made up my mind.

As Mike was reading out the names of the bidders, a bit of background on them and what they intended to do with the business, I was mentally putting myself into the position of the staff. How would they take the business to the next level of £200 million turnover in a very short time, and integrate our website with the buyers? By the time Mike had finished presenting, which only took him about ten minutes, I immediately gave my decision; I knew Marilyn would trust whatever I said, and my decision was final - it took the responsibility from her.

I decided on Morrison's supermarket, because I felt that they had the same principles as us and they wanted our Internet experience, which Scott could do standing on his head. They also had about a £billion in reserves, and I liked the idea that they were going to leave Kiddicare as an independent brand and business.

They would keep Kiddicare separated from their main business; it would be run by our own staff, headed up by Scott, who would be the Chief Executive Officer - one of our main stipulations, that we had discussed with Mike when putting the business on the market, was to sell to someone who would keep the business intact, keep the staff, and keep the suppliers.

I had thought, but of course I was only thinking of a win-win, common-sense solution, and common sense is in short supply. Elaine would carry on heading-up the buying of goods as, in my opinion, she was the best in the industry; and I imagined, but again, imagination is a great thing, that Joanne would continue getting involved in just about everything that goes into running a successful business.

I also had a suspicion that Morrison's hadn't got a clue about the Internet world; well, I was told that they had already spent £500 million in the last 3 years trying to get online so, for one thing, spending another £70 million was an absolute bargain for them. And the most important thing as far as I was concerned was that Scott would not be under any pressure, because they wouldn't know whether it would take 3 months to get online or 3 years, giving Scott a bit of leeway if he needed it. But I didn't think he would need it, anyway.

I had come to the conclusion that if Scott and I had been of the same age-group, things would have been a lot different; maybe we could have created a longer-lasting business, who knows?! All I do know is that there's nothing better in life than when people gel together, like we all did for those few years.

## My Risk Assessment

My risk assessment was done in my head in seconds, as Mike read out all of the bids. I knew that, with Morrison's, it was possible for Scott to get the food business online within 12 months; click and collect was in its infancy in 2011, and I imagined that he would have implemented that within days of Kiddicare being affiliated, because that's how fast things moved along in Kiddicare. Putting our stock into 500 Morrison's supermarkets would have been easy too. As I said, within seconds this all went through my mind, and I was certain that it could and would be done; I was happy to make that choice.

## Could Have, Should Have, Didn't Think

I understood, after I had made my decision, that Scott and Mike had been talking to all of the bidders along the way and that, with Morrison's not being online, buying our business was the way to catapult them into the mainstream of the Internet alongside all of their competitors.

I was told that they were not really interested in the shop. If I had known that, I think that I would have just sold to them a copy of the operating system that we had developed, and carried on with the business. Sounds simple, but that's all we did, simple things. In the end, after just 3½ years, they spent another £217 million on renting the Ocado platform and never used ours.

The little shop that Marilyn had started all those years ago, in a two-up-two-down house, then developing and growing it every day over those years, had now gone to a company with a £billion in the bank. Those 35 years had gone in a blink of an eye.

Marilyn had spent all of that time in that business, at the same time bringing Elaine and Jo up to want to be with her, selling millions of pounds' worth of stock and, in the process, creating and selling four nursery equipment businesses; and this, the last one, was achieving a record £70 million in cash.

## Probably a World Record Price

I think £70 million must be a world record price for a single nursery equipment shop business, owned and sold by the founders; something to be very proud of, not just for the price of the shop but to have also accumulated over the years 20 million pounds' worth of property as well.

Now, hopefully, with taking the biggest independent out of the equation the independent trade would settle down; we were the ones, according to everyone, who were causing all of the problems as far as the trade was concerned. I was wondering who would be next to take on the title from us as the biggest independent in the UK and yet, in the last 3 years, I still haven't seen any changes; maybe we should go back into it again, or maybe not!

# Deal Done, or Was It?!

I had made the decision in the morning and, in the late afternoon the CEO, Dalton Philips, and CFO, Richard Pennycook, came over to sign the paperwork, although the deal wouldn't be completed until 14$^{th}$ February, so there was a 14-day window where things could go wrong and we could be left still holding onto the baby. We spent those 14 days making sure that we were leaving everything in place so that people could carry on without us.

# Oh No, a Bank Transfer

It was a bank-to-bank transfer, not actual cash in suitcases. Oh boy, would I have liked to hear the sound of that night safe banging each time £5,000 went into the wall; I think I might just have lost count, but what a great feeling.

What an unbelievable journey it had been; not only a roller-coaster ride from, as people would say, rags to riches, but a moment in time when, over the 30-odd years, groups of people crossed each others' paths as they passed the same way in life, their lives running in parallel for just a short while. Some were really bad, some really good and lots were amusing, but the vast majority were lovely people who just seemed to want to make other people happy - that's retail for you.

# What's a Serial Entrepreneur?

I wish there had been a book on the market to tell me what to do, or how to get from A to B without upset and conflicts - maybe I am now in the position to write one. We had built both businesses over 36 years, seen it, done it and, as they say, got the t-shirt. That cost a bloody fortune, getting all those t-shirts every week; that's part of creating a business and, when you have already done it, you don't want to do it again. Well, not for at least 24 hours - then you see something and think you can do that better, and off you go.

# Marilyn Couldn't Have Tried Any Harder

## That Journey Over, Never To Be Forgotten

*The smiles certainly didn't show all of the true feelings. From left: back row, Joanne with Heidi, Scott, Me, Elaine, Sophie; front, Marilyn, Charlie.*

When Marilyn sold her business she instantly made Elaine, Joanne and Scott multi-millionaires which, I must say, they certainly had all earned and deserved. She also made many others, including some staff, very happy, enabling some to buy cars or houses if they wanted to, and others to clear their debts.

This also gave Elaine, Joanne, Scott and Andrew the opportunity and freedom to pursue anything that they wanted to do, as Marilyn starting that business when she did paved the way for us all to have such a fantastic life. Having said that, Marilyn and I are so grateful to them for stopping with us for so long; they became our inspiration to carry on over the years. We will always miss working with them, and especially miss seeing the grandchildren as they are growing up, running into Nanny's office every day wide-eyed in expectation that Nanny will still have some sweets for them in her sweetie cupboard, which she always had. But who knows what the future will bring?

***Our grandchildren: Sophie 20, Heidi 4, Charlie 11, Finlay 18 months***

## What's Next?

We had thought that Scott, Elaine and Jo would take the business forward, which would make the expansion a lot easier with Morrison's compared to any of the other bidders. Also, I knew that they could start to physically implement the supermarket onto the Internet the very next day; well, Scott could, anyway, because he had the knowledge and the staff to do it without any fuss or bother.

I also knew that if they were to put our Kiddicare kiosks into their 500 stores, in the appropriate areas and with the right advertising surrounds, Kiddicare would double their £40 million turnover within probably 6 months. I also thought that if they had just one pallet of our "special offer" products a week in each store, which would be nothing to them, it would have been another £20 million a year through Kiddicare and, within a week, Kiddicare could have been selling all of Morrison's homeware products through a Morrison's branded website after that; every day, the offering would increase until everything was online. **"Well, you know what thought did."**

Working for a PLC with a billion pounds in the bank and all of the resources that they had to hand should have been child's play. With Scott now head of the business, Morrison's made him CEO; the process of climbing to the £200 million that we had set would be fine - I just wish that we could have stopped to help see it through, as we had got to do something and, to be honest, I would have rather made money for someone who had just given us £70 million than for strangers.

## Letters After My Name - What?!

I couldn't have stopped anyway, because someone would have put letters after my name, which in my mind would have meant, **"You don't own the business."** All I knew was what was in our dreams, our hearts and our souls, that had got us all to this point in our lives. I think staying would have never worked, as I know, deep down, that all of our knowledge would never have been taken on board and exploited for the good of the business going forward.

Every day had been different; we were used to selling businesses, or creating new ways to do things and taking most things in our stride, but this was an exception, this was "The End," and we had got to find a new beginning, and most people thought the word "retirement" would be in there, but our close friends said, "You two will never retire; if you do, you will go mad."

## An Announcement from the City

14th February 2011 was a day full of mixed emotions; we didn't want to go into the office as it would have been too emotional for us, knowing we were leaving. When the announcement was made to the City and on the TV news at 8am that morning, I was with three of our property maintenance lads cleaning drains on one of our commercial estates which we own in Peterborough.

I was jet-washing inside a main drain when one of our tenants came out of his unit and asked me what we were doing. I looked up; I was covered in muck. I said, "We are just doing the maintenance, mate." He took another look at me and said, "Is that you, Neville?" I said, "Yes, mate; how are you doing?" He replied, "I've just heard the f***ing news that you have just sold your business for £70 million; what the f**k are you doing cleaning f**king drains?"

Of course, working was the only way that I could cope with the loss of not working with our friends and our family any more, except, that is, for David Fulcher; he was with me that day, cleaning drains. I had worked with him for some years, and still do today.

***3<sup>rd</sup> November 2015. Just going to lay 8 metres of concrete - Ginger, as he is known, is in the book because he is exceptional, turning his hand to virtually anything; oh yes, and for being on call 24/7 for us for the last 14 years. I really don't know anyone else like him.***

## The Emotional Bank Account

Everybody has an emotional bank account, it's something that's invisible; you receive deposits and you give them. I am not talking about pulling in favours, by the way; there is not much that I don't like, but one of them is the phrase "they owe me one." Steve Best rang me one day asking if I needed any maintenance work doing, as he knew a person called Ginger who used to work for Steve's dad. Ginger was looking for a job and, to cut a long story short, he got a full-time job and is still with me today.

Several times over the years people have asked me for things which I have refused; their reaction has been, "Well, Ginger would get it," whatever it was - time off, a loan, or a new vehicle. I would say, "But Ginger keeps putting deposits into the emotional bank account of my life, and they are overflowing in his account, but yours is overdrawn; therefore, it is impossible for me grant you any request, and it's also impossible for me to refuse any request from Ginger."

You see, for about the last fourteen years he has worked for the business 24/7, every single day in his mind, but when I have asked the other person what they came to work for us for, they generally say the figure that they get an hour; then I say, "Well, Ginger came to work for the company and he can have anything he likes."

## You Have To Do Something

Now the loss of not working with our family was so hard to understand, as this was what we had worked for from the first day that we went into business in 1974, after "saying" in that dole office, ***"I will look after my family myself."*** But of course, babies grow up and create families of their own, and I had forgotten this point; well, not forgotten, I just didn't want it to happen.

## A World of Our Own Once Again

We were now on our own. I am not an "on-my-own" person; I want people around me creating something that would help people to get what they want, like I suppose we had done. Even now it seems odd, more like I'm not wanted. ***"Funny feeling"*** I have always been curious as to why so many people have died shortly after retirement, but now I think I have figured it out; in their eyes, they are not wanted or needed any more - simple as that.

For a very long time, well, that's what it felt like, maybe it was days. After the sale we were just getting on; people saw us going through the normal motions of life but, secretly, we were lost in **shitworld.** I don't think anyone will understand what I mean, unless they have been in the same situation and, if they have, they probably would be too embarrassed and wouldn't admit to the feelings anyway.

## Why Build Only One Store?

It's a question that people have asked us a thousand times over the years - why have one shop? Marilyn wanted to be with her family, and one way was to keep things simple; concentrating all of our energy in one place made it simple. Hold a magnifying glass a few inches away from paper, align it with the sun, and see what concentration does. To us, having one shop was easy, convenient and very profitable. We have seen people with a hundred shops still not make as much money as we did, although that's not always the case; it was just that we preferred it that way - different people, different things.

Earlier in the book, in the chapter on **Mind Over Matter**, I put a word of caution; I said, "Understand, and know why you are doing it," as enthusiasm in the moment can carry you away on a journey that can take you far away from what you first wanted in life.

I have to say that the journey we have been on has sometimes taken us far off our track, causing problems and, at other times, fulfilling our wildest dreams so, over the years, it's been better to throw caution to the wind rather than just sitting on the fence all of our lives, playing it safe; we knew that we could always start again.

I wouldn't normally advise this unless you are the only one who has any say in your business, or have the backing of a partner, or you are doing this together; either way, you have to be aligned or one day you will come home to an empty house, as I nearly did.

## We Needed Some New Goals

Now we were "In-betweeners;" in between work, projects, people, just everything. We needed to find our place; all the normal thoughts went through our heads, just like they did in 1974 when we had nothing, and our thoughts now were the same - what shall we do? And why, and when, and how? And on and on it went, day after day after bloody day. We had been so used to knowing that today we would have something to do, but now "sod all".

Marilyn told me in no uncertain terms that she couldn't stay at home and do nothing all day, but she also said she didn't want to be committed to being the head, in charge of a new business. Marville Properties would take only 20 minutes a day to run, that's less than a minute per million pounds of assets; no wonder the taxman says it's unearned income and taxes us at the highest rate.

She needed an office, and I needed to get out and do some physical, manual labour. Well, as you know by now, it wasn't going to stop at that; one thing leads to another and, with eyes and ears open and the urge to create, we were on our way in record time. In fact we went from our office in Kiddicare, across the road to an office that we had bought in an auction a week or so earlier, so we never missed a day; but, I must say, it was boring.

I would chastise my children if they ever said that word as they were growing up, yet here I was at the age of 60 saying it. I was lost in "shitworld" and pining for the familiar; well, not just me - Marilyn is a very private person; where I could tell my life story to a stranger at the bus stop and then ask them for advice, Marilyn told no one of her pain, and has only recently admitted that she cried just as much I did, but in private.

## We Had Hit a New Low

Mentally hitting a new low, now we were on our own, sitting in that godforsaken office in silence, shuffling bits of old paper from the past into files that would never be used, but thinking that we might need them. This was like being in prison, in contrast to just a few days earlier. We had come down from an exhilarating roller-coaster of a business, where the adrenaline would be racing every day and, of course, our children were across the road where the new party was just getting started. Can you imagine the biggest party in the world going on and everyone you knew being there and, although you had instigated it, you weren't invited? Well, we did want our cake and eat it, I suppose.

## The Life and Times of Reginald Perrin

Then the thought of Reginald Perrin kicked in; as CJ would say, ***"I didn't get where I am today by being low,"*** and that was it - off we go again. I've learned over the years that it takes just a few seconds to change your thinking and direction as, most of our lives, troubles are all in our minds, which are really easy to alter if you are determined.

## Well, It's Your Baby

It seems daft to me why it should have affected us like that. All through the journey, when we were talking to people, we would naturally be showing our enthusiasm about the industry; people would say, "I can see that you are very passionate, not only about the industry, but also about your business; and, of course, that's to be expected - after all, it is your baby."

I used to say to people, "I don't consider this business to be our baby; we just shift boxes. It doesn't matter what the products are inside of them." But of course, I had never really thought about this as we had been busy; anyway, at the time, we weren't going anywhere to make us think that way, as this was our life, and all of the people connected with us were our lives, so it was bound to affect us eventually.

# Money Isn't Everything

Naturally we were happy with an enormous amount of money, but not for money's sake. A great many people initially think money is everything and equates to happiness; well, it does contribute somewhat, but money isn't everything - does not buy you happiness. We needed to feel needed, part of a team; we needed to help, to teach, and to protect the vulnerable, to encourage the strong-willed, and we needed to be a constant in peoples' lives. If that makes sense, we needed to contribute something of ourselves.

***2013 - New Year in Switzerland. From left: Natasha and Andrew, Marilyn and me, and our good friends Carol and Trevor who we met in Australia, "who live in Yorkshire." This picture is on the mountain above our chalet.***

Our friend Andrew Killingworth, who owns a business called Yours Clothing, has just said to me, "Neville, I spoke to you about a week after you sold the Kiddicare business. You looked miserable; you told me that you had nothing in your life. I nearly felt sorry for you, but then I remembered that you had got £70 million in cash."

Andrew is one of the wealthiest people I know, and understands that money is just an asset that you use in your business, working it like any other asset, and certainly knows money is nice but it's far from everything. But it still doesn't stop him from ribbing me about it.

# What's Happening With Your Old Shop?

People would ask us what was happening with our old shop as, after we had left, we were told that apparently people were put into positions that they had no experience of, or training in for what their new responsibilities were; others were given letters after their names that denoted their position in the business. Although they could talk the talk, they still didn't know what they didn't know, as some had never been in a situation of real responsibility before, which I could see would have a compounding effect on what were to be developing problems that were easy to see.

The door to Kiddicare opened wide on all sides; from whatever angle I looked at the business, I could see that the philosophy, ethos, structural and financial direction of the business were not what we had worked on for the last 35 years. It was like someone had put a bomb into the body and blown it apart, separating all of the vital organs that each one of us had played, and breathing life into this great family business.

## Why Stay?

The business was not like any other, it was unique and, when we left Joanne could not understand why anyone would change the successful formula that we had sold. In her opinion, the ethos changed into following the same models of businesses that at that time were failing on the High Street by expanding into more shops.

Circumstances within no time at all pushed Joanne in another direction. She had expected that things would continue in the business in the same direction that it had taken 35 years to perfect, with "Marilyn's culture" and winning formula that had inspired Jo.

She was under the impression that, with Scott at the helm, he would be able to keep this intact with the teaching and philosophy and the technology integrated into the new owner's business.

Well, that's what Jo thought, but she found that she wasn't in the inner circle of management like she had been with us, so it was difficult to know who the puppet-master was in the business. She had been working with us all of her life, and had a vision of what was right and what felt wrong.

The direction that it suddenly went in was not what Joanne wanted; then, by 4th March, Kiddicare's website was being launched in three Scandinavian countries. Joanne had not been consulted on this, although she had been involved full-time from the beginning in overseeing the planning and construction of the new building, including the distribution of goods internally and to the customer's final destination. She was concerned about the operation of the logistics of serving those customers' needs so far away, as she knew communication in the UK is bad enough, and any returns very costly, in fact prohibitive, from another country.

There now seemed no reason for her to stay, as she hadn't the influence now that she had before; working twelve hours a day, six days a week and taking responsibility for the things she did in the business counted for nothing. Luckily, we had brought her up to make a difference in whatever she was doing and, of course, once she couldn't do that there was no point in her staying.

## I'm Working With You

One day, about a month after we had sold Kiddicare, Jo walked into our new office around lunchtime. We said, "Hi, Jo; have you come for a coffee?" She said, "No, I've left; I have come to work with you."

By September, Kiddicare was looking to expand by acquiring 10 Best Buy stores and developing them into mega-flagship stores, and increasing the staffing levels to 1000. In Jo's, and indeed our, opinion this was leading to a path of destruction, and counter-productive to the continued success of the business.

After a while, from what I read in the papers and on the Internet, Scott was put in charge of Morrison's non-food division as well as Kiddicare. In my opinion, at that point Elaine should have taken the helm in Kiddicare, as she had been there since day one. She was the one who really knew the business inside out and, under her leadership, I personally think that the business would not only have survived but would have prospered.

By March 2012 Morrison's had moved four of its most talented senior directors into Kiddicare - Hilary Lean as Commercial Director, Grant Henley, Operations Director, Simon Eastwood, Retail Stores Director, and Mandy Flatley, HR Director, along with a lot more.

Scott went on to develop Morrison's cellar, which took twelve weeks to complete in-house, all from scratch; this operation was all run out of Kiddicare, Peterborough, which shows just how versatile the Kiddicare team was. I believe this was a huge success until Morrison's had to abandon it when going into Ocado.

I am sure the £200 million would have been achieved if the principles and format that we had developed had stayed the same. I do not think it helped the business by taking on the 10 new stores from Best Buys in the depth of the recession, but I think they certainly knew what they were doing, getting rid of them.

From what I read, by 13<sup>th</sup> March 2013, just one year after bringing in the senior directors, Scott's position as head of Kiddicare had gone. Also, they had no use for Elaine, even though she had been in the business since it started.

Personally, I think that if Elaine had stayed and then persuaded Jo to return, they could have saved the business in a week by closing the 10 shops and going back to what they knew worked; this they could have done standing on their heads. Scott should have returned to manage the Internet and then the whole value would have been retained.

## All Basic Stuff

This is all basic stuff that my girls, Scott and the Kiddicare staff had done before, but there you are! I've said it before - different people have different agendas for all sorts of reasons. It was a shame to see the business sold by Morrisons after just 3½ years for £2 million, after suffering a £170 million loss; how the hell does that happen?

It took 35 years of priming the pump and sowing the seeds every day without fail; it took focus, dedication, and input from passionate people to build this fantastic business, and then it took just a blink of an eye by FOY people to destroy it. **Look up the words (Full of yourselves) on Google.**

# 2011 - When One Door Closes

**_"Ten more will open, but you really have to hunt for the keys"_**

## Another Milestone

**_Joanne and Andrew's wedding, 19<sup>th</sup> August 2011_**

Before Jo joined us we were just going through the motions every day, investing in new businesses, which should have been exciting, but they were just time-fillers; they were meaningless, we hadn't created them, and we weren't responsible for them. We couldn't influence their paths to success because, in a lot of cases, the people in whom we had invested knew it all, yet knew nothing; they wanted our money, but ignored our advice - well, that's what I thought then.

# Make Work an Adventure

Make work an adventure. When it becomes work it is not an adventure any more. Although I have said "work" in this book many times, work was not in our mental vocabulary, it was our life, and it was doing all the things that we wanted to do.

Why clutter our minds thinking about work, when we could think about building a life from our dreams? We had been on a journey that turned into an incredible adventure, not only for us and, hopefully, for our children as well, but for those we met on the way, as they touched our hearts, our minds and our souls.

## *"Don't dwell on what went wrong. Instead, focus on what to do next."*
Denis Waitley

## Business Stops for No One

Money is just a by-product of doing a series of things that are repeated over and over for many, many years, accumulating into a business which provides products and/or services that are wanted by others. Once that is forgotten, or not even learned, the business will fail.

So when Jo joined us, we set about creating another business together and, as normal, one thing led to another. Jo's husband, Andrew, who worked in London as a building surveyor, also came to work with us and, before we knew it, we had created several profitable businesses. Sadly, by now, Kiddicare had lost its way and a fortune, and that really made us want to go and help them, but we knew they would never have the courage to ask. *"Pride can be an awful thing"*

I tell this story to help the reader who is in, or is thinking of going into, business, to stop frequently, stand still and think, "Is the thing that I am doing taking me nearer to, or further from, my goals in life? What are my goals? Why are they my goals right now? And have they changed since starting on this current path that I am taking." And if they have, repeat the process and move forward.

# Another door opens

Two of our businesses came from a chance meeting, one with a guy called John Barrett, which has led to creating multiple associated businesses, forming one of the biggest independent house-building businesses in the Midlands. A mutual friend was in my office in January 2011 when he asked if we still bought investment properties. I said we did, so he arranged for us to meet up with John, who had just built a Tesco's and about 20 other shops and some offices in Northampton, which he now wanted to sell.

Marilyn and I met John at the site. We were in the new coffee shop having our meeting, when he asked what we did for a living. I said we had a property investment business and that we were just about to start expanding into house-building, because we were selling our shop and would have a bit more time on our hands; that was on 3$^{rd}$ February 2011.

John said, "Why go to all of the trouble of finding the people and creating a business, which will take years, when I have the experience of the building industry and the knowledge of building housing estates with up to 280 houses? I have a team of 12 incredible people in my office in Milton Keynes." John said to me that, unfortunately, they had run out of work, land and money, because of the worst building recession since the 1930s, and he was going to close if he couldn't find any work immediately, or someone to invest in the business. We both thought it was just the right time to start building spec houses ready for when the recession was over.

On 3$^{rd}$ February 2011 we shook hands with someone whom we had known for 30 minutes and, apart from a dream, Marilyn and I made a commitment to invest and arranged for the paperwork to go ahead. By the time the solicitors had got it done Andrew, our son-in-law, Jo's husband, and Jo had joined us in the partnership. Andrew had been a Chartered Surveyor in London for eleven years and wanted a different lifestyle. Once again, we were gathering the right people to create another spectacular team for this new business.

First, we established a completely new company to build spec houses. We then acquired land and started to build; it took us 18 months before we had got the first fifteen houses built and sold. In the meantime, we had started to build the next three sites, consisting of 40 two-, three-, four- and five-bed houses.

**John in the middle, Andrew left, and me, at our site in Milton Keynes**

After 4½ years, still laughing and still using the same principles as those behind Kiddicare, "The answer is yes; now, what's the question?"

**A sample of the houses that we are building**

18 months after we started, we added another building company to our partnership, specialising in building social and Council houses. As I write this, on 30th August 2014, we are working on many projects; some are in the planning stages that will see 582 units built, worth well over £90 million between both of these two

businesses which we had started from nothing more than trust and respect for each other, and a model that we have replicated with others specialising in niche sectors of the building industry. Our aim is to sell the business as a going concern within five years of starting it.

## Marville Properties

***In 2012 we built a bespoke computer headquarters for 350 people***

Since leaving Kiddicare, we have carried on expanding Marville Properties. There are pictures below of some of Marville's buildings that we have either built or acquired. To me, it doesn't matter whether it's selling prams or property, business is about trusting the people you are associated with; that's what counts, knowing that they are there watching out for you as you watch out for them.

***135,000 sq ft building was on the market for around £10 million; we bought it in the recession for £4½ million.***

**Office building that was sold for conversion to 97 apartments. This is an £8-million project, which will be completed in 2016 by GKL of Peterborough.**

**Under construction: 30 apartments from existing offices; a joint BW/GKL project.**

# Public Speaking!!

After selling Kiddicare, requests came in to me for public speaking; banks, accountants and business clubs asked me to tell our story of how we built a family business, with all of the stresses and strains, together with the emotions of keeping it together as we went on our journey of building the largest independent nursery retailer in the UK. They said that others could then use our knowledge and experiences in their own businesses.

I received an email on 27th September 2012 from two lads called Mark Homer and Rob Moore; they own a company called Progressive

Property and had moved into a building a few doors away from us. I had contacted them to ask them to get rid of their clients' cars, which were blocking the estate roads every day, and which were sending other people owning offices there mental. I did offer them an area of parking about 2 minutes away, that I owned, for I think £1.50 a car per day rent when they wanted it, but, sadly they didn't take the offer up, and yet still alienate themselves from their neighbours years later.

They had done some research on me and asked if I could meet up for lunch. I went along, although lunch is a waste of time for me; I wanted to be polite as they were neighbours. I was immediately struck by their positive attitudes - Mark reminded me of myself, with his strategic thinking, and Rob reminded me of how I was when I was his age, full of enthusiasm and wanting to help everybody.

Talking to them made me realise that the last few years of our 36-year journey of being in business had worn me down; I was still like Rob in my mind, but what came out of my mouth was Mr Grumpy. During lunch they asked if I would be the keynote speaker on stage with Frank Bruno for them, at Wembley Stadium in London.

There would be 23 speakers, mainly specialising in one subject or another regarding property. I became the latest in a long line of keynote speakers who had spoken at this conference over the years, people like Sir Bob Geldof, Lord Alan Sugar and Baroness Karren Brady.

Maybe at the time I thought that I was being classed in their league but, since seeing the others perform, I think that they were just scraping the barrel as I'm not that good at it - I get too emotional about the things that I talk about then, afterwards, I chastise myself for it. I know that I should back away and become the third person because, when I talk about the beatings I had as a child, I get transported back and I feel the pain as I did all those years ago.

# Why Bother With the Pain?

I do it for four reasons really: (1) to face the fear that I have of not being as confident as I would like to be, (2) to inspire other people to follow their dreams, (3) to encourage others not to procrastinate over the things that they want to do in their lives, and (4) to help people accept that what they want to have, be, and do, is in line with their expectations, and not the expectations of others.

**Left to right: Myself, Rob Moore and Frank Bruno**

**Left to right: Mark Homer, myself and Rob Moore at Wembley Stadium.**

## Money Makes Money

I think everyone has said this sentence before: "Money makes money." Well, it's right, but only if you take care of it by investing in things that you are familiar with and you are confident will increase in value in the long run, at the same time producing an income stream so you don't need to work. But very few have done it for themselves - I wonder why? Anyway, enough said; I have just achieved another one of my goals. On 9th October 2015 I have finished the book, 3½ years from when I started, to the relief of everybody around.

# Final Words

It has been an absolute pleasure writing this book, a brief history of our family business, but it is really to recognise Marilyn's dedication to family and business in creating Kiddicare, from the first day to the sale in 2011.

This book is from my own personal viewpoint only, and I have not asked any other person's opinion with regard to the content but, without Marilyn's steadfastness, loyalty and her need for stability, I would not have written it.

Also for the people who asked me why we started the business, and how we succeeded through turbulent times.

Not forgetting the ones who say, "It's all right for you." I'm not holding my breath, thinking they will read it.

I am pleased you have got this far, and I do hope now you have a better understanding of how normal business people act, think and do things, very often just getting by "by the skin of their teeth."

If you truly want to be rich, like millions of people do, I do hope that you have gained some insight into how we got there, as it was mostly a by-product of the whole family doing things that each one of us loved to do, and making the final decision to sell very easy.

I sincerely wish all of you the very best of luck on your life's wonderful journey. By the way, does anybody want to buy a used piece of scrim that's not needed any more?

Thank you

# Neville Wright Nevillewright.com